Moral Crisis in the Ottoman Empire

Moral Crisis in the Ottoman Empire

Society, Politics, and Gender during WWI

Çiğdem Oğuz

I.B. TAURIS
LONDON • NEW YORK • OXFORD • NEW DELHI • SYDNEY

I.B. TAURIS
Bloomsbury Publishing Plc
50 Bedford Square, London, WC1B 3DP, UK
1385 Broadway, New York, NY 10018, USA
29 Earlsfort Terrace, Dublin 2, Ireland

BLOOMSBURY, I.B. TAURIS and the I.B. Tauris logo
are trademarks of Bloomsbury Publishing Plc

First published in Great Britain 2021
This paperback edition published 2023

Copyright © Çiğdem Oğuz, 2021

Çiğdem Oğuz has asserted her right under the Copyright, Designs
and Patents Act, 1988, to be identified as Author of this work.

For legal purposes the Acknowledgments on p. ix constitute
an extension of this copyright page.

Series design: Adriana Brioso
Cover image © BOA.I.DUIT.101/101 (4/1). Map of the Ottoman Empire showing
military and civilian administrative divisions during the First World War, 1917

All rights reserved. No part of this publication may be reproduced or
transmitted in any form or by any means, electronic or mechanical, including
photocopying, recording, or any information storage or retrieval system,
without prior permission in writing from the publishers.

Bloomsbury Publishing Plc does not have any control over, or responsibility for,
any third-party websites referred to or in this book. All internet addresses given
in this book were correct at the time of going to press. The author and publisher
regret any inconvenience caused if addresses have changed or sites have ceased
to exist, but can accept no responsibility for any such changes.

A catalogue record for this book is available from the British Library.

A catalog record for this book is available from the Library of Congress.

ISBN: HB: 978-1-8386-0709-8
PB: 978-0-7556-4253-3
ePDF: 978-1-8386-0712-8
eBook: 978-1-8386-0711-1

Typeset by Integra Software Services Pvt. Ltd.

To find out more about our authors and books visit www.bloomsbury.com
and sign up for our newsletters.

To Alberto

Contents

Illustrations	viii
Acknowledgments	ix
A Note on Transliteration	xii
Abbreviations	xiii
Glossary of Non-English Terms	xvi
1 Introduction	1
2 The Intellectual Contest over Morality, and Interpretations of Moral Crisis: Secular versus Religious Morality	23
3 The Public Morals, Prostitution, and Cultural Perceptions	65
4 Morality between Discourse and Daily Realities	97
5 Family at the Center of Moral Decline: Legislation Targeting the Regeneration and Protection of Ottoman Muslim Families	115
6 Conclusions and A Discussion on Moral Crisis from Past to Present	149
Notes	163
Bibliography	204
Index	222

Illustrations

3.1 Canadian recruitment poster from the First World War   69
3.2 Martial law was abolished in the area inside the borders of the thick line drawn with a pencil (except for Istanbul)   75
4.1 "The World of the Nouveau Riche" as depicted in Sedad Simavi's cartoon album   106

Acknowledgments

This book is a revised version of the dissertation that I prepared at Boğaziçi University's The Atatürk Institute for Modern Turkish History and Leiden University's Institute for Area Studies, Turkish Studies Program. I wrote the last parts of the dissertation in August–September 2017, but I could only defend it in June 2018, after completing all the requirements at both universities for the co-tutelle degree. Since then, many new studies appeared in the field owing also to the attention that the war's centenary generated worldwide. I include some of these newly published works here.

This research, for which I have spent more than seven years, witnessed a list of difficult moments that surely must have impacted its quality. During this time, I moved constantly in the middle of writing process, which left me away from the books that I collected in the last fifteen years. My attempt to include more sources from the military archives in Ankara (which takes two months to receive the ordered documents) was interrupted due to the bombings that took place around the area where the archives are located in 2016. Later that year, I moved in the Netherlands and then moved again in Italy, where I finally completed the study. As Covid-19 hit Italy hard, the last revisions had to be done under lockdown conditions without accessing the libraries. Yet the enthusiasm for a heretofore unexplored topic and the stories that it unveiled has never stopped. I am thankful to many people and the institutions that helped me keep this spirit alive and made this study possible.

I would like to express my thanks to the supervisors of my dissertation, who expertly guided me and provided an intellectual orientation throughout this study. M. Asım Karaömerlioğlu encouraged me to focus on the topic of morality and provided me with invaluable insight with which to evaluate the sources. He read the drafts meticulously and persuasively conveyed a spirit of intellectual curiosity with his comments. Conversations with Erik Jan Zürcher in Leiden enriched my thinking on the topic and led me to ask new questions. His challenging, insightful critiques on the drafts greatly contributed to this study. I feel privileged to have their support to date in the preparation of the book.

I am grateful to my Boğaziçi thesis committee members: Zafer Toprak for his valuable comments and recommendations, and to Mehmet Ö. Alkan for his comments and support. The dissertation committee at Leiden, Ben Schoenmaker, Dick Douwes, Nicole A.N.M. Van Os, Hans Theunissen, and Uğur Ümit Üngör provided me with great insights that contributed immensely to revise the study.

I owe thanks to the staff of the Atatürk Institute: Kadriye Tamtekin, Dilek Arda, and Leyla Kılıç. I thank Jonathan Philips, the in-house editor of the Atatürk Institute who edited the earlier version of this study. I also thank the staff of Prime Ministry Ottoman Archives, Boğaziçi University Library, Leiden University Library, and The Women's Library in Istanbul.

I thank the Turkish Historical Society for the fellowship it provided in the first four years of my PhD at Boğaziçi. I am grateful to the American Research Institute in Turkey for the grant it provided in 2017. EHESS-CETOBaC granted me an affiliation that allowed me a short research visit in Paris and provided me with the opportunity to discuss my research at a meeting co-organized by CETOBaC and INALCO.

Many dear friends stood with me in this journey. I thank my "Friends without Borders" Sinem Kavak and Ceren Deniz for reading and commenting on parts of this book. My friends as talented scholars helped me in so many different ways during the preparation of this work, and I am thankful to them: Ebru Aykut, Seçil Yılmaz, Fırat Kaplan, Gizem Tongo Overfield Shaw, Mehmet Polatel, Melih Yeşilbağ, Maral Jefroudi, Gözde Orhan, Deniz Pelek, Selin Pelek, and Barış Zeren.

From February 2019 to January 2020, I have worked as a postdoctoral researcher at the University of Naples Federico II for the project "War and Citizenship: Redrawing the Boundaries of Citizenship in the First World War and Its Aftermath" under the supervision of Daniela L. Caglioti. I revised the dissertation thanks to that position. I am thankful to Professor Caglioti for providing me with this opportunity and encouraging me to prepare this book while leading me into another fruitful research area. I had the chance to discuss a part of this work in our "Naples Group" meetings, where I received insightful feedback from many talented scholars.

I am thankful to the two reviewers of the manuscript, whose comments contributed greatly to the improvement of the quality of this study. I am grateful to the the I.B. Tauris editors, Rory Gormley and Yasmin Garcha, for the efforts to help me throughout the publication process.

Finally, I thank my sister Özge Oğuz, my brother Bora Oğuz, my aunt Meliha Karslı, and my grandmother Hesna Türkan Ekmekçioğlu for believing in me all these years and sharing my enthusiasm. I thank Malù Caiazza, Alfonso Siani, and Paola Russo for their support and welcoming me into the family in Italy. The memory of two wise people, my mother Mediha Oğuz and my grandfather Kemal Ekmekçioğlu, is always with me. I thank Alberto L. Siani for his patience, companionship, and love and his great comments on the drafts. I dedicate this study to him.

A Note on Transliteration

In the transliteration of Ottoman Turkish, I chose the simplest form of Latinization and indicate long vowels. For the sake of simplicity, names and terms that are well known in contemporary English are rendered in conventional form. Therefore, I use *Sharia* not *Şeriat*, and *Jihad* not *Cihad*. For a similar reason, I prefer *Şeyhülislam* to *Sheikh-ul Islam*. Names and terms in Ottoman Turkish are generally transliterated in their modern Turkish form.

Abbreviations

AKP	Adalet ve Kalkınma Partisi
ATASE	Genelkurmay Askeri Tarih ve Stratejik Etüt
BOA	Başbakanlık Osmanlı Arşivleri
CUP	Committee of Union and Progress
MMZC	Meclis-i Mebusan Zabıt Ceridesi

Abbreviations of Archival Catalogs

A.) DVN.MKL.	Sadâret Divan-ı Hümayûn Kalemi Mukâvele Kısmı
BEO	Bâb-ı Âlî Evrak Odası
DH.ŞFR	Dahiliye Nezareti Şifre Evrakı
DH.EUM	Dahiliye Nezareti Emniyet-i Umumiye Müdüriyeti
DH.EUM.ADL	Dahiliye Nezareti Emniyet-i Umumiye Müdüriyeti Takibât-ı Adliye Kalemi
DH.EUM.ECB	Dahiliye Nezareti Emniyet-i Umumiye, Ecânib Kalemi
DH.EUM.EMN	Dahiliye Nezareti Emniyet-i Umumiye Müdüriyeti Emniyet Şubesi
DH.EUM.MEM	Dahiliye Nezareti Emniyet-i Umumiye Kalem-i Umumî Müdüriyeti
DH.EUM.MTK	Dahiliye Nezareti Emniyet-i Umumiye Muhâberat ve Tensikat Müdüriyeti
DH.EUM.SSM	Dahiliye Nezareti Emniyet-i Umumiye Müdüriyeti Seyrüsefer Kalemi

DH.EUM.THR	Dahiliye Nezareti Tahrirat Kalemi
DH.EUM.VRK	Dahiliye Nezareti Emniyet-i Umumiye Müdüriyeti Evrak Odası
DH.H …	Dahiliye Nezareti Hukuk Evrakı
DH.İ.UM.	Dahiliye Nezareti İdare-i Umumiye Evrakı
DH.İ.UM EK	Dahiliye Nezareti Evrakı Dosya Usulü Envanter Kataloğu
DH.İD	Dahiliye Nezareti İdare Evrakı
DH.MTV	Dahiliye Nezareti Mütenevvia
DH.ŞFR	Dahiliye Nezareti Şifre Evrakı
DH.UMVM.	Dahiliye Nezareti Umur-ı Mahalliye ve Vilayat Müdürlüğü Evrakı
HR.İD	Hariciye Nezareti İdare
İ.DUİT	Dosya Usulü İrade Tasnifi
MV.	Meclis-i Vükela

Abbreviations of Hicrî and Rumî Months and Days

M	Muharrem
S	Safer
Ra	Rebiyyu'l-evvel
R	Rebiyyu'l-ahir
Ca	Cumade'l-ula
C	Cumade'l-ahir
B	Receb
Ş	Şa'ban
N	Ramazan

L	Şevval
Za	Zi'l-kade
Z	Zi'l-hicce
Ka	Kanun-i evvel
K	Kanun-i sani
Ta	Teşrin-i evvel
T	Teşrin-i sani

Glossary of Non-English Terms

Âdâb	Manners
Ahlâk	Morality
Ahlâk-ı Umûmîye	Public morality
Ahlaksız	Immoral
Ahlaksızlık	Immorality
Bâb-ı Meşihat	Office of the Şeyhülislam
Dar'ül-Hikmet'il İslamiye	The School of Islamic Philosophy
Diyanet İşleri Başkanlığı	Directorate of Religious Affairs
Esbâb-ı Mûcibe Lâyihası	Justificatory Memorandum
Fuhuş	Prostitution
İctimâîyyat	Sociology
İdare-i Örfiyye	Martial law
Medrese	Islamic learning institutions
Şeriat	Islamic law
Şeyhülislam	The supreme religious authority
Terbiye	Upbringing
Ulema	Ottoman religious scholars (collectively)
Zina	Adultery

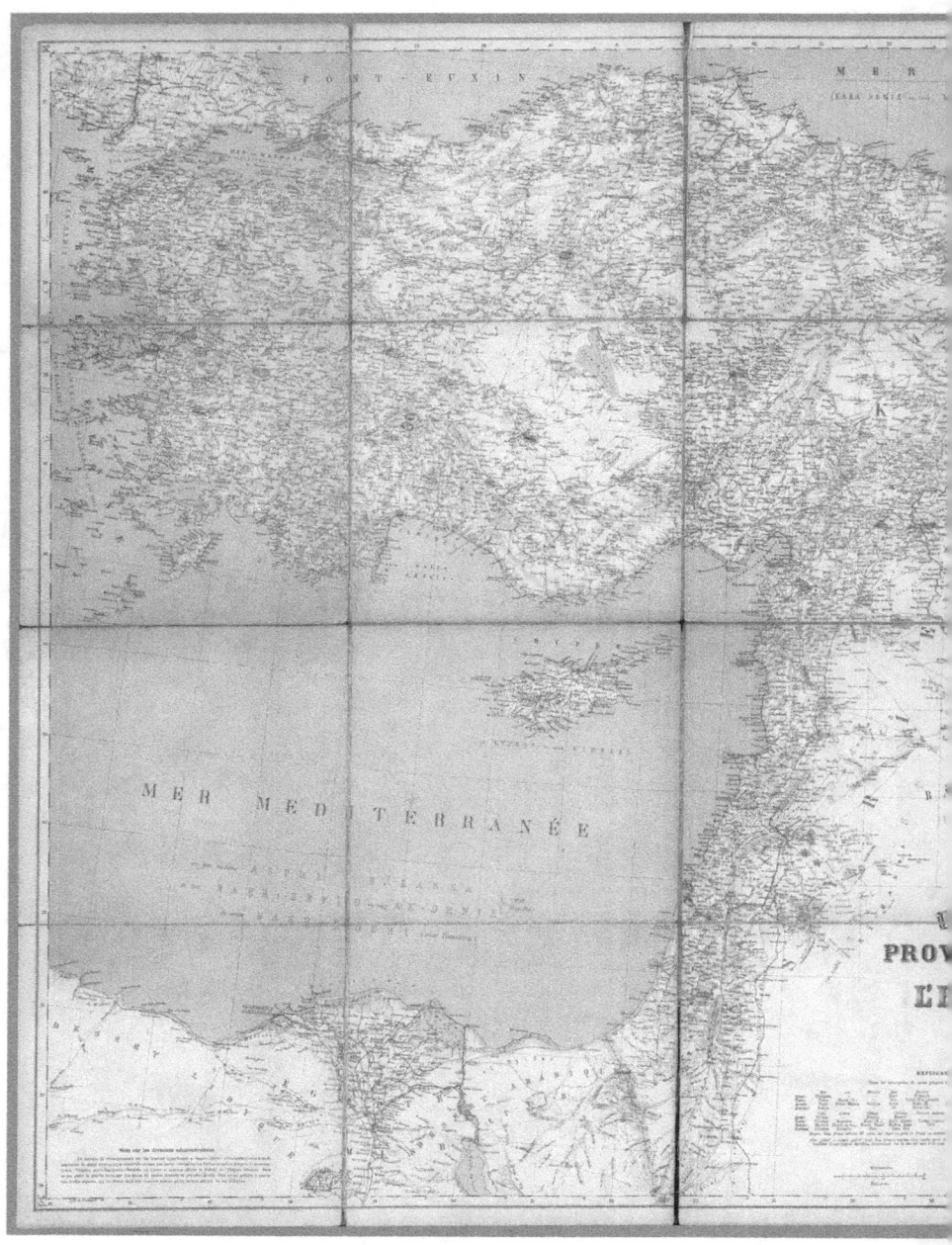

The Ottoman Empire (the provinces Hedjaz and Yemen are not shown) 1917 edition of "Nouvelle carte generale des provinces asiatiques de L'empire Ottoman: sans L'Arabie," by Heinrich Kiepert and Richard Kiepert, Berlin, 1883. Credit: David Rumsey Map Collection, David Rumsey Map Center, Stanford Libraries.

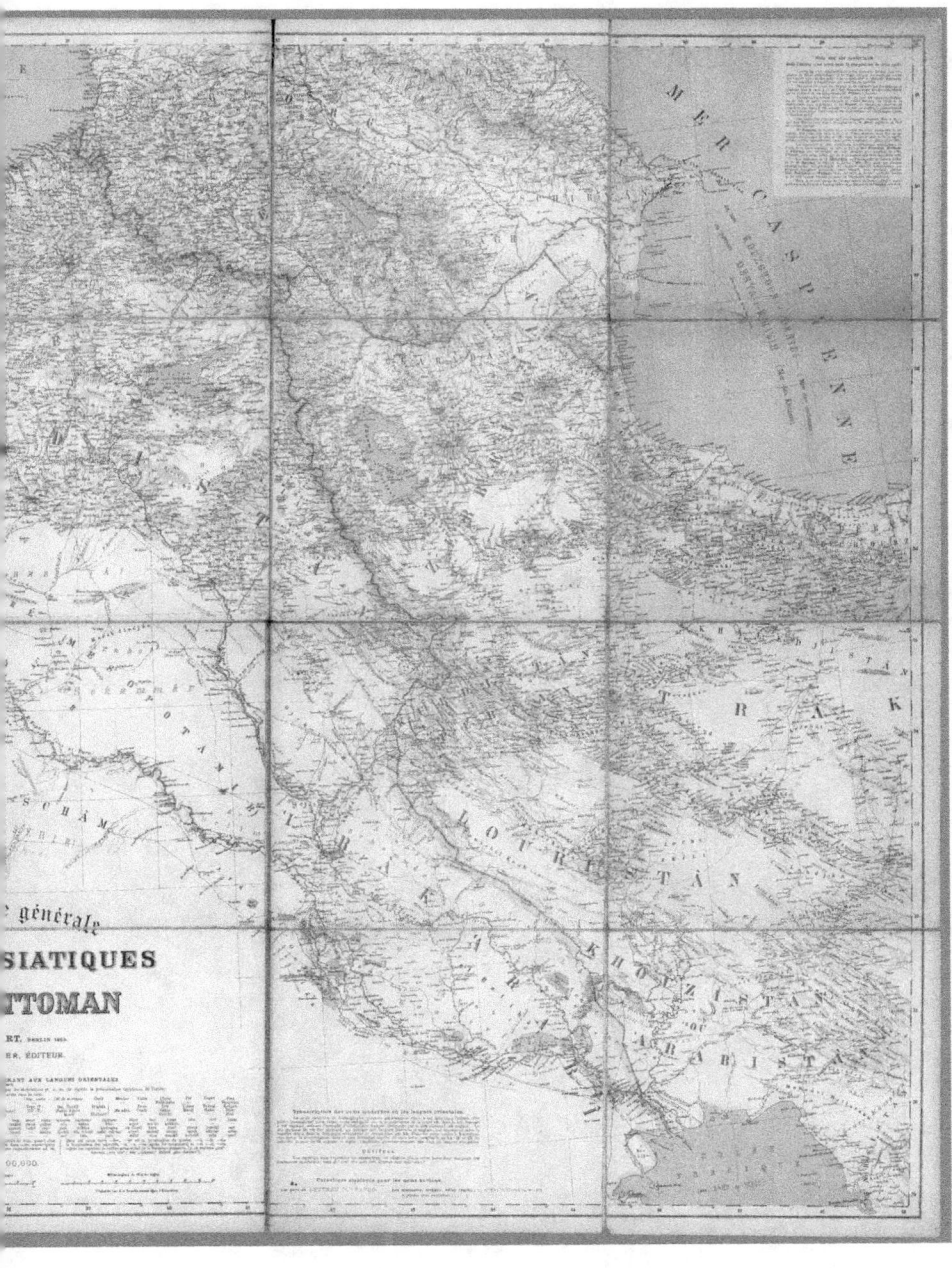

1

Introduction

Long before the rising scholarly interest in the home front in the historiography of the First World War, a Turkish academic and journalist as well as a witness to the war, Ahmed Emin (Yalman), wrote a chapter entitled "War Morals" in his well-known work *Turkey in the World War*. He asserted that "people in Turkey were, from the viewpoint of morality, less prepared to resist the social and economic effects of the war than any other belligerents" and the privations of war brought about a moral breakdown in society.[1] Many other Ottoman Turkish intellectuals of various ideological backgrounds continuously mentioned the problem of moral crisis at the turn of the twentieth century, which, according to them, reached a peak during the First World War. But what did it mean, and how did it happen? And how can we make sense of discussing morality in the midst of a war that eventually led to the dissolution of a centuries-old empire?

This study aims to shed light on the polemics of moral crisis and their preconditions on the Ottoman home front during the First World War. It argues that debates about morality had important political, social, and cultural implications in this particular period. Morality was a key concept to see through the social and cultural transformation that the late Ottoman society experienced in times of political and social turmoil.

My interest in the topic also arose from the central place of morality in the political and social environment of contemporary Turkey. Intermingled with discussions about lifestyle, a powerful discourse on morality, it can be argued, is part of Turkish identity. Every Turkish citizen knows the motto: "We will adopt the technology of Europe but not European morality." In addition, moral discourses employing the terms of "religion," "patriarchy," and "tradition" prevail in daily life—particularly in provincial towns of Turkey—thereby constituting an important dynamic that suppresses potential challenges to the extant social order. The following chapters sketch, in different ways, how fault lines in today's Turkish society are grounded in the sociopolitical context of the late Ottoman Empire.

The First World War not only paved the way for the territorial dissolution of the empire but also contributed decisively to its sociocultural transformation on which the Republic of Turkey would be founded. Despite the constant debates among late Ottoman intellectuals on morality as an important aspect of Ottoman-Muslim identity, this field has remained largely untouched in Ottoman-Turkish historiography except for a few studies. On the other hand, the topic has been studied at great length by theologians because morality debates are closely associated with religion, in particular with Islam.[2] A recurrent characteristic of such studies is that they treat late Ottoman texts on morality (especially texts written by the Ottoman Islamic scholars, *ulema*) as if they are timeless, ahistorical works to be taken as guides for life for all time. However, a close look at these morality texts reveals the context of intellectual disputes following from the social and political conditions of the period in question. This does not imply that the effects of these discourses remained limited to the time of their emergence. These historical disputes over morality have shaped the manner and tone with which social and cultural conducts are discussed today. The contest over morality still prevails in Turkish society (and also in other Middle Eastern countries) in line with ideological and cultural confrontations.

As I started to work on the so-called moral crisis in the context of the late Ottoman Empire, I had two assumptions in mind that came to be challenged as the study progressed. My first conviction was that the concept of "moral crisis" was a reflection of anxiety in society resulting from increasing prostitution due to economic hardships. My second assumption was that I would find many punitive measures regarding the protection of public morality on the Ottoman home front. This was partly because a single party—namely the Committee of Union and Progress (CUP)—ruled the Ottoman state as an authoritarian power deriving its power from the extraordinary nature of wartime. With respect to my first assumption, prostitution was indeed a major topic in morality discussions; however, the direction of the causal link between immorality and prostitution was not as I had assumed. In most contemporaneous accounts, prostitution was not regarded as the reason for moral decline; rather, it was treated as one of the consequences of it. Also, the definition of prostitution was broader than I had assumed and encompassed several kinds of misconduct. This also means that prostitution per se was only part of a broader discussion on moral decline. With respect to my second assumption, the CUP government truly attached great importance to the protection of public morality, but it never introduced punitive measures—at least not measures as harsh as expected—no matter how heated the debate became. Despite many rumors during wartime about the introduction of new measures, the government defined the violation of public morality broadly and left final decisions to the discretion of the courts.

However, moral anxieties indeed played an important role in the penetration of the state into the realm of family. Protecting the honor of Ottoman citizens was important as part of mobilization efforts. While eliminating prostitution and related vices went hand in hand with anxieties about fading Muslim identity and imperial prestige, fears over the destructive effects of the war on society constituted the precondition for rethinking the limits of the state intervention. In some cases, immorality in the forms of prostitution and trafficking in women was prosecuted on grounds of national security. Yet, surprisingly, it was not the wartime CUP government but the Ankara government and the Turkish republic that would realize the expected punitive measures in the name of protecting public morality, including the prohibition of alcohol in 1920 and of prostitution in 1930. Before presenting the detailed arguments of this study, I would like to present a conceptual and contextual framework to the reader.

The *Oxford Dictionary* defines morality as "principles concerning the distinction between right and wrong or good and bad behavior."[3] In Ottoman Turkish, the word for morality is the Arabic *ahlâk*, the plural form of *hulk* or *huluk*. Şemseddin Sami's famous dictionary *Kâmûs-i Türkî* defines *ahlâk* as a "spiritual and inner condition that humans possess either by creation or education."[4]

While keeping these basic definitions in mind, I avoid giving a strict definition of morality as well as an analysis of moral philosophy. This is for the sake of contextualization purposes. Instead of limiting the reader's perspective of morality with a strict definition, this study maintains a broad concept of morality that transcends the Hegelian distinction between ethics and morals. As a work of social and cultural history, anything described or referred to as morality or immorality in primary sources falls under the scope of our analysis. This does not mean that the study negates the importance of philosophical and sociological analysis; instead, it utilizes them to enhance the understanding of the works of Ottoman intellectuals, for sociological analyses have a distinctive place in the study of morality. Throughout this study, I consider morality to be a contested area in which several actors were involved encompassing both external and internal developments in the broader context of the war. These actors ranged from intellectuals to military men and from ordinary people to state elites.

In a similar vein, this study avoids presenting a single definition of "moral crisis." Instead, I argue that this concept is abstract in form yet understood when employed to define certain phenomena. Contrary to the common view that moral crisis is merely a consequence of increasing prostitution; this study offers a broad understanding of morality and a novel perspective that encompasses political, cultural, and social dynamics. Broadly speaking, the term "moral crisis" was often used to refer to degradation of social and moral values among the Ottoman Muslims, resulting in pursuing individual interests at the expense of common good. To my knowledge, no intellectuals of the time who were commenting on morality denied the existence of moral crisis. However, the definitions of that decline and the solutions for it varied. As the context of the First World War provides a deep insight into the points of debates, I attempt to limit certain preconditions of moral decline with the war context.

A glimpse at the history of the Ottoman Empire shows that morality discourses had a significant place in political and social life long before the nineteenth century. The *nasihatname*s (advice letters), for instance, exemplify the motives and context of moral discourse in the early modern Ottoman Empire. This literary genre, which appeared in the second half of the sixteenth century and continued up until the eighteenth century, sought to teach manners and advise statesmen on various issues. They were similar to European literary products such as Machiavelli's *The Prince*.[5] The authors of this genre employed a strict moral discourse with an emphasis on growing corruption and the degradation of moral and social life that accompanied a discourse on the decline of state power and the disruption of the world order (*nizâm-ı âlem*). Abou-El-Haj argues that the "moral polarization" between the virtuous and avaricious characters in these stories actually referred to political struggles among the ruling elites. *Nasihatname* writers such as Koçu Bey and Mustafa Ali manifested their discontent as they were losing political power to new social classes.[6] The *nasihatname*s and the rise of moralistic discourses were the products of a socioeconomic context in which great transformations and crises were emerging in terms of the land system, taxation, and the rise of commercialization.[7] In addition, gender relations were central to these moralistic discourses. This was clearly depicted in one of the most popular *nasihatname* of the sixteenth century, Kınalızade Ali Efendi's *Ahlâk-ı Alâî* (Supreme Morality). As discussed by Baki Tezcan, Kınalızade's work was based mainly on the "idea of equilibrium" among social "classes" and associated the continuation of the political order with the preservation of the patriarchal family, as the latter was essential for establishing the hierarchy among members of the household.[8] Equally important was the social hierarchy in expectations of high standards of morality from the elites.[9] In a similar vein, moral discourses that accompanied clothing laws in the eighteenth century emerged from the considerations of the ruling classes, hoping to preserve the social order on the basis of gender, class, and ethnic separation.[10] In this way, the Ottoman state institutionalized moral authority as a means of restoring order, particularly after crises that were followed by loss of territories.[11] Kırlı emphasizes the importance of the context of political crisis for the emergence of sumptuary laws targeting public spaces such as coffeehouses, taverns, and similar venues.[12]

Selim III's reform program, the New Order (*nizâm-ı cedid*), involved moral renewal in its agenda underlining moral laxity as a signifier of the need for reform in Ottoman society.[13] The first constitutional movement in the empire, the Young Ottomans, also utilized moral criticism in their opposition targeting the Tanzimat elite in the 1860s and 1870s. They held the Tanzimat bureaucrats responsible for the poverty of people with their use of state budget in a corrupt way.[14] The Young Ottomans successfully employed the new literary genre of the time, the novel, to juxtapose characters with regard to their moral qualities. The vicious protagonist was represented by a figure of snob (*züppe* in Turkish, while the terms *fop* or *dandy* are also used) as an upper-class character who appeared "Europeanized" only from outside, a "wannabe," who was completely estranged from his own society. He was depicted as an anomaly of excessive Westernization. On the other side, there was an exemplary character who appeared as an ideal person in society with a vision of informed Westernization finding equilibrium between the old and the new. The most famous example of this genre *Felâtun Bey ile Râkım Efendi* was written by the pioneering novelist Ahmed Midhat.[15]

The Young Ottomans' contribution to the moral discourse of their time also involved the debate over the reception of science.[16] A viewpoint that would survive up to now was put forward defending that the Muslims had to adopt the new knowledge, that is, science that was produced by Europeans, but they had to preserve Islamic moral values. The addition of Islamic emphasis in adopting scientific knowledge originated not only to utilize moralistic criticism toward the Tanzimat elite and to popularize the idea among the masses; this science and morality formulation was also developed as a shield to protect the social order against possible consequences of modernization that came to the surface with the social crises and revolts in all over Europe in the 1830s and 1848. Therefore, Yalçınkaya states, their solution was a synthesis of "a sufficient amount of properly understood new knowledge, coupled with an understanding of one's place that should not be challenged, that is, the combination of science and morality."[17]

When considered altogether, it is possible to argue that transitory periods had a significant role in the rise of moralistic discourses. However, each period must be evaluated in light of its own peculiarities. I believe that the point about late nineteenth-century polemics of moral crisis that distinguishes them from those of early modern discourse was their inclusivity. Owing partly to the development of the press, the rising literacy rate, and the wide circulation of the newspapers, particularly after the Young Turk Revolution of 1908, morality debates had become more polyphonic with the participation of new authors and audiences coming from different social backgrounds. The popularity of these debates also contributed to the changing nature of morality discourses from monologues to dialogues, particularly with the participation of women in the discussion. This implied that the monopoly over moral authority by the ruling elites and their entourages became vulnerable and open to challenge. The growing economic integration of the Ottoman Empire with European capitalism increased social and economic conflicts, and the consequences of this integration manifested itself in increasing cultural polarization too.[18] Particularly apparent in literary works, morality came to be identified with these problems, and it was translated into a common discourse of anxiety.[19] As shown in the following sections, the discourse of moral decline in Ottoman reformist circles also reflected intellectual debates about decadence, degeneration, and regeneration in late nineteenth- and early twentieth-century Europe.

Along with sumptuary laws and various measures, public education in the Ottoman Empire in the nineteenth century has become the subject of scholarly attention in terms of its emphasis on morality. Given that education was central to the Ottoman bureaucratic and military modernization process, Somel discusses the fact that public education during the Tanzimat and Hamidian eras was an instrument for inculcating modern notions such as order, discipline, and material progress together with the ideology of the Ottoman state and Sunnism in provincial areas.[20] According to him, until the 1860s, Ottoman educational reforms retained "the ancient tradition of viewing education as a means of inculcating religious and moral values," through which "obedience and loyalty" for the central authority were reproduced.[21] He asserts that, particularly during periods of political crises, children and adults were forced by the central authority to frequent mosques and attend Quranic schools.[22] On the other hand, morality textbooks such as *Ahlâk Risalesi* by Sadık Rıfat Pasha were representative of educational policy during the Tanzimat era and provided both religious and rational justifications for shaping ideal social norms.[23] During the Hamidian era, additional emphasis was put on moral and religious values in school curricula. Benjamin Fortna examines the gravity of "Islamic morality" in "secular" schools and argues against the "presumed split between 'religious' and 'secular'" while drawing attention to the combination of the traditional Islamic "underpinning that had been crucial to official Ottoman legitimation for centuries" and "the optimism engendered by the relatively new conception of education as worldly or profane science (*maarif*)."²⁴ Moral instruction in public education, according to him, was a general trend in the nineteenth century instead of being unique to the Ottoman or Hamidian cases.²⁵ Hamidian public schools thus sought to instrumentalize moral instruction to fight "foreign encroachment and internal moral decline."²⁶

Betül Açıkgöz, in her doctoral thesis on Ottoman school textbooks between 1908 and 1924, argues that moral instruction was central to public education even after the Hamidian era but in a different way: "In the Constitutional years, morality was needed not only to make God content and the other world secure, but also for the purpose of this world's rescue and happiness, which was prosperity and progress. The latter was overemphasized and prioritized the former."²⁷ During the Balkan Wars and the First World War, a "regeneration thesis" that argued that the loss of morality in the Ottoman Empire resulted in the loss of lands in the battles was also integrated into school textbooks.²⁸

An emphasis on gender roles and sexual norms constituted a major part of the moral crisis debates.²⁹ As a matter of fact, this is also peculiar neither to the nineteenth century nor to the First World War period. Başak Tuğ's study demonstrates that as a result of socioeconomic transformations in the late seventeenth and early eighteenth centuries and the rise of competition between central and provincial/local authorities, public and social order came under scrutiny of the Ottoman state in which sexual crimes, as an important indicator of disorder, constituted one of the major subjects of surveillance in early modern sense.³⁰ She argues that the themes of sexual order built a legal discourse on the notion of "protection of honor" through which a new relationship between the Ottoman state and its subjects was established in moral terms. Balsoy's study shows that female sexuality and morality were in the forefront of the state agenda even in the early nineteenth century as a result of population concerns of the Ottoman state.³¹ The economic, military, and political crises of the state were attributed to the population decline, as a result of which the pronatalist policies came to be applied, including abortion bans and legal and medical control of pregnancy and childbirth, since the 1840s. In this framework, female morality was under scrutiny as an important element to support these policies. Balsoy also draws our attention to another significant point in Ottoman pronatalism: it was concentrated only on the decline of its Muslim population. Accordingly, it was the Muslims whose population was in decline because of widespread abortion, and it was Muslims who had to serve in the army, while non-Muslims had higher population growth rates owing to the absence of these two unfavorable factors.³² This also explains largely why moral crisis was only concerned with Muslims in my study.

Elizabeth Thompson identifies a certain "crisis of paternity" in Syria and Lebanon to describe the "widespread gender anxiety" that emerged during and after the First World War to which French rule added another dimension.[33] Years of famine and war brought about the dissolution of traditional authority at home and in community.[34] As a matter of fact, the footsteps of this crisis can be observed in debates over "crisis of family" voiced by intellectuals and novelists of the 1910s and the decades that followed. As Zafer Toprak notes, the novels of these decades are particularly important for historiography because they fill the vacuum of what history books have excluded.[35] In this respect, Behar and Duben's study of Istanbul households evaluates late Ottoman and early Republican novels with specific emphasis on the "crisis of family." They reach out to the conclusion that the discourse of crisis increased during the war years and encompassed themes of moral decline, the clash of generations, and the lack of paternal authority.[36] This crisis also offered reformist intellectuals the opportunity to demand social change in line with the idea of creating a "national family."[37]

Some political and ideological developments in the aftermath of the 1908 Young Turk Revolution further politicized the concept of morality. The CUP government was challenged in the immediate aftermath of the constitutional revolution by the liberals (*Ahrar Fırkası*) that sought to decentralize the empire and the religious class—the *ulema*—that organized around the idea of "restoring the Islamic Law"—although the Sharia had not been abolished at all. In 1909, the opposition against the CUP turned into an armed movement, with bloodshed in the streets of the capital city and voicing of demands that Islamic principles (including prohibition of bars and theatres, the prohibition of photography, and imposing restrictions on the freedom of movement of women) be imposed along with some other political demands such as marginalization of some of the Unionists. The event, known as the Uprising of 31 March, left its mark on the collective memory of the late Ottoman Empire and the Early Turkish Republic as a counterrevolution. Moral crisis was central to the calls of Sheikh Vahdeti, the leader of the uprising: "The empire is collapsing; the foundation of this collapse is in the Western morality."[38] With the Uprising of 31 March, morality discourses gained a new political meaning.

The years following the event were characterized by bitter political struggle up until 1913. In 1913, the CUP took the power via a military coup known as *Bâb-ı Âli Baskını*. The CUP leadership aimed at establishing absolute authority in order to prevent further territorial loss after the outbreak of war in the Balkans. From then on, the Ottoman government was under the control of the committee. Amit

Bein calls this period as the period of "political marginalization of the ulema."[39] In this period, a discourse on the similarity between European clergy and the *ulema* accompanied radical steps to eliminate the jurisdiction of the şeyhülislam over sharia courts and remove his seat from the cabinet. The administration of religious endowments (*evkaf*) was transferred to the newly established Ministry of Religious Foundations (*Evkaf Nezareti*). Islamic schools (*medrese*) were brought under the authority of the Ministry of Education, and their curriculum was modernized.[40] Throughout the history of the Ottoman Empire, family law had remained a stronghold of the *ulema*. With the introduction of the new Family Decree of 1917, its religious tone notwithstanding, the *ulema* lost its monopoly over the formation and the dissolution of the marriages. Also, the *ulema* traditionally had the right to officially answer moral and ethical questions in the Ottoman Empire. Such moral judgments were not mere intellectual exercises; they constituted the basis of both religious and secular lawmaking.[41] In this respect, morality discourses had political implications. This explains how and why tensions regarding moral polarizations escalated so quickly and occupied such an important position in political conflicts. In addition, while the CUP eliminated the political power of the Ottoman *ulema* to an extent, it adopted a pragmatic approach to the relationship between politics and religion. The declaration of jihad as part of the war effort during the First World War clearly shows this. The committee's grand vizier was Said Halim Pasha, who was a declared political Islamist. Such paradoxical attitudes were the result of complex political relations and developments. At the end of the war, when the CUP lost power, Mustafa Sabri, the new şeyhülislam and an opponent of the CUP regime, dedicated his office "to revers[ing] the emasculation of the religious establishment and reassert[ing] the observance of traditional Islamic norms and practices in the public sphere."[42] He used the anti-CUP political atmosphere to revive the moral authority of the *ulema*. Through a "morality commission" established under the Islamic Academy (*Dar'ül-Hikmet'il-İslamiye*) in 1918, he prioritized the regulation of public morality by issuing official decrees and "guidelines" as well as the reporting of cases of violated morality to police and necessary institutions.[43] Such cases ranged from alcohol consumption to the violation of the fast during Ramadan, to immoral content in theater plays and the press, to disregard for gender segregation, and to women's attire and public appearance.

The terminology of moral crisis, indeed, speaks for itself. Several expressions were used to define this phenomenon in the works of Ottoman Muslim intellectuals: moral crisis (*ahlâk buhranı*), moral decay or decline (*ahlâkî çöküş*), social crisis (*ictimâî buhran*), movement of immorality (*ahlâksızlık ceryanı*), social ills (*ictimâî hastalık*). On the other hand, state documents referred to the phenomenon in a rather different way: acts against morality (*ahlâka mugâyir hareketler*), violation of public morality (*ahlâk-ı umûmîyeye hıyânet*), and breaking public morality (*ahlâk-ı umûmîyeyi iskât*). The point these expressions had in common was an emphasis on "acts" or "behaviors" that promoted decadence. In this respect, state documents treated immorality more concretely and approached it within the wider scope of protecting public order.

The Context: The Ottoman Empire in the First World War

The Ottoman state declared its mobilization on August 2, 1914, and entered into the war in late October on the side of the Central Powers—Germany and Austria-Hungary—against the Entente Powers—namely Britain, Russia, and France. At the time, the ruling party was the Committee of Union and Progress, the organization behind the victorious Constitutional Revolution that had overthrown the regime of Abdülhamid II in 1908. After the Tripoli War with Italy in 1911 and the subsequent outbreak of the Balkan Wars, the empire was on the verge of territorial dissolution. Faced with a difficult decision when European powers started to mobilize following the murder of the Austrian Archduke Ferdinand in June 1914, the Ottoman government hoped to restore its previous territorial losses with the help of the Central Powers by entering into the war. In Turkish historiography, the decision of the Ottomans to enter the war to side with Germany is discussed at great length with emphasis on the role of the "triumvirate," the three powerful men in the CUP: Enver, Talat and Cemal. In his book, Mustafa Aksakal presents a complex picture of the Ottoman Empire's entrance into the war that employs both internal and external dynamics.[44] In political circles of the empire, the war was an opportunity "to transform the empire into a politically and economically independent, modern country by removing foreign control and cultivating a citizenry that would be loyal to the state."[45]

Expecting to revive opposition in the Muslim colonies of France and Great Britain, as well as in the Muslim territories of Russia, and to establish a religion-based unity with Arabs and Kurds in the empire, the Ottoman government proclaimed jihad in November 1914. Hence, the war became "sacralized" both at home and abroad to legitimize and popularize the mobilization among the Muslim masses.[46] The declaration of jihad added to concerns about morality and strengthened moral discourse in both international and domestic debates regarding the legitimacy of the holy war. Acting in line with the Islamic principles and morality became a standard to test the legitimacy of an Ottoman-led jihad.

The Ottoman Empire succeeded on two fronts at the First World War: Kut al-Amara and Çanakkale (also known as Gallipoli or Dardanelles). The conquest of the Transcaucasian region in 1918 and the successful campaigns in Galicia and Romania in 1916–17 could be counted among the military achievements of the empire. Especially Çanakkale became the symbol of Ottoman resistance and blessed in public as a moment of national revival. However, on other fronts, significantly on the Caucasian front against Russian troops, the Ottoman counteroffensives resulted in disastrous defeats. The Arab Revolt in 1916 led by Sharif Huseyn in Mecca with the support of British forces as well as attacks by British troops in Palestine and Mesopotamia broke the Ottoman resistance. Furthermore, Ottoman soldiers were poorly equipped and suffered from starvation and diseases, including malaria, typhus, typhoid, syphilis, cholera, and dysentery.[47] Desertion was a significant problem caused by both harsh conditions on the battlefront and conditions on the home front that made Ottoman soldiers and their families vulnerable.[48] In October 1918, with the defeat of Bulgaria, the Central Powers lost their territorial connections. The Ottoman government immediately resigned and the new government started the process that resulted in the Armistice of Mudros on October 31, 1918.[49]

A significant amount of the scholarly work on the war points out that the home front inquiry is as important as the battlefield. The very concept of "total war" implies the central role of domestic mobilization. The Ottoman Empire was no exception in this regard. However, as detailed by Akın in his compelling account on the Ottoman home front, there were some significant dynamics on the Ottoman home front making the country's war experience unique with respect to other belligerent countries. These dynamics included: first, the empire's inadequate infrastructure that stood in the way to wage an advanced war; second, being less connected in terms of accessing global resources while fighting within the borders of the country; third, the cycle of war that the empire entered already before the First World War (the Balkan Wars being the most destructive bringing an influx of Muslim refugees); and last, the CUP's ambitions over redesigning the demography of the empire.[50]

When I told a philosopher friend of mine that I study morality in time of war, he laughed and asked me if there was morality in war. Among the main developments on the Ottoman home front, as genocide literature deals with in great length, first and foremost comes the destruction of Armenian community. On April 24, 1915, some 300 people among elites of Armenian community in Istanbul were arrested and deported, which was followed in May by mass deportations and killings en route to their final destination of Deir ez-Zor in today's Syria. Their properties were confiscated.[51] Many Armenian girls and women were kidnapped, forced into prostitution, taken to work in Muslim households, or absorbed in Muslim houses as wives.[52] Gender violence was an integral part of the destruction.[53] But the Muslim commentators of morality debates that I evaluate in this book did not deal with the "Armenian issue" as part of the moral crisis in the country. As Uğur Ümit Üngör states, "the war caused a moral lapse, if not collapse, for surviving Armenian women," yet the accounts of conservatives or others that I study did not mention Armenian prostitution, which emerged as a direct consequence of genocide. One reason to this could be the wartime censorship which did not allow any debate on this matter. Another reason could be that the "Armenian issue" as a whole was excluded from the moral world of the Muslims and they did not see a moral problem that could be evaluated as part of the moral crisis. Yet, in the aftermath of the war, there would be some voices bringing forward the debate. I discuss these at the end of this book.

As part of distributing the population in a way to make the country's demography homogenous to rule out any sovereignty claims, more than one-third of the Muslim population too (including the Balkan refugees, Arabs, Albanians, Bosnians, Kurds, Turcoman nomads, Lazes, etc.) was resettled throughout the war. Some Greeks were also settled from coastal towns to inner Anatolia under suspicion of possible collaboration with the Allies.[54] In Syria an exceptional military regime was applied under the command of military-governor Cemal Pasha. Although the official aim was to prepare an attack on Suez Canal and recapture Egypt from the British, it soon became clear with deportation and persecution of influential Arab leaders that his reign aimed also to break all foreign influence in Greater Syria and make the Arab *vilayet*s an integral part of the Ottoman Empire.[55] The blockage in the Mediterranean and lack of transportation means (and the use of existent ones only for the army) left important port cities such as Beirut deprived of all kinds of resources, eventually turning the situation in Mount Lebanon into famine claiming hundreds of thousands lives.[56]

Privations, hunger, poverty, compulsory labor, and the heavy taxation of agriculture and husbandry as well as the constant attacks of deserters and plunderers on villages defined the living conditions of the Ottoman people on the home front. The urban population was affected by economic privation due to the lack of access to transport. Istanbul was significantly affected by such privation with its reliance on imported goods. At the beginning of the war, the city met consumption needs with existing stock, but as the war went on, speculation, black marketeering, and rising inflation accompanied shortages. Eventually, a new class of war profiteers emerged from this scene.[57]

The concept of total war highlights the role of the state in total mobilization by which it gradually expanded its power, but the concept also refers to the reciprocal relationship between state power and society.[58] Also, the need for "mass participation" in the war increased the state's reliance on the people.[59] This point addresses the changing nature of the relationship between the state and society. Yiğit Akın explores this point in his work on soldiers' families by referring to the changing relationship between women and state authorities in the absence of male family members.[60] Through an analysis of women's petitions submitted to state authorities, he states that women "clearly displayed their awareness of the moral obligation that the state had towards soldiers' families, whom it promised to shield in the absence of their protectors."[61] In this study, I discuss this point with reference to morality and family with respect to protection of soldiers' family members from sexual assaults. In addition, I highlight the importance of polemics on social values in the formation and dissolution of families, which, in turn, constituted the reason for the promulgation of the Family Decree of 1917.

The Armistice of Mudros stipulated that the Allies could occupy any place in the empire in case of a security threat. Soon after that the occupations began. The occupation of Istanbul and some parts of Anatolia was marked by moral discourses that juxtaposed the occupiers and their collaborators with the national resistance movement in Anatolia. Together with occupation forces, the arrival of refugees from Russia who escaped the Russian Revolution brought about a change in the public sphere, entertainment, and leisure in Istanbul that for some contemporary observers—such as the famous neuropsychiatrist Dr. Mazhar Osman—resembled the Pompei of the Roman Empire.[62]

Between Progress and Decline: The Intellectual Context of Discourses of Moral Crisis in the Late Nineteenth and Early Twentieth Centuries

The "sense of decadence" has a long past, dating back to the political thought of ancient Greek and Roman civilizations, but at that time, the discourse was part of a cyclical understanding of history that presupposed that "what goes up also come down."⁶³ Koenraad argues that the decline of the Roman Empire particularly influenced European thought to the extent of obsession "in the hope of finding an answer to the question of how their own society could escape a similar fate."⁶⁴ Moral decay in a society attracts intellectual and political interest as it was believed that such a decline in virtue constituted the major reason behind the decline of the Roman civilization. This thought is well expressed in Cicero's famous exclamation "O tempora, O mores!" by which he referred to corruption of his age.⁶⁵

The idea of decadence prevailed in the medieval ages, as well; however, it was not perceived as integral to a natural course of events in which things "go up and down." Rather, it was part of a "divine scheme preceding the ultimate salvation of the elect."⁶⁶ With the Renaissance, this gloomy understanding of history began to transform into an optimistic approach to future.⁶⁷ Although complaints about the current state of affairs continued in later periods, what made the nineteenth century unique was the insistence on the inevitable victory of progress despite the intrusion of decadence. Moreover, decadence was treated as a necessary step; the old system had to diminish to open up space for the "birth of a new superior phase of civilization."⁶⁸ At this point, we should also take into account nineteenth-century discourses of "degeneration" which also applied to morality. Initially coined in psychiatry to define a deteriorated mental condition, the term *dégénérescence* had a powerful appeal in the natural sciences, particularly with reference to the theory of evolution.⁶⁹ Darwin's followers expanded the theory of evolution to cultural and social realms in search of affirmation of progress in human populations from a scientific point of view. In the context of the nineteenth century, such views became popular, and references to physical and moral degeneration led to infamous biological determinisms and eugenics.⁷⁰ Daniel Pick notes that by combining the ideas of evolution and progress, the language of degeneration in the nineteenth century had a different connotation from that of early sentiments that insisted on "the notion, or at least the question, of things getting worse": the language of degeneration "moves from its place as occasional sub-current of wider philosophies and political or economic theories, or homilies about the horrors of the French and the Industrial Revolutions, to become the center of a scientific and medical investigation."⁷¹ However, it needs to be underscored that the term "degeneration" was used not only to characterize racial differences but also to identify internal dangers and crises within Europe involving moral decadence in terms of crime, alcoholism, prostitution, and suicide.⁷² Paradoxically, these so-called social pathologies emerged from rapid urbanization and industrialization as a consequence of "progress." Finding the "pathologies" to remove obstacles to progress came to be regarded as the scientific solution for degeneration. Degeneration and progress developed dialectically in a way that "civilization, science and economic progress might be the catalyst of, as much as the defense against, physical and social pathology."[73] Koenraad also draws attention to how paradoxical concepts—progress and decadence—combine: "It is, for example, not at all illogical to be convinced that in certain fields like religion or morality serious decline has taken place and yet to believe at the same time that in other areas like science and art great progress has been achieved."[74]

The language of degeneration is strongly connected to tensions and constant conflicts in the society that emerged in the course of the nineteenth century. The case of France is representative and important given the vast influence of French scholars on Ottoman intellectuals. Late nineteenth-century French republicans were inspired by the ideas and methods of Auguste Comte's positivism and anticipated the triumph of progress over religion: "Thus, a lay Republic that sought to replace religion with a 'scientific' morality, while preserving the 'natural' structures of the social order, could be regarded as a progressive force in history."[75] Auguste Comte, the leading figure of sociology and positivism, condemned the French Revolution in his search for social order, authority, and an organization to facilitate progress.[76] Emile Durkheim studied the years of tension between the revolution and the counter-revolution during the Third Republic.[77] Durkheim developed his theories as a means of overcoming political and social disintegration in French society and sought the means of "national regeneration."[78] In this respect, morality and moral values were important for reinforcing the ties among individuals that would eventually lead to the "division of labor" and harmonious social life.[79] This point, indeed, is crucial for understanding the approach of Ottoman Turkish intellectuals who regarded science as an ultimate guide and sociology as the queen of the sciences with respect to coping with the problems of moral decline and establishing a new understanding of morality.[80]

Interestingly, fin-de-siècle discourses on "decadence" together with the decadent movement in literature had lost its influence in France by the eve of the First World War. "A new state of mind" emerged among a new generation "who became known for their realistic attitude toward life, their interest in action and sport, and their antipathy to excessive speculation and self-analysis."[81] The war was welcomed as a step toward further regeneration.[82] Ottoman intellectuals such as Ziya Gökalp guided by the sociological insights summarized above continued to believe that Ottoman Muslim society was experiencing the same sense of crisis, though in a belated fashion. Like the French case, they argue that the crisis was a sign of progress and a signifier of an upcoming national regeneration. On the other hand, a divine understanding of moral decay continued to dominate religious circles intermingled with contests over moral, political, and social authority. While discourses on "decadence" corresponded with discourses on moral decline in the late Ottoman context, "degeneration" had more to do with early republican eugenics, another—albeit more biological and medicalized—approach to morality.[83] Yücel Yanıkdağ's analysis of the concept of degeneration among Turkish neuropsychiatrists demonstrates that Turkish neuropsychiatrists such as Mazhar Osman, Fahrettin Kerim, and İzzettin Şadan approached the First World War as a watershed moment that revealed inherited pathological conditions among prisoners of war, including the mental disorders.[84] In this sense, their medical claims served the ideals of reviving the nation by equating the health of the nation with the health of individuals.

The First World War brought about profound changes in the social, cultural, and political realms that had a long-lasting impact on intellectuals and public opinion. During the war, more than 8 million men lost their lives on the battlefield.[85] The number of civilians killed during the war may have been even greater given that they were exposed to systematic violence by enemy countries through sieges, deportations, forced labor, mass executions, and bombardments targeting civilians.[86] Civilians were also targeted by their own governments and exposed to similar violence, including massacres such as that of the Armenian population living in the Ottoman Empire.

"For communities at war, military casualties predominate. The fundamental reality is loss of life and limb. All other considerations are secondary," wrote Adrian Gregory, drawing attention to the moral power of sacrifice evoked in the new ideals in society: "The needs of 'total war' subverted the dominant idea of political economy, the idea that the common good was served by the pursuit of self-interest. In its place it resurrected new forms of older ideals, those of Christian martyrdom and 'republican' civic humanism in which self-interest was contrasted to the common good."[87] On the home front, hunger and famine overshadowed other concerns, adding to the moralization of everyday life. "Moral judgment" worked well to distinguish between "profiteers and the nation at war" and reinforced senses of collective solidarity and the common good.[88]

On the other hand, significant loss of young men during the war put great pressure on the traditional family given the high number of widows and orphans left behind. Those men who returned home were "destroyed" by the physical and mental effects of the war. Many of them committed suicide; some found solace in alcohol or, as Mazower wrote, "tried to reassert their authority by beating their wives and children."[89] "A newly fatherless community" had emerged, further provoking the sense of moral and social disorder.[90] At the end of the war, the rate of population decline triggered governments to increase not only the quantity but also the quality of their nations' populations.[91] For contemporary observers, the war broadened the reach of the idea of degeneration from psychiatry to different contexts.[92] In this context, family and family values—with a strong emphasis on motherhood—came to be more central to interwar European politics and ideology than before.[93]

Plan of the Study

The study explores discourses of public morality and moral crisis at four interrelated levels. The first is the intellectual level and focuses on polemics of moral decline among Ottoman Muslim intellectuals in juxtaposition with each other. Considering morality as a contested space among the conflicting ideologies of the period, I examine journals that represent these ideologies, namely the Journal of Islam (*İslam Mecmuası*), New Journal (*Yeni Mecmua*), and Straight Road (*Sebilürreşad*). Through the analysis of several articles on morality, I aim to show that morality played a vital role in ideological conflicts of the time. Although reflecting on this conflict through the labels such as "political Islamist" or "Turkish nationalists" sounds problematic due to many thin lines separating the two, I still find it useful in the analysis of moral viewpoints. Here, I use the labels of "nationalist" or "nationalist reformist" to indicate intellectual circles who wanted Islam to be adjusted to the needs of society, and of "political Islamists" for those who wanted society to be adjusted to the rules of Islam.[94]

Following the intellectual debates on morality, I turn my interest to the second level: political regulations and their limits regarding the protection of morality. In this regard, two dimensions of the Ottoman home front call for careful analysis: the abolition of the capitulations and the expansion of military power due to the extension of martial law. Only after the unilateral abolition of the capitulations at the outbreak of the war was the Ottoman government finally able to control brothels and take action to prevent the "trafficking in women" by foreign citizens in the empire. The proclamation of martial law expanded the power of the military to undertake measures to ensure public morality. Based on archival research conducted in the Prime Ministry Ottoman Archives (Başbakanlık Osmanlı Arşivleri, BOA), this chapter reveals the deportation and banishment of those engaged in prostitution. Their cases were considered an issue of national security during the mobilization. The citizens of the Allied countries who engaged in sex work fell under the status of "enemy alien," and they applied for Ottoman citizenship to avoid the consequences of this status. All citizenship applicants were subject to an investigation also with respect to their moral backgrounds, and many were declined due to immorality fames. Such wartime measures enabled the dismissal of "undesirable" elements in the society and also became a tool in presenting Ottoman citizenship as an honorary title to be "deserved" by the applicant. The fact that none of these applicants obtained citizenship shows how moral judgment and national security concern intersected.

Obviously, the Ottoman government's motivation for eliminating prostitution in certain areas concerned the spread of venereal disease. As discussed in this chapter, this was also the case in many belligerent countries in the First World War. I consider prostitution as one of the realms through which one can observe the cultural rivalry that intensified over the course of the war. For many contemporary writers, prostitution was not the reason for moral decline but rather the result of it.

For state authorities, the violation of public morality was a part of the concern for public order. Despite heated debates that even involved state elites, the Ottoman government kept the definition of public morality offenses under the discretionary authority of the courts and never attempted to define the limits of violations of public morality.

In daily life, the protecting public morality had broader implications than counteracting prostitution. Therefore, I reserved a chapter on the sumptuary laws, war profiteering, regulation of entertainment venues and conspicuous consumption, and official approaches to alcohol and gambling. By juxtaposing the popular perceptions of immorality and political measures, I argue that the Ottoman government's pragmatic approach toward "vices" intensified during the war. This was partly due to limitations on the state power that accompanied financial concerns, as such "vices" constituted a good amount of the state's budget.

In the final chapter, I focus on the Ottoman Muslim families and dynamics in provincial areas that contributed to the involvement of the state in the family vis-à-vis morality. I examine rape, sexual assault, and adultery cases that involved soldiers' families. Throughout the war, soldiers, the women of their families, and locals such as village elders and military officers continuously sent complaints to the Ministry of War, the Ministry of Interior Affairs, and in some cases to provincial authorities or the Ottoman parliament. I consider these petitions as instruments calling state authorities to take measures to prevent rapes, abductions, assaults, and threats. I argue that moral concerns lay behind the attempts at legislation regarding the protection of families. Hitherto in the historiography, these laws are examined separately. Moreover, researchers often suppose that the motivation of the state for penetrating the family was as a means of modernization. However, a close look at individual cases shows that given the circumstances of war, state involvement in the family showed a reciprocal character. In line with the previously discussed point on the changing relationship between the state and society, I argue that state intervention not only stemmed from the keen interest of the state or military alone but was also shaped by demand from below in cases concerning honor.

Although statistics of morality-related crimes are not available, the frequency of attempts to legislate them along with the immense interest of Ottoman intellectuals shows that crimes violating morality resulted in the questioning of existing social norms and moral values in society. The willingness of state authorities to regulate family formation and dissolution and intellectual concerns about the moral codes of society are interrelated. The ruling elite as well as ordinary people were thereby convinced that it should no longer be taboo to regulate the family realm. As the focus of these regulations was "protecting the honor of the soldiers," social unrest caused by sexual assaults contributed to these regulations. The sexual assaults, rapes, and abductions targeting soldiers' relatives not only contributed to concerns about morality but also contradicted official war propaganda regarding the protection of women in soldiers' families. In the long run, state intervention paved the way for more radical but legitimate steps to be taken. I evaluate the topic together with debates on social reform that were based on the degeneration of Muslim families. When advocates of family reform questioned the degeneration of Muslim families, they ended up struggling with existing moral values. Can legislation change the norms in society? Apparently, Ottoman intellectuals and reformers believed so and introduced legislation as a means of introducing new family values. The advocates of family reform linked the well-being of adolescents, women, and men to those of the nation, legitimizing the need for reform.

Finally, the scope of the study is limited to the First World War and mostly to the Muslim community of the empire other than cases of foreign prostitutes and topics such as intercommunal prejudices that played a role in moral labels. The reasons for the choice of wartime are various. First of all, the period of the First World War brought about an urgency to discussions of social problems in Ottoman society. For moral decline polemicists, the war served as a laboratory in which to ground their theories on the destructive effects of immorality. The war exacerbated a sense of anxiety both about diminishing traditional values and about the so-called corruptive new adaptations. There was also a dilemma that came to the surface during the war: while the Ottomans were at war with the Entente Powers, they admired the progress and advancement of those enemy countries. The influence of yet another country, Germany, was growing in the Ottoman Empire. As a result, fears about the growing influence of European culture and the loss of authentic Muslim identity solidified. Second, particular political and ideological developments such as the rise of Turkish nationalism added to these tensions. It was the nationalist challenge to traditional Islamic thought that triggered the heated debate on morality when Ziya Gökalp invented the concept of "national morality" and theorized a "new life" for Ottoman Turks. Third, and related to the second, was the declaration of jihad during the war that made the Ottoman Empire more vulnerable to critiques, targeting lifestyles within the empire that were "incompatible" with Islam. In this framework, morality was of broad and intense interest in discussions of the legitimacy of the caliphate. The sensitiveness of the political situation increased with defeat at the end of the war. Finally, as the war progressed, social problems became even more visible and this caused a gradual increase in the morality discourse. Female sexuality, as a central topic to moral order, fell under further scrutiny at a time when Muslim women's participation in social and economic life increased while prostitution spread widely due to harsh economic conditions. The state's interest in moral order was also a consequence of concerns over deteriorating public order, a vital issue for an empire that relied heavily on its human power, a phenomenon which eventually would break the ties between the government and society.

Sources of the Study

Besides the current literature on the First World War, this study is based mainly on documents in the Prime Ministry Ottoman Archives in Istanbul and on periodicals and newspapers that were published during the period in question. Especially Chapters 3, 4, and 5 rely on archival sources. Among the catalogues in the archives, I benefited from the documents of the Ministry of Interior Affairs (*Dahiliye Nezareti*) which include files belonging to the Interior Administration (*İdare-i Umumiye*) and the Police Department (*Emniyet-i Umumiye*). I could only benefit from the First World War collection in the Archives of Turkish General Staff (ATASE) in a limited way. Besides the archival documents of state officials, I examined letters and petitions from people banished from martial law areas to central Anatolia in order to better present the lives of people who carried the stigma of immorality. Given that petitions are among the very few sources in social history that present the voices of ordinary people, I consider the letters from soldiers and the women in their families to various state departments as primary sources that reveal how moral anxieties played a role in state intervention in the family. In addition, such letters indicate the bilateral nature of this intervention. The stories in these documents also expose the wartime circumstances on the home front that contributed decisively to social and political transformation in the empire. Along with archival documents, the newspaper articles and the minutes of the Ottoman parliament cited in this study help to frame the morality discussion. Articles from various journals that represent the views of the Ottoman intelligentsia offer details on how morality became contested in the turmoil of the war. The term "morality" was itself a battlefield.

2

The Intellectual Contest over Morality, and Interpretations of Moral Crisis: Secular versus Religious Morality

> [T]he ones who are responsible from the persistence of today's moral crisis are firstly those scholars who do not elaborate and write on the new morality, and secondly the conservative forces who insist on the imposition of the old morality.
>
> –Ziya Gökalp, *Ahlâk Buhranı*

Moral crisis was a highly debated topic among the Ottoman intelligentsia within the context of the First World War. Despite the difficulty of contextualizing a relatively abstract topic such as morality—or more precisely, immorality—the following pages attempt, in various ways, to assess the implications of discourses of moral decline with regard to wartime conditions and to investigate the reasons for the preoccupation with morality during the period in question. In this study, I consider morality as a contested space; therefore, representative, competing ideological perspectives from the Ottoman political spectrum are chosen to grasp a better understanding of this contest. The journals evaluated here put forward polemics of moral crisis and morality with several volumes and articles in their pages. These journals are, namely, *İslam Mecmuası* (Journal of Islam), *Sebilürreşad* (Straight road), and *Yeni Mecmua* (New journal).[1]

Intellectual discussions about moral decline show us how morality was politicized in the context of the war. The rise of materialism, the declaration of jihad, ideological contests over political and public space, critiques of previous reform movements in the empire, the search for a new life, the war-induced social problem of profiteering, and women's participation in social and economic life constituted the major topics of polemics of moral decline. Moral decline debates offered several prominent intellectual figures an opportunity to discuss and question extant daily and social practices in their quest for social reform and a new spirit to revive the empire from within. What is more interesting is the fact that morality in traditional sense was once an obstacle to progress; then it became an ideal starting point to discuss the future of the empire like a Trojan horse to penetrate in its previously untouched institutions. The First World War, on the other hand, constituted the setting for testing out the contesting ideologies over morality in Muslim society.

İslam Mecmuası: A Theological Perspective on the "New Morality"

The Islamic reformists publishing *İslam Mecmuası* were mostly Turkish nationalists including ones who had emigrated from Russia. They sought new interpretations of religion to create new possibilities for the revival of Muslim society. The chief editor of the journal was Halim Sabit, a Turkic émigré from Russia. He published *İslam Mecmuası* from February 1914 to October 1918, in the very years of the First World War. Without the benefit of hindsight, one may find it odd publishing a theological journal during the war years. However, a closer look provides a better understanding of this choice. As the Turkish nationalist ideology was consolidating its power, this group sought to clarify their perspectives on religion. This was also important for war propaganda, in part due to the agenda of jihad. Masami Arai, a prominent author who studied nationalist journals of the Young Turks, argues that since nationalists believed their relation to Islam was not sufficiently set out in other journals such as *Türk Yurdu* (Turkish homeland), they founded *İslam Mecmuası* to voice their views on religion.[2]

The issue of "finding true Islam" was at the core of the themes with which authors in *İslam Mecmuası* had dealt.[3] The names appeared as authors in this journal will sound familiar to scholars of late Ottoman intellectual history: M. Şerefettin (Yaltkaya), Mansurizade Said, M. Şemseddin (Günaltay), Ziya Gökalp, Mahmud Esad, Musa Kazım, Ahmet Agayef (Ağaoğlu), Musa Carullah, Rızaeddin Fahreddin, Abdürreşid İbrahim, Bereketzade İsmail Hakkı, Ispartalı Hakkı, Besim (Atalay), Bursalı Mehmed Tahir, Köprülüzade Mehmed Fuad, Aka Gündüz, and Ömer Seyfeddin. As Arai puts it, the writers for *İslam Mecmuası* "had one characteristic in common: They obtained a modern school education alongside a traditional one; they could thereby see into Islam and its conditions in an informed way."[4] They searched for the reasons for the decline of the Muslim world and agreed that while Islam itself was not a barrier to progress, superstition was.⁵ Accordingly, Islam could be progressive if "foreign" elements falsely regarded as religious rules could be eliminated. Therefore, they pioneered the translation of Quran into Turkish and promoted the delivery of sermons (*hutbe*) in Turkish. The fields with which the writers dealt varied from jurisprudence (*fıkıh*) to sociology (*ictimâîyyat*) and from history to literature. The final pages of the journal were reserved for news from the Muslim world and jihad.

The journal sparked significant discussions on four topics: polygyny, nationalism in Islam, the sociology of Islamic Jurisprudence (*İctimâî Usûl-ü Fıkıh*), and the delivery of sermons in Turkish (*Türkçe hutbe*). These topics became heated discussions when writers for *Sebilürreşad* harshly criticized nationalist and reformist interpretations of Islam. For instance, İsmail Hakkı wrote seven articles to refute Gökalp's arguments on the vast place of mores (*örf*) in Islamic Law and on the reinterpretation of jurisprudence under the heading of *İctimai Usul-ü Fıkıh*.⁶ Some of these debates, such as the one on the place of nationalism in religion, provoked such heated discussions that the government intervened to silence both sides.⁷ Broadly speaking, the conflict between the Islamists in *Sebilürreşad* and the nationalists in *İslam Mecmuası* was exacerbated by the question of the source of law since the nationalists were attempting to open up space for reform in religious thought.⁸ By attaching importance to mores (*örf*) and national culture (*hars*) and claiming that there is a distinction between culture and civilization, the nationalists interpreted religion and Islamic law anew. Through these interpretations, they touched upon the realms that were previously dominated by traditional *ulema*, such as family formation and dissolution, social conduct in everyday life, religious education, and religious practice.

On the issue of morality, *İslam Mecmuası* published a column titled "*Ahlâk*" (Morality), which accounted for 14 of the total of 362 articles published over its four years.⁹ However, many other articles—for instance, ones in the columns "*Jurisprudence*" and "*Sociology*"—also dealt with the issue of morality. Besim Atalay (1882–1965), a teacher and director of several schools of education, was the primary commentator on morality.¹⁰ Other writers who wrote on morality in *İslam Mecmuası* included Ziya Gökalp, Halim Sabit, and Kazım Nami (Duru). Much has been written on Gökalp and his social and political thought in the formation of Turkish nationalism and secularism.¹¹ While his views on religion, culture, nation, Turkism, and Turkish history are among the most studied topics in Ottoman/Turkish historiography, his understanding of morality has remained less explored so far. Zafer Toprak touches upon Gökalp's views on morality in his works on the emergence of sociological thought in late Ottoman Era. Taha

Parla's work also offers an analysis of Gökalp's understanding of morality. However, he focuses more on political modeling and the system of thought (corporatism and solidarism) in Gökalp rather than the context and contest (with other writers and ideas of the time) that Gökalp's ideas about morality were based on.[12] Throughout this chapter, I focus on Gökalp's attempt to create a "national morality" and contextualize what this prominent figure of the time meant by moral degeneration as well as how he responded to conservative arguments on morality. Generally, his articles on morality were published in *Yeni Mecmua*; however, he wrote several articles that also touched on morality in *İslam Mecmuası*. Another author, Kazım Nami is famous for the volumes containing his memoirs which he published in the 1950s.[13] He was a pedagogue and his articles were on upbringing and pedagogy rather than morality. In 1925, he published a book for teachers on moral education in schools.[14]

With respect to morality discourses, the importance of *İslam Mecmuası* stems from its theological approach. Instead of looking for arguments completely opposed to Islamist thinking, my aim is to see whether a different approach to morality was possible within the theological framework, and if so, how? What was the place of morality at the intersection of nationalist and religious thought? Indeed, the themes, questions, and views that were elaborated upon under the heading of morality in *İslam Mecmuası* had points in common. The idea of rejecting European morality was shared by *İslam Mecmuası*'s writers who emphasize the superiority of Islam over Christianity and Judaism with respect to moral thought. They shared the viewpoint of Islamists on the destructive effects of modernist reforms during the Tanzimat era and of Westernist thought on Ottoman Muslim society.[15] They claimed that Tanzimat reforms brought about an obscure ideology of Europeanization and it created a generation that sought the reasons for decline in Islam. Referring to the emergence of Islam and the times of the prophet Mohammed, the authors attempted to revive the moral purity of Islam and to apply it to contemporary Muslim society. For Islamic reformists, the problems of false traditions and superstitions resulted in the degeneration of religion and moral values in society. For them, the Ottomans remained backward because of superstition. They argued that contrary to the emphasis on morality discernible in theological works, morality was never considered as important as other religious practices in Islam.

As a distinctive point, the authors in *İslam Mecmuası* attempted to combine religious views on morality with nationalism in order to create a new understanding of morality based on the duty of individuals to their nation. In line with the catchphrase of the journal—"lively religion"—they tried to make Islam useful in society. Contrary to the argument that morality sets individuals' responsibility to God, they emphasized the social aspect of morality. In this framework, morality became a matter of national survival; its decline brought about the decline of the nation. Morality is collective, and the fact that all the calamities were the result of moral degeneration only confirms this argument.

The authors of the journal considered morality to be central point for the construction of a new understanding of good and bad to be pursued in the daily lives of Ottoman Muslims. For them, morality was a point of departure for discussing conflicts between the necessities of modern times and the old doctrines of tradition and religion. Questioning the limits of Islamic Law was their ideological strength, and morality was a great weapon to control this debate. The Turkish nationalist formulation of the modernization of the Ottoman Empire—"adopting the technology of the West but not the Western morality"—served for the purpose of avoiding being associated with "imitators of the West." Here, for the sake of analysis, first I begin with what the old morality meant for the authors and how they criticized it. We should note that old morality mostly referred to doctrines of religion but was not limited to them. The concept also referred to the principles of the Tanzimat era, which nationalists resented because of its European-oriented character. Second, I compare the concept of a new morality to the old, presenting their views on contemporary morality in order to assess their definition of the moral crisis. *İslam Mecmuası* was a theoretical journal that set out the ideas of Turkish nationalists on Islam and made theological interpretations of Islam in line with the nationalist principles. Therefore, it would be misguided to expect many references to day-to-day events or practical issues. Instead, such references were abundant in *Yeni Mecmua*.

Eventually, I demonstrate how the discourse of morality crisis was used and manipulated by the authors for the purposes of advocating reform to the religious mentality. The nationalists embraced the concept of a moral crisis—which was frequently claimed by political Islamists to emphasize the troubling consequences of modernization—and took it in the opposite direction in critique of conservatives. It is possible to summarize this view as a theological approach that claimed the moral sphere, but this time to use morality in the service of profane affairs.

As mentioned earlier, Ahmed Besim Atalay was among the prominent figures writing on the relationship between religion and morality. Although his writings remained within the theological framework, he developed an alternative understanding of morality to the understanding that he called "old morality."

The old morality was originated from a mixture of several sources. Ahmed Besim, in his article "Morality and Religion," argued that up to then all the moralists in the Muslim world adopted the morals in the ancient Greek and Indian philosophy.[16] He said Muslim scholars reproduced this "archaic perspective" in their so-called Islamic and religious works.[17] He divided Muslim society into three according to their perspectives on morality: The philosophers constituted the first group in Muslim society that adopted the ancient Greek and Indian morality. This group consisted of prominent figures in Islamic scholarship including İbn-i Rüşd, Farabi, İbn-i Sina, or Nasiruddin Tûsî. The second group consisted of *sufi*s who appreciated spiritualism and discovered the virtues of high morality. However, they represented only a small group, and despite some original views that they derived from Islam, they too were inspired by a foreign philosopher, Pythagoras. The third group was the common people (*avam*), and their understanding of morality did not rely on rational thought, experimentation, or self-improvement. Their understanding of morality relied only on certain false traditions (*eğri doğru birtakım görenekler*) and teachings (*telkînat*); hence, it is impossible to assess the morality of the masses and identify the sources feeding their moral judgments.

He argued that the morality understandings of the first two groups were under "foreign influence," primarily that of Greek and Indian philosophy.[18] Therefore, he claimed that Muslims never developed an independent thought on morality; on the contrary, among the three principles of Islam (*ahkâm-ı İslamiyye*) Muslims neglected conscience and social principles (*vicdâni* and *ictimâî*) and corrupted jurisprudence and theology (*fıkıh* and *kelâm*) by simply turning their communities into "praying machines" and spreading relativity and materialism among them.[19] Consequently, Islamic scholars did not develop an authentic Islamic morality. According to him, by defining morality as "habitual" practices that need no further consideration (*nefs-i nâtıkanın bir melekesi*), Islamic scholars made the mistake of removing "reason" and "cogitation" behind human action.[20] These scholars' wrong interpretations on religious morality and the conspiracies of immoral clerics brought about most calamities in both the Orient and the Occident.[21] Ahmed Besim, quoting from Rousseau and Gustave Le Bon, wrote that such "scholarship" based on poor interpretations did not advance humanity.[22] Ahmed Besim used Islamist claims—such as "being moral is superior than to making scientific discoveries" or "without morality, knowledge is useless"—and turned their arguments upside down. His formulation was that "religious scholars or clergy (*ulemâ*) are useless without morality."

As a defender of "true Islam," Besim argued that upright morals constitute the foundations of Islam. For him, the hadith (the advice of the Prophet Mohammed) of Prophet Mohammed, "I was only sent to perfect moral character," summarizes the essence of religion. Islam gained power thanks to its emphasis on high moral standards that prioritize virtues. He referred to the importance of the historical context when Islam was initially spread. The Roman Empire was on the verge of destruction due to the moral failure of the Romans. In contrast, Islam announced morals as fundamental to human life and thus gained popularity among those who resented the corruption in the Roman Empire. Islamic principles were based on the fact that morality is the only difference between a human and an animal.[23] For him, it was this emphasis on morality that had given rise to the advancement of Islam.

İslam Mecmuası had a mission to redefine ideals of morality according to the needs of modern times. First of all, the new morality had to serve collective (ictimâî) benefits, not individual ones. Ahmed Besim defined the rituals and practices in Islam (such as prayers and fasting) as part of a "habitual" understanding of morality. He condemned those "who feel sorrow if they wash their nose with their left hand [by mistake] during ablution but feel nothing when destroying the lives of orphans' or accepting bribes."[24] "Evil behavior harms everyone, " he claimed, "if we search for the sources of calamities that human beings—especially Turks—have experienced, we find that they were the moral corruption of some people who acted inconsiderately and did not even deem their acts to be petty sins."[25] Claiming that the basic reason for religious practice was to remind people of their moral duty, he frequently quoted the Quran and hadith to support the idea.[26] Ahmed Besim argued that adhering to high moral standards is more important (and useful) than religious practices such as praying: "God will forgive us if we do not perform physical practices of religion, and such sins do not harm social order (ictimâîyyat). However, if we do not fulfill our moral duties, we disregard both the rights of God and the rights of his vassals."[27] He criticized the current understanding of "religious practice" which, according to him, was only limited to "bodily" activities. Instead, he claimed there is another "spiritual" way of religious practice—namely, being moral.[28]

As morality is a spiritual religious practice, it serves both the purposes of being religiously upright and the welfare of society. In fact, the new morality focused on society and collectivity rather than individual and self. In İslam Mecmuası, "saving the nation" was central to the effort to formulate a new morality. Ahlâk had to have a reason (gaye). Ahmed Besim was convinced that "nations that had survived so far absolutely possessed a solid moral and spiritual foundation."[29]

He considered morality to be a precondition for "progress" and "civilization," because it was not law that prevented (or encouraged) people to behave correctly but morality.[30] He insisted that the decline of the nations, especially Muslim nations, was due to the adoption of the ancient morals of defeated nations.[31] The rise of the Roman Empire, he argued, was a result of the Romans' moral strength symbolized by resignation of the senate to return to farm.[32] For him, an upright morality was similar to military training that encourages people to resist bullets.[33] All physical religious practices, in his opinion, should serve the needs of society. Fasting, for instance, produces empathy with the poor. Therefore, one should think the social benefits of religion while performing religious duties.[34] Ahmed Besim and a few other writers commented on the question of whether morality changes over time. As making social values compatible with the modern age, space (*mekân*), and community was their ultimate goal, the reformists in *İslam Mecmuası* agreed that morality changes over time. Or to put it more precisely, they argued that morality had to change and indeed, this was the genesis of the idea of social revolution (*ictimâî inkılab*).

In the first issue of *İslam Mecmuası*, Muallim Vahyi (Ölmez) wrote an article titled "Muslim Morality."[35] Instead of engaging in a theoretical discussion, he briefly summarized how Muslims should behave in order to be morally upright. He posited four conditions for ideal Muslim morality: "strength [of the body], wisdom, diligence, and fairness."[36] He emphasized how important it is for Muslims to accumulate capital, become involved in trade, and increase their wealth as these were among the good deeds. He recommended Muslims to find practical solutions in every sphere of work, use machine power, make scientific discoveries, and be good at their jobs. He formulated new Muslim morality as such: "the heart of a Muslim beats with God while his hand works continuously."[37] One may find his advice generic; however, it is possible to read his statements as expressions reflecting the drawbacks to progress in Muslim society. He summarized these drawbacks in contemporaneous morality as: "seeing the world's despair, being hopeless, [and] falling into idleness."[38] Most probably, this pessimistic description was related to the war and psychological atmosphere of the wartime. Ahmed Besim also mentioned a pessimistic attitude among Muslims in the Ottoman Empire and he advised Muslims to turn their faces toward the future not the past.[39]

An interesting point that deserves attention in the writings of "reformists moralists" is their emphasis on happiness (*saadet*). In almost all the articles, references to happiness accompany the discourse of "progress"; it is the ultimate goal reached by means of ideal morality. Being happy was used as a contrast to pessimism and asceticism. Ahmed Besim argued that despite the firmness of Islamic morality, it is also capable of rendering happiness to humanity.[40] Being Muslim, accordingly, is to be happy through self-purification. On this point, he combined his efforts of changing moral rules with achieving happiness: "We Turks were not able to generate a solid social life because initially we imitated the Persians and then the Europeans. Our morality should stem from our religion, law, customs, and contemporary mores so that it will appeal to our souls and minds and make us happy."[41] He formulated this ideal morality as a key to happiness as well as to progress: "In short, it is a morality that meets the necessities of [modern] times yet is grounded in national mores that will make human beings happy."[42] This led him to the topic of upbringing (*terbiye*) through which the new generation would gain a new understanding of morality. Once future generations received a proper education on religious morality (in line with his interpretation), "finally, real happiness will be manifested in this destitute country."[43] This brings us to the issue of *terbiye* through which an ideal morality bears fruit. However, before moving on this topic, a discussion is vital to understand the philosophical ground on which a new education policy was built on.

Moral change (*tebdîl-i ahlâk*) was one of the most debated topics in *İslam Mecmuası*. In line with the idea of reform, "Islamist Turkists" reserved a space to put their understanding of the new morality into practice. Once the argument that "morality can change in time" was proven (from a historical point of view), this space could be created and reserved for reform. Although Ahmed Besim supported his arguments with references to the Quran, hadith, and biographies of the prophet (*siyer*), on the issue of moral change he also cited philosophers such as Schopenhauer and Spinoza. In his article "Does Morality Change?" he argued that this is a philosophical discussion yet there is a conventional—and wrong—assumption among the people concerning the unchanging nature of morality.[44] He claimed this understanding creates wrong views with respect to upbringing and discipline. To illustrate his point, he argued that God sent prophets to correct people's morality. According to him, the understanding of morality was based on three things: milieu, heredity, and education.[45] As these are subject to change, so too is morality. In this framework, he developed a theological argument on how to reform morality. In another article, he defended renewing the current morality by emphasizing its role in regenerating societies. Accordingly, morality serves the purposes of regenerating a nation and bringing it to the point of progress. Therefore, morality needs to be progressive. By referring implicitly to the Islamists' ideal of "going back to the *asr-ı saadet*," he argued that the proposal to adopt medieval morality in contemporary times was nonsensical.⁴⁶ His illustration to show the drastic change in morality was—not surprisingly—the rise of nationalism and the adoption of nationalism and patriotism as great ideals of morality.⁴⁷ The question was how to change the established understanding of morality and practice the ideals that Ahmed Besim theorized. On this topic, more so than to Besim himself, the articles of Gökalp, Halim Sabit, and Kazım Nami need to be taken into account.

The writers for *İslam Mecmuası* focused on the issue of *terbiye* as a way of dealing with moral decline in Ottoman Muslim society. The term *terbiye* played a key role in their understanding of the education of the masses. However, the term does not refer to scientific education—rather it translates to upbringing, discipline, or instruction. They formulated *terbiye* for the adolescents of future generations as a key to progress: only through education could the Ottomans catch up to modern standards and carry the mores of a nation as well as the essence of Islam. On this topic, too, their starting point was a critique of old (and current) forms of *terbiye*. However, the critique targeted not only medieval understandings of education but also the policy of education initiated in the Tanzimat era. Accordingly, Gökalp wrote an article in the first issue of *İslam Mecmuası* titled "Islamic Terbiye: The Nature of Islamic Terbiye," in which he claimed that the schools of the Tanzimat inculcated modern education (*asrî terbiye*) improperly while Islamic education was under the influence of Arabic nations.⁴⁸ In his opinion, the crucial problem was a lack of a purpose (*gayesizlik*) that caused degeneration and moral decline in youth. He argued that the purpose of *terbiye* should be to make life meaningful and give it a purpose so that the future generations would rely on it. This education would eventually bless their souls with higher virtues and self-sacrifice in the name of the nation and religion. Modern education would provide people with the necessary tools for national progress.⁴⁹

Kazım Nami, in his article titled "Islamic Terbiye, Religious Terbiye," made more radical critiques of the "so-called Islamic morality."⁵⁰ He targeted the Muslim idea of an "other world": "Those who carry the idea 'every man for himself' by calculating only their comfort in the after life are harmful burdens on social life."⁵¹ The reformist but theological perspective of *İslam Mecmuası* on education is important with respect to their ultimate goal of penetrating religious discourse and conquering this realm from within. Education was crucial because it would eventually become the only way to instruct an "ideal morality" in society. What is interesting (and new) in the discussion of education that took place in *İslam Mecmuası* is not an emphasis on reforming school or university curricula but introducing a new religious body responsible for developing a new understanding of *terbiye* in Muslim society. To put it briefly, they sought to reform the institution of the Office of Şeyhülislam (*Meşihat*) and establish an office of Religious Affairs (*Diyanet İşleri*)—which would be established indeed in 1924—for these purposes.

Halim Sabit wrote two groundbreaking articles on this issue in *İslam Mecmuası*.⁵² In a Durkheimian view of "division of labor," he suggested a reconsideration of the role of the *Meşihat* in society. Accordingly, he proposed two main bodies for the *Meşihat*: a religious advisory organ (*dinî teşrî' heyeti*) and a religious education commission (*dinî terbiye heyeti*). He argued that the duties of the *Meşihat* should be limited to these two within a framework of the division of labor in order to achieve a division between the religious and secular realms. On the one hand, by saying that the *ulema* was the sole authority in religious affairs, he courted and flattered them. On the other hand, he narrowed down the definition of "religious affairs" and questioned "unholy" things with which the *ulema* was dealing, such as legislation, and thus limited their area of jurisdiction. He quoted the following statement from the Quran: "obviously, God orders you to command [his] entrusted realms to competent [people or institutions]"⁵³ and continued, "henceforth, the religious realm will be clearly defined by relieving it of its [worldly] burdens."⁵⁴ He based his arguments on the "orders of God" as well as on early practices in Islam, claiming that there was separation between religious and legislative (*dinî* ve *kazaî*) orders. By using religious references, he avoided formulating his views as anti-religious statements; on the contrary, he presented his ideas as the savior of the religious realm that would bring its holiness back by lifting off worldly burdens. Strikingly, he categorized the implementation of justice as among the burdens of the religious realm and claimed them for secular institutions: "henceforth, jurisprudence, with all its institutions, including family law, should be transferred to the Ministry of Justice, while legislative power should be handed over to the sultan, the assemblies of the senate and the deputies."⁵⁵ Eventually, *terbiye* would be central to the duties of *ulema*. In accordance with the logic of the "division of labor," a hierarchy among religious offices should emerge and work for reviving religiosity and increasing the moral standards of Muslim people. In this hierarchy, the caliph was first, followed by the Şeyhülislam, and then the Directorate of Religious Education (*terbiye-yi diniyye müdüriyeti*). In towns, muftis (*müftüler*) would be in charge of these duties, in districts preachers (*va'izler*), in *nahiye*s orators (*hatipler*), and in villages and neighborhoods the imams.⁵⁶ He asserted that his solution was an antidote to diminishing religiosity in society because "the mosques are silent, prayers are cold, and requests are selfish."⁵⁷ Therefore, he offered this education project to revive religion.

Gökalp discussed the project of Diyanet İşleri in his writings to distinguish religious affairs from government ones, to limit the authority of *ulema* and to claim their sphere for reform.⁵⁸ However, as in the articles of Halim Sabit, reformists in *İslam Mecmuası* used the Islamist discourse of morality crisis itself to remind the Islamists of "their real duties." Instead of interfering in worldly affairs, they should withdraw from legislation and jurisprudence and increase the spiritual awareness of the Muslim people. As Parla argues, religious organization as a spiritual "ethical corporation" was central to Gökalp's model of society. Religion, in this view, had a social function rather than a theological one in the fight against the materialistic positivism which Gökalp found particularly destructive.⁵⁹ These arguments would attract harsh criticism from the Islamist conservative circle represented by the journal of *Sebilürreşad*.

Sebilürreşad: In Defense of Religious Morality

The journal *Sebilürreşad* had a longer publication history than *İslam Mecmuası*.⁶⁰ The journal was published right after the declaration of the constitutional regime in 1908 with the title of *Sırat-ı Müstakim*. The chief editor was Serezli Hafız Eşref Edib, a graduate of the law school. The journal is considered one of the "Islamist modernist" journals in the empire, as it published translations of famous Islamist reformers, such as Muhammed Abduh and Ferid Vecdi. As discussed by Somel, the writers for the journal had strong ties to the Committee of Union and Progress.⁶¹

When Ebul'ula Mardin quit the editorship in 1912, the name of the journal was changed to *Sebilürreşad*, and the chief editors became Eşref Edib and Mehmed Akif. While *Sırat-ı Müstakim* was more tolerant of non-Islamist voices, the political perspective of the writers for *Sebilürreşad* became more radical after events such as the Balkan Wars, the Tripoli War, and the First World War.⁶² Although the journal supported the War of Independence, it became a stronghold of opposition to the secularist reforms of the Early Turkish Republic. Eventually, the infamous Law on the Maintenance of Order (*Takrir-i Sükûn*), which was enacted to suppress the Sheikh Said Revolt of 1925, spelled the end of this journal because of its Islamic, oppositional stance.

The *Sebilürreşad* writers published dozens of articles on morality and Islamic morality starting in the journal's early volumes. Here, I only consider articles published during the First World War and some others from the year 1919.[63] Also, instead of evaluating articles in *Sebilürreşad* that posited generic and ahistorical statements to emphasize the importance of morality in Islam, I focus on direct references to moral decline and its setting in order to assess the viewpoint of *Sebilürreşad* writers. *Sebilürreşad* editorial reviews of morality-related articles from other newspapers are emphasized because through these reviews, one can best see references to wartime realities and contextualize the intellectual debates about morality. In some cases, the *Sebilürreşad* acted as an informant vis-à-vis dubious morality and published the names of writers, journals, and articles—including some excerpts from the works—to urge the government to act against immoral content. Articles on dancing, coeducational meetings, anti-veil propaganda, cinema, theater, and love poems were among these "immoral" publications listed by *Sebilürreşad*. In addition, the editors also published pieces from other papers that they appreciated from a moral point of view. I evaluate some of these in here as these reviews also apprise us of other articles on moral decline in the Ottoman press. Pages of *Sebilürreşad* were generously given over to morality issues even before the war. This vast interest in morality stemmed from the fact that Islamists approached morality, the protection of morality, and moral education as one of the last strongholds of their intellectual, social, and political superiority.

The authors who dealt with morality in *Sebilürreşad* included, variously, Mehmet Akif (Ersoy), Ahmed Naim (Babanzade), Prens Said Halim Pasha, and Ahmed Hamdi (Akseki). However, most commentaries and reviews written in response to other journals and newspapers were penned by the editorial staff and signed simply as "Sebilürreşad."

Before delving into morality debates in *Sebilürreşad*, a few introductory words need to be said about the figures mentioned above. Mehmet Akif (Ersoy) (1873–1936), the writer of the Turkish National Anthem, famously carries the title of "national poet" of Turkey. A strong supporter of the CUP (during the First World War he served in *Teşkilat-ı Mahsusa*, the underground paramilitary organization of the CUP), he supported the War of Independence with famous sermons in the mosques. Later, he was disappointed by secular reforms of the Republic of Turkey and thus abandoned the country and settled in Egypt.[64] Ahmed Naim (Baban/Babanzade) (1872–1934) received degrees from Galatasaray High School (*Galatasaray Mekteb-i Sultanisi*) and the School of Civil Administration (*Mekteb-i Mülkiye*) and subsequently became a member of the Ottoman bureaucracy. During the war years, he worked in the Ministry of Education. In the early republican years, he became the rector of Istanbul University until the forced resign during a 1933 purge that targeted academics.[65] His work opposing ethnic nationalism, titled *İslam'da Dava-yı Kavmiyet* (Nationalism in Islam), became a manifesto by which Islamists defended the unity of the Muslim *ummah* under the caliphate against Turkish nationalists.[66] Said Halim Pasha (1865–1921) was the grandson of the founder of modern Egypt, Muhammed Ali. He worked in the Ottoman bureaucracy during the Hamidian regime but was eventually exiled following a denunciation report (*jurnal*). In 1913, he became grand vizier as a member of the CUP despite his criticism of the 1908 Constitution. He remained grand vizier until his resignation—or most accurately, his removal from office by the CUP—in 1917, after the Arab Revolt of 1916. He was a known Islamist and supporter of the idea of Muslim unity, and this revolt cost him his career.[67] His works, most of which were published as series of articles in *Sebilürreşad*, were brought together as a book titled *Buhranlarımız* (*Our crises*) in 1919. Among the crises he mentioned, I examine the social and ideological crisis with respect to which he harshly criticized Westernists and advocates of European morality. Ahmed Hamdi (Akseki) (1887–1951), a graduate of a madrasa, worked in many madrasas as lecturer (*dersiam*). He became the head of the Directorate of Religious Affairs (*Diyanet İşleri Başkanlığı*) in 1947.[68] He wrote many books on morality, some of which were composed of the articles he wrote in *Sebilürreşad*.[69]

The main concern of *Sebilürreşad*'s writers was to underscore the fact that Islam is the only source of morality and that Islamic practices are the instruments to reach a higher moral standard. In this line of thought, moral decline was the result of divergence from Islam, because religion was the source of morality. Accordingly, all the empire's calamities, including loss of land, dissolution, and social problems, stemmed from moral decline. For them, the strength of Muslims came from faith in the greatness of God and respect for the sharia law; once religion lost its power, defeat was inevitable.

An examination of *Sebilürreşad* is also important to see how morality became politicized both among rival ideologies and in the international context. Provoked by an article published in the *Times* concerning the increase in venereal disease and moral decline in the Ottoman Empire, the issue of moral crisis became a significant discussion of the legitimacy of the caliphate and of lifestyles that are incompatible with Islam. One of the main concerns of *Sebilürreşad* was that moral decline might harm the future of the caliphate and thus the future of political Islam. Emphasizing that other Muslim nations were following the news about the Ottoman Empire, the writers pointed out the importance of constituting a "good example" for the Muslim world for the success of jihad. At the end of the war, this concern became more concrete thanks to the establishment of the School of Islamic Philosophy (*Dar'ül-Hikmet'ül İslamiye*), which had advised on press censorship in the name of "protecting Islamic morality." Along with debates over the *Times* article, I present a conflict that emerged following a concert that took place in the Turkish Hearths (*Türk Ocağı*), over which the contest over morality between nationalists and the Islamists transpired. For *Sebilürreşad* sexual morality, and its demise, was a principal issue in shedding light on moral decline. Yet the topic was not limited to prostitution or adultery; the issues of the place of women in the society, of family, of gender roles, of veils and women's clothing, and of the feminist movement were also discussed with respect to moral decline.

In his introduction to a series of articles on the literature of morality (*ahlâkiyyat*), Aksekili Ahmed Hamdi used two concepts to define which behaviors were moral and immoral: *fezail* and *rezail*, which I translate as "virtues" and "vices."[70] In his view, morality can be studied within the borders of religious scholarship under the heading of *ilm-i ahlâk*—the science of morality and the concepts of "virtues" and "vices" constitute the backbone of this science. The science of morality leads people to the path to happiness and virtues and helps them distinguish the good from evil. An individual is granted "salvation" and "happiness" in exchange for complying with Islamic practices and remaining within the borders of Islamic law. Not only Ahmed Hamdi but also other writers for *Sebilürreşad* referred to the concepts of *rezail* and *fezail* while defining morality and immorality. Said Halim Pasha stated in his article on Islamization: "Islam is the most complete religion. Its morality is based on its creed, and its sociology derives from these moral principles… The Islamic credo is the key to human happiness, as long as Muslims feel, think, and act according to the fundamental principles of this religion."[71] These two spheres, religion and morality, were therefore inseparable. Leaving one and embracing other, according to *Sebilürreşad* writers, was impossible. Şeyhülislam Musa Kazım also asserted that "it has been argued that old religions can be replaced by a new quasi-religion, 'humanism.' According to the advocates of this new ideology, religions belong to the past and are outdated. What is needed for the modern world is a new, non-religious, secular morality: humanism. For me, such a thing is simply not possible."[72]

The biggest threat to religion that *Sebilürreşad* writers identified was materialism. Indeed, Mehmet Akif and Ahmed Hamdi translated a series of articles in *Sebilürreşad* by Mehmed Ferid Vecdi (1878–1954), a contemporaneous Egyptian scholar known for being a follower of the Islamic modernism movement, on the attack of the philosophy of materialism (*felsefe-yi maddiyun*), on the philosophy of spiritualism (*felsefe-yi ruhiyyun*).[73] The Bolshevik Revolution further increased concerns over the future of religion.[74] In this context, spiritualism and morality stood out as notions to become the strongholds of political Islam. Identifying immorality and showing its cure were the tasks for the Islamists to undertake in order to maintain political power. To defend Islam in every sphere, they resorted to the moral decline argument in their explanations of the backwardness or progress of nations.

Many writers in the journal discussed the question of whether Islam was a barrier to progress. Dr. Ismail Hakkı Milaslı wrote a series of articles in which this question appeared in the title.[75] In the last of the series, he argued that there were three conditions for the progress of nations: physical, mental, and moral strength. Since Muslims derived their moral principles from Islam, their source of moral strength was Islam. He contended that "religion and morality are the same" and that when Muslims lost faith, they lost their morality and thus their strength to progress.[76] He agreed about the need for a new morality in contemporary Muslim society; however, the divine referents of morality had to remain unchanged. To achieve the task of "defending Islam as the source of morality," *Sebilürreşad* directly confronted other intellectual circles particularly in the editorial reviews.[77]

On August 8, 1918, *Sebilürreşad* editorial congratulated the newly appointed Minister of Interior Affairs, Ismail Canbulat, for his interview in the newspaper *Tasvir-i Efkâr*. The interview was titled "The Necessity of Improving Public Morality," and in it, the new minister expressed his interest in reforming the organization of the municipal police to more effectively combat violations of public morality:

> Indeed, not only the Ministry of Interior Affairs but the entire government establishment attributes great importance to this [morality] issue. Especially the grand vizier [Talat Pasha] is concerned about the gradual decline of morality. And he firmly agreed to take all necessary precautions against this situation. Actually, in my opinion, government is always interested in morality issues. In every country, governments have moral, intellectual, and behavioral influence over society. The power of this impact is more than that of our [government]. The government has to be the one showing the right path, protecting and restoring public morality by being an example. More than anywhere else, our people need guardianship and tutelage. People slavishly imitate all the behaviors and actions of the government."[78]

Strikingly, the minister likened the ideal role of government in Ottoman society to a father in the family—the chief exemplar of good manners and morals.[79] Moving on from the role of government to correct public morality, he continued: "Henceforth, during my term of office, I will deal particularly with public morality. I will endeavor with great attention and care to make sure that the municipal police execute their duty with respect to the protection of morality."[80] Eventually, he indicated the new gambling houses and the gradual increase in prostitution were initial problems to be addressed. He emphasized his resentment about permissions to open new brothels. Citing examples of European countries that had abolished brothels (such as Switzerland and Prussia), he concluded that government has to put obstacles in the way of immorality: "We will try to reduce the causes that produce or pave the way for moral degeneration. We expect success because in our society, the public's affinity for moral sentiment is more than other societies' disposition and nature."[81] These statements of the minister brought joy and pleasure to *Sebilürreşad*'s editorial board, and they emphasized that the new minister is famous for his views about applying the law equally for everyone; thus, finally, an "honest and ambitious person had arrived to serve the Muslim nation and prevent its disgrace."[82] It appears that *Sebilürreşad* shared the thoughts of the minister on the causes of moral decline—the selective application of law in cases of the violation of public morality. The date of this interview coincided with the last months of the war, and it can be interpreted as a critique of corruption among CUP circles. Indeed, this critique is clear in one *Sebilürreşad* editorial review focused on the article of the famous Turkish nationalist, Necmeddin Sadak, an author for *Yeni Mecmua* and a follower of Ziya Gökalp and Durkheimian sociology.

Through the end of the war, it is possible to see that *Sebilürreşad* increased its emphasis on morality. In some cases, half the pages of an issue were reserved for *Ahlâkiyyat*. In December 1918, immediately after the war, *Sebilürreşad* cited the article of Necmeddin Sadak titled "The Considerations on Morality" written in his own newspaper, *Akşam*.[83] At the end of the war, thanks to the lifting of censorship, the time had come to target Turkish nationalists "for their role in moral decline" in the journal's pages. Before giving details of the editorial review in *Sebilürreşad*, I briefly present the main points Necmeddin Sadak explored in the aforementioned article. His article is also the statement of a "new life" advocate on moral decline as the outcome of war:

> Obviously, over the last four years we saw that things had changed. Among these, morality is the most remarkable. Many of us have changed our consideration of morality [and] what to take from it; the borders of the concept of morality

have widened. We have seen this transformation in every kind of morality. The morality of profession and duty, women and sexual morality, civil morality, etc. all gradually failed. I don't know if there is any other country in which morality had declined so quickly.[84]

Necmeddin Sadak accused this new consideration of morality of corrupting the morality and honor of the Turkish family and Turkish women because its eclectic perspectives on the concepts of progress, civilization, and modernization were incomplete. He continued: "Today we have reached the end. It is difficult to assess the damage that the homeland has witnessed just because of moral corruption. What is done is done; that whirlpool is left behind."[85] Finally, he explained what he meant by the "damage" caused by moral corruption:

> Here are the biggest and most catastrophic ones among these damages that need our attention… On the one hand, there is the prosperous lifestyle that can be observed among the war profiteers and among those who currently live in comfort, apparently as a result of easily earned wealth at the expense of the country. On the other hand, there appeared a new form of womanhood, completely emancipated from sexual and familial morality, that is a so-called representation of the life of the European woman with its manners and liberal and extreme desires.[86]

Sadak put war profiteering and the emergence of a new womanhood at the core of moral corruption. According to him, because these two "damages" remained unpunished, the upbringing (*terbiye*) *of* young girls and boys was extremely affected. He complained that the new generation is following the example of this comfortable, easily earned life and tends to be ignorant and lazy. He urged families, schools, and the press to take action.

> If considerations of a new and moral life do not appear soon—in other words, if the *terbiye* of the family and school do not decry this and the press does not take control of this morality, there will be a more significant and final decline. Let's work to keep moral considerations in their natural, reasonable boundaries. Only then can we save the future of homeland.[87]

The *Sebilürreşad* editorial review appreciated these lines and accepted these statements as an apology.

> No doubt, it is a success to see an author of *Yeni Mecmua*—the journal that desired to overthrow our entire religious, national, social, and moral basis and replace it with fake institutions; the journal that expressed joy by chanting "a space is opening for the new life" after the gradual fall of our old religious notions of chastity—on the right path, making confessions under the heading "Considerations on Morality."[88]

Sebilürreşad concluded the review by expressing the wish that those intellectuals unite against present calamities (*felâkât-ı hâzıre*) and work for the correction of morality.

Actually, competition over morality had increased between the Islamists and Turkish nationalists at the end of the war. As mentioned earlier, the abolition of censorship played a role in direct confrontations, but also the loss of the war and increasing political tensions with the occupation of the empire created an atmosphere in which morality became a tool in political confrontations. *Sebilürreşad* deliberately followed the activities of nationalists and used the argument of immorality whenever possible. An example to this moralized political contest was a debate that followed a concert that took place in the nationalists' Turkish Hearth (*Türk Ocağı*). On December 18, 1919, *Sebilürreşad* quoted an article by the owner and chief editor of *İkdam* newspaper, Ahmed Cevdet Bey, titled "Orient and Occident," in which he focused on the "undesirable" consequences of Westernization on women of the Orient (including Greek women).[89] The aim of the editorial review was expressed as embarrassing the other writers in *İkdam* who appreciated the concert that took place in the Turkish Hearth.[90] The editors harshly criticized the event since women and men were sitting mixed without gender segregation, women took the stage and sang songs, and above all since the concert for *Sebilürreşad* presented a contrasting image of the misery of the people under occupation and the pleasure of "modernists" in concert halls: "While hundreds of our Muslim brothers, orphans, desperate women, sick, old people are groaning and suffering in the mountains of Izmir, the Turkist clubbers, who give moral lectures to others, are giving concerts with women and men mixed, chanting and singing in the name of the 'celebration of Turkism.'"[91] The *Sebilürreşad* continued to criticize Turkish nationalists in a sarcastic way: "Obviously, the club will try to reveal why it was established and attract audiences by continuing the activities of pleasure and concerts."[92] Debates over "concerts" in the Turkish Hearth would continue. Accompanied by a sarcastic tone, the *Sebilürreşad* editorial board's comments and reviews had a political agenda, as well.

The role of ideology in moral decline was debated in all intellectual circles both during and after the war. Each side blamed the other for the "intellectual basis" for defeats in battle and the backwardness of Ottoman society. However, the end of the war brought another political dimension to this debate: the future of the caliphate. As the Ottoman Empire was defeated on the battlefield, the ideology surrounding the caliphate, jihad, was questioned, as well. This counter-propaganda was particularly evident in the British press, which openly argued that the Ottoman Empire did not qualify for "holiness" due to immorality observed among the common Ottoman Muslims. This increased the anxiety of Islamists over moral decline and added a dimension that can be formulated as "the whole Muslim world is watching us." Here, I cite an important event that shows how the issue of moral decline and the discussion on morality escalated quickly and marked an important point of departure for a political conflict.

On September 11, 1919, the *Times* published an article titled "Decadent Turkey: Muslim Virtues Fast Disappearing," claiming an "alarming increase of venereal disease in Turkey, and especially in the capital during the last few years."[93] The *Times* correspondent declared that although "long established" in Anatolia, venereal diseases were now becoming a big problem in the capital, Constantinople, with some 40,000 women and girls undergoing medical treatment "in a population of about 1.100.000 inhabitants of both sexes." The correspondent based this information on a "well-informed Turkish source." As discussed by Seçil Yılmaz, it appears his source was Abdullah Cevdet, the director of the General Health Administration and the chief editor of *Ictihad*, who was a prominent "Westernist" figure.[94] Before detailing the "fight" that took place between *Sebilürreşad* and Abdullah Cevdet, we should focus on the rest of the newspaper article to see the process of the politicization of public morality and why it became so important in that historical context.

Moving on from the increasing number of venereal diseases among Muslims, the correspondent of the *Times* depicted the situation of public morality in the Ottoman Empire.

> The Government has ceased to recognize Moslem prostitution and to enjoin the medical inspection of Moslem prostitutes, which was some slight check on the dissemination of disease, but takes no steps to close Turkish houses of ill-fame or to punish the food profiteering which is one of the chief causes of the evil. It is also handicapped by the inefficiency and venality of too many Turkish doctors, the lack of drugs and hospitals, the increase of alcoholism, and many other difficulties. It has not been able to check the growth raki drinking among the Turkish working class or the increase in the number of private gambling clubs run by effendis to any appreciable extent, and its chances of tackling the redoubtable problem of the social evil seem small.[95]

After summarizing the circumstances of "decadence," the correspondent eventually proceeded to the political ramifications of these circumstances and addressed the petition by prominent Indians that had been sent to the Prime Minister of Britain. The petition was written in solidarity with the Ottomans and expressed concerns over the future of Constantinople, a city that was considered "the center of Islamic civilization and morality." The correspondent found it "a pity" that "highly distinguished Indians, such as the Aga Khan," joined the solidarity with the Ottomans. Quoting from the petition in which the Indian Muslims expressed concerns after the occupation of Istanbul about the replacement of Islamic civilization "by alien civilizations with all their concomitants, casinos, gambling dens, liquor shops, and other undesirable adjuncts," he stated that the writers of this petition were either ignorant or infected by "early Victorian cant in its most odious and hypocritical form." Based on the immorality argument, the correspondent argued, "there are good reasons enough for the maintenance of some form of Turkish sovereignty at Constantinople, but it is ridiculous to urge that its present civilization is Islamic, or indeed anything but Levantine." He concluded his article with the advice to the "Indian friends of Turkey" to offer medical help to Turks suffering from syphilis and consumption (as well as a loss of manpower due to war) because, quoting a British doctor, "in a few years the Turkish problem will be medical rather than political."

This article had a great impact on the Ottoman press. Especially *Sebilürreşad* took up arms against Abdullah Cevdet, who had proposed licensing Muslim prostitutes in order to combat venereal diseases.[96] The debate led to his dismissal as director of the General Health Administration a year later.[97] "Those Westlovers (*Garpperestler*) who lead our women to an evil path shall read this," wrote the editors of *Sebilürreşad* when reprinting a two-page article by Cevdet, the chief editor of *Ikdam*, in which he evaluated the article in the *Times*. Here, I briefly present Ahmed Cevdet's view on the causes of moral decline because his article on the topic was written in a surprisingly explicit fashion and *Sebilürreşad* quoted it in its entirety, despite its length.

According to Ahmed Cevdet, the path leading to the *Times* newspaper article resulted from several mistakes that took place in the Ottoman Empire. First off, any civilization project in the Orient had to take religion into account because it was nothing if not religion from which the people of the Orient derived their moral principles. Accordingly, it was a mistake to disregard Islam. A good religious education had to be in place in school curricula. The second mistake was government legislation in various fields. Economic policies needed to prevent poverty because people sacrifice their chastity due to poverty. Another legal action that the government needed to consider was military service. Recruiting men and separating them from their wives for years, leaving them away from their families in a country that lacked adequate means of transportation, had become a problem from the perspective of morality because in the end, the situation corrupted the morality of both men and women. In addition to this, another legal issue that impacted morality was divorce law which gave husbands a monopoly over divorce. Men exploited this right, Ahmed Cevdet argued, and used it extensively to remarry. He also contended that women should obey Islamic clothing rules if they expected to be respected in society. However, since times had changed, they should also have access to the university education and earn their own livelihood. "In our society the number of women is more than that of men," he said; therefore, it was no longer possible for women to "sit at home and make a living."[98] Furthermore, Ahmed Cevdet pointed out the role of contemporary literature on moral decline. He claimed novels, stories, and European literature had poisoned people's sense of spirituality; they not only caused moral decline but also spread a misunderstanding of real European civilization. He asserted that none of the authors in these genres had visited Anatolia, and none had an idea about the essence of Turks. All these works were materialistic—based solely on profane ambitions. He added a critique of CUP rulers who had not paid enough attention to this issue.

According to Ahmed Cevdet, there was an obvious problem of moral decline in Ottoman Muslim society for the aforementioned reasons. Therefore, the article in the *Times*, despite its exaggerations and political agenda, had a point. He referred to a "morally degenerate class" in Istanbul that had emerged in a time of social dissolution along with the declaration of the constitution. According to him, such phenomena were natural in times of turmoil; however, this class needed to be replaced by a new ruling elite, which had not yet happened in the Ottoman case. Therefore, he concluded, "we [Ottomans] are in *fetret devri*, time of troubles."[99] But he argued that the *Times* correspondent had not analyzed the situation as closely as he had, and he urged the office of the Şeyhülislam (*Bab-ı Meşihat*) to take action, particularly against publications that violate public morality.

The declaration of jihad during the First World War made modern lifestyles more vulnerable to critiques. In this framework, morality was of broad and intense interest in discussions of the legitimacy of the Ottoman caliphate. The sensitiveness of the political situation had increased by the end of the war when the Ottomans were defeated. Therefore, the fight over morality became more explicit among intellectuals, particularly between Turkish nationalists and political Islamists.

We can also consider the famous dispute over the concert that took place in the Turkish Hearth in this context. The Islamists in *Sebilürreşad* had political motives when they informed authorities of immoral activities that were taking place in the country. In this case, they had a special office with which to collaborate: the moral censorship commission in the *Dar'ül-Hikmet'il İslamiyye* (the School of Islamic Philosophy), which was established under the authority of the Şeyhülislam on March 5, 1918. The council was founded "to promulgate and circulate the high virtues of Islam, to protect religious institutions in the best possible way, and to work towards the accomplishment of a variety of goals, such as reforming the medreses (madrasas) and providing religious advice to the general public."[100] Three commissions operated under the office: the first one was called catechism (*akâid*), charged with the task "to protect Islam against philosophical attacks and superstitions"; the second one was jurisprudence (*fıkıh*) commission, which "examined the legal opinions of the Muslim jurists"; the third, and most important for our topic, was the morality (*ahlâk*) commission, "charged with promulgating Islamic morals."[101] This commission would become the main censorship mechanism during the armistice period. The commission, after discussion among board members,[102] would issue declarations urging the Ministry of Interior Affairs to take action against immoral publications.

Sebilürreşad resorted to the morality commission to complain about immoral activities and publications. The concert in the Turkish Hearth club was one such activity; thus, from this moral mindset, publications that praised the event needed to be censored. Eventually, the School of Islamic Philosophy published a declaration titled "On the Inappropriateness at the Turkish Hearth," which was also reprinted by *Sebilürreşad* in appreciation of the commission's statement. An interesting aspect of this declaration was the emphasis on "the house of the caliphate, the place where the whole Muslim world is watching,"[103] where the immoral events would "incite the feelings of Muslims and surprise their enemies."[104] Finally, the commission called upon the ministry to take necessary measures against the organizers of the event as well as against the publications promoting it.

The School of Islamic Philosophy mainly operated after the war; however, I believe that intellectual discussions that took place during the war together with political circumstances of the time were the actual catalysts for the establishment of this institute. During and after the war *Sebilürreşad* reported "immoral" publications to authorities, urging the latter to take action against what the journal labeled "disgusting publications" (*iğrenç neşriyat*) and "propagandas of immorality" (*ahlaksızlık propagandaları*).

As mentioned earlier, through the end of the war the ideological contest between Turkish nationalists and Islamists increased. *Sebilürreşad* considered it a "duty" to inform authorities of publications violating public morality and spreading immorality. The editorial board published excerpts from articles as well as literary works in its pages under the headings of "immoral publications" or "immorality propaganda." The editors also commented on them, warning both readers of *Sebilürreşad* and authorities how harmful these publications were. Unsurprisingly, others would label this activity on *Sebilürreşad*'s part as denunciation (*jurnalcilik*), a label denoting the oppressive years of censorship under the Hamidian regime (1876–1909). However, *Sebilürreşad* would claim that its readers were demanding it that they have "to do something" to stop such immoral publications. For instance, on August 8, 1918, *Sebilürreşad* published a letter from a reader that was sent to the journal penned by "a member of the *ulema*" from Konya.[105] The letter complained that a local newspaper, *Türk Sözü*, had published an article that "invited youth to fight against Muslim veils and marriage practices and encouraged women and men to have a lengthy relationship before getting married."[106] The author asked *Sebilürreşad* to respond to this article. *Sebilürreşad* stated that it had taken notice of the mentioned article; however, responding to it "would be superfluous," though the editors wished the article's author had read the series in *Sebilürreşad* titled "Diseases in the Islamic World and Their Cures."[107] Other reasons *Sebilürreşad* presented for the "denunciation" of immorality were to protect the religion and Muslim women by revealing the "real face" of its political opponents.

For our analysis, it is important to understand what was labeled "immorality" or "things causing immorality" from the perspective of *Sebilürreşad*. In December 1918, *Sebilürreşad* published a two-page list of excerpts from other, mostly nationalist, journals.[108] With a sarcastic title, *Sebilürreşad* was attempting to draw attention to the "contrast" between circumstances in the country and the topics with which the press was dealing. As an incipit, the *Sebilürreşad* editorial complained about the lack of regulation of such publications and asserted that "one would be ashamed of humanity after seeing this situation. Even enemies would be saddened by this much degeneration and decline."[109] *Sebilürreşad* continued with an apology to readers because it was necessary to publish excerpts of this *iğrenç neşriyat* in order to show the degree of the "calamity."[110]

The first journal targeted was *Fağfur*, which was a journal of the time published between August and November 1918. *Sebilürreşad* considered two love poems in the journal—Faruk Nafiz's "*Baş Başa*" (In private) and Selami İzzet's "*Beyoğlu'nun Hanımlarına*" (To the ladies of Beyoğlu)—to be among the disgusting publications. The second example was the article "*Büyükada Hayatı*" (Life in Büyükada) in *Serbest Fikir Mecmuası*, from which these lines were quoted in the editorial: "This luxurious life is the only thing that keeps people alive. I laugh at those who don't think in this way: To those people who want to see life as misery, sorrow, and poverty brought on by the war, I pity them."[111] Another article from *Serbest Fikir* was quoted to show how the authors of such works pursue or wish to pursue the world. For instance, instead of looking for sorrow and misery, one author emphasized the beauty of women's attire in an article titled *"Kadın Tuvaletleri ve Hayat"* (Women's attire and life):

> I was looking for the joyful and entertaining sides of life this week. It seems it is easier to find than an abundance of misery! Today we are living a luxurious life. Especially our women; we cannot find anything more interesting and exciting than their carefully chosen elegant dresses, colors, socks, and attitudes.[112]

Lastly, *Sebilürreşad* targeted a love poem published in *Yeni Mecmua* by Enis Behic, who was also an adherent of the Syllabist Movement (*Beş Hececiler*), a new movement in Turkish literature. *Sebilürreşad* introduced the poem sarcastically: "And here is *Yeni Mecmua*, the journal that gives social and moral lessons to the Turkish community on the 'New Life.'"[113] The title of the poem was *"Bir Çift İskarpin"* (A couple of shoes), telling of the harmony of a man and woman's footsteps on the sidewalks.[114] Considering that *Sebilürreşad* found advocating "getting to know each other before marriage" to be immoral for Muslim couples, the "harmony" of which the poet wrote might have led its editors to label this poem immoral. Note, however, some among the authors of the "calamities" to which *Sebilürreşad* referred—such as Faruk Nafiz Çamlıbel—are in the contemporary Turkish literary canon and famous for creating the national literary genre. While establishing a fresh, nationalist genre in Turkish literature during and after the war, these poets attracted the critique of the conservatives of *Sebilürreşad*.[115]

This contest over morality revealed other facts regarding wartime censorship. *Sebilürreşad* published a list of articles that, according to it, were "against the sacredness of Islam."[116] In this list, there were articles from *Serbest Fikir*, *Hürriyet-i Fikriye*, and *Sıyanet* that questioned the practice of veiling women in Islam. These journals claimed that *Sebilürreşad* was acting as an informant (*jurnalci*) and violating freedom of speech in the country. According to Ahmed Hamdi Akseki, who wrote in answer to these critiques, it was the "duty of *Sebilürreşad* to protect Islam" against false statements about the practice of veiling. Therefore, *Sebilürreşad*'s editors drew such articles to the attention of the military administration (*askerî hükûmet*). Ahmed Hamdi also noted that the military government had intervened in the dispute and asked that the topic be closed.[117] Apparently, the wartime government asked newspapers to end discussions on some "sensitive topics." It is possible to argue that due to intervention by the wartime government, disputes over morality remained relatively few compared to the postwar period. This also means that intellectual debates during the war had certain limitations.

As mentioned, the problem of "immorality" for Islamists was of equal importance with irreligiosity. Their statements on morality served to link morality and religion and keep it within the limits of Islamic law. According to *Sebilürreşad* writers, among the many versions of immorality, prostitution, or sexual immorality in general, was the worst. The argument that "God sends calamities to those who are immoral" was frequently espoused; however, I dig beneath the arguments to provide the peculiar context of the war and the ensuing years of armistice marked by the Allied occupation and the national resistance against it.

On December 16, 1919, the *Sebilürreşad* editorial board published an article titled "The Problem of Morality in Our Homeland," in which the editors reviewed wartime developments together with intellectual debates that—according to them—had paved the way for immorality and particularly for prostitution.[118] The article appreciated that the Ottoman press, after "ten years of destruction," had finally recognized how evil immorality was and had realized that "immorality or prostitution and adultery were social wounds" to be healed.[119] Most of the complaints by the press proposed no real solutions to the immorality problem and there were common misconceptions on the issue. *Sebilürreşad* was proud of its own perspective on morality, which had never changed from the beginning despite accusations of its "bigotry."[120] While others recognized the importance of morality only after the war, *Sebilürreşad* had known the sources of the problem from the beginning: "Now, we shall say it again. The reason for the rapid spread and dissemination of all this immorality and especially prostitution and adultery was the death of religious grace—more precisely, humans forcing the destruction of spiritualism with their many words and speeches."[121] Moving on, the article presented an overview of the sources and definitions of immorality from a historical point of view. Accordingly, the problem first started with the misunderstanding of the concept of "freedom" that was announced with the proclamation of the constitution in 1908; "some people thought freedom means being free from religious duties and doing whatever they like."[122] The initial phase of this misunderstanding was revealed with respect to the issue of veiling, the most rooted religious practice among Muslims with a history of thirteen and a half centuries. The article went on to refer to "they" without detailing to whom "they" refers. "As they anticipated that once the obstacle [of veil] is removed, the remaining religious duties would collapse more easily; they discovered that they could achieve their plans by destroying the woman's *çarşaf*[123] and pulling down the wooden curtain between *haremlik* and *selamlık*."[124] Thus, changes in clothing and gender segregation acted as triggers in the development of moral decline. The article continued listing the "sources of evil": the opening of cinemas and theatres to women, and organizing events where women and men were mixed. Keeping in mind the critique that *Sebilürreşad* made of nationalists regarding concerts in the Turkish Hearths, it is possible to assume that "they" referred to nationalists. The argument continued that the source of "immorality" was the modern understanding of life (*asrîlik*) and the project of creating the modern human (*muasır insan etmek*), to which we are familiar from the works of the prominent figure of Turkish nationalism, Ziya Gökalp. The second issue was women's participation in economic activities. Although the article did not explicitly argue against the idea of women working, it emphasized that "they" indicated that Islam was an obstacle to women's participation in economic activities but Islam's only concern was with protecting the honor of Muslim women. Eventually, as argued in the article, young women and men "lost the control of their minds"[125] after such provocations. "Women took the *çarşaf* off saying it was too heavy and jumped into the streets wearing dresses that are reserved for sleeping"[126] and men started to engage in acts disapproved of by God (*münkerat*). The article harshly criticized the notion that "foolish women" who were obedient to their husbands were therefore under their yoke.

Unlike other accounts that considered poverty to be the main reason for prostitution, the article asserted that while "poverty might be one reason for prostitution," it was not "as significant as bringing women and men together under the same roof."[127] They blamed "so-called vanguards" in society who helped unite women and men in *Darülfünun*'s (imperial university) conferences and organized concerts in halls with women and men together. These "so-called vanguards" sent "young, uneducated" girls alone to European universities. They encouraged the government to employ women and eventually "filled the chambers of the state with unqualified, useless women" (*devâir-i devleti vukufsuz işe yaramaz kadınlarla doldurup*) and wasted public money.[128] All these constituted "the first stage of prostitution." *Sebilürreşad* was proud of its view, which, according to the article, had never wavered since the beginning. The article asserted that Muslims had a pure morality bound to religion "despite shortcomings in public morality that prevented our progress." Apparently, it was not modernization that Islamists considered harmful to morality but the "path" that Turkish nationalists had followed to achieve modernization. For the sake of modernization, "they" made people forget God and destroyed the "holy source" of morality. The editorial board of *Sebilürreşad* concluded with these lines:

> One should know well that this nation is Muslim. Its source of morality is Islam. It received all its graces from there. And the disgraces have been instilled in its soul and body by foreign hands. And the cure for the immorality microbe from which it suffers is to vaccinate religion at the heart of it.[129]

Another writer for *Sebilürreşad*, Mustafa Sabri, summarizes this line of thought more precisely:

> The idea of our religious reformers is, "Since we are not able to build our world, we must at least destroy our afterworld." I can only say I am not one of those who deny the material and moral decline of the Muslims, and I neither want to prevent their awakening nor the methods of reform that could improve the situation of the Muslim world. But if the progress and advancement of the Muslim world is to be obtained at the expense of their religion, by destroying Islam as a religion, I would rather Muslims stay in that miserable and wretched condition than to benefit from material advancement.[130]

The article above was indeed a summary of what Islamists thought about morality and immorality. As is clear, the problems of women's employment during the war, their participation in social life, their veiling and clothing, and their new rights to education were at the core of "immorality" arguments. In general, the "women issue" stood at the center of the "immorality microbe." Aggressive and exaggerated statements such as "jumping into the streets in night dresses" and claims that modernist nationalist elite projects were the reason for prostitution constituted the ways that Islamists attempted to reclaim moral authority. In fact, *Sebilürreşad* depicted these elites as "inexperienced doctors" with no idea about curing the "immorality microbe." Therefore, they could do everyone a favor by "leaving the patient in bed" and stepping aside.[131]

The issue of women, and its relation to immorality, was a prominent topic in *Sebilürreşad*. The basic idea was that a Muslim woman's principal duty was to protect her own morality. Women also had power over men to correct their husbands' behaviors. Another article in *Sebilürreşad* titled "The Conditions and Duties of Women" explicitly stated that "the reason of prostitution is not economical, but spiritual."[132]

Even at the end of the war, *Sebilürreşad* continued accusing Turkish women of immorality and evilness. Unlike nationalist statements depicting Turkish women as the "heroines" of the war, *Sebilürreşad* recalled the widespread "prostitution and immorality" during the First World War. On October 16,

1919, *Sebilürreşad* reviewed an article published by the nationalist newspaper *İstiklal*. The latter article had praised the sacrifices of Turkish women during the war and celebrated their steps on the path to emancipation.[133] *Sebilürreşad* wrote a sarcastic commentary manifestly accusing Turkish women of having been corrupted. The review stated, in a sarcastic tone, that "we know what the path of emancipation has been for Turkish women in the last four or five years, especially during the Great War."[134] *Sebilürreşad* used the passive voice to depict the situation of women instead of blaming them directly. The journal held an unstated subject (implicitly the nationalist and Westernist intelligentsia) responsible to the situation of women, thus disregarding their own agency:

> In recent years, as nobody can deny, prostitution has increased among our women and it has been observed that Muslim women are secretly engaged in prostitution. These women, abandoning and neglecting family life and their duties, were sent to the streets. Men's duties were saddled on the shoulders of these women in exchange for salaries that were unquestionably insufficient to make a living.[135]

Strongly arguing against the idea of women's struggle for emancipation, *Sebilürreşad* asserted that there was no such struggle between men and women in Muslim society.[136] It advised *İstiklal* newspaper to "think first" before publishing such articles. As can be seen clearly, unlike many contemporary observers, *Sebilürreşad* articles claimed that the real reason for prostitution was not economic hardships but lack of adequate religious morality.

Yeni Mecmua: The "New Morality" as a Cure for Moral Decline

The sixty-six issues of the weekly *Yeni Mecmua* were published between July 1917 and October 1918, the time marking the end of the First World War. It began publishing again upon the foundation of the Republic of Turkey for a short time. Yahya Kemal Beyatlı, who was among the writers of the journal, asserted that the chief editor, Ziya Gökalp, sought to publish a politically independent, financially self-sufficient journal; however, after just a few issues, he was faced with financial problems. A leading CUP member, Küçük Talat (Muşkara), offered help to finance the journal while guaranteeing the independence of its content. From then on, the journal was published with the sponsorship of the CUP.[137]

The writers of the journal are among prominent figures in Turkish intellectual history: Mehmed Fuat Köprülü, Ahmed Ağaoğlu, Ömer Seyfettin, Yahya Kemal Beyatlı, Halide Edip Adıvar, Avram Galanti, Refik Halid Karay, Tekin Alp, and Necmeddin Sadak. As discussed by Erol Köroğlu, this journal brought together many intellectuals, including those with different views in order to increase the efficacy of the cultural output of war propaganda.[138] Together, these authors contributed to the formation of a "national culture" by creating a new literary genre called National Literature (*Millî Edebiyat*) in the pages of *Yeni Mecmua*.[139] Gökalp's articles in sociology columns constituted the principles of the Turkish nationalist movement. Some of the series of articles in *Yeni Mecmua* (including those on morality) would become part of Gökalp's handbook on nationalism titled *Turkification, Islamization, Modernization*.[140]

Yeni Mecmua advertised itself as "weekly journal on scholarship, arts and morality" (*ilim, sanat ve ahlâka dair haftalık mecmua*). In line with this claim, articles on morality appeared in almost every issue. This journal provides a precise understanding of what those prominent nationalists of the time thought about moral crisis, how they correlated it to the war, and how their solutions differed from those of theological and religious approaches. Morality was a central topic throughout this journal, as a concept carefully analyzed by Necmettin Sadak and Ziya Gökalp in their attempts to formulate the idea of a "new life."[141] They envisaged a new understanding of morality—"the national morality" that would constitute the backbone of Turkish political, economic, and sociocultural life.

The articles on morality were frequently in the sociology (*ictimâîyyat*) column and occasionally under the title of the problem of upringing (*Terbiye Meselesi*). Necmettin Sadak and Ziya Gökalp were the chief commentators on morality—either Gökalp or Sadak wrote on morality on a weekly basis.[142]

In this study, I primarily take the articles of Gökalp and Sadak in *Yeni Mecmua* into account with few exceptions. Gökalp and Sadak shared common views on morality; however, Sadak had more practical insights when contrasted with Gökalp's historical, theoretical analysis. In his articles, Gökalp argued that only through sociological analysis could the Ottoman society overcome the crisis of morality. On the other hand, Sadak usually expressed his ideas on morality vis-à-vis the issue of upbringing. Gökalp and Sadak shared a mission that can be summarized as correcting the contemporaneous views on morality and establishing a theory of secular national morality.

This formulation of a new morality was a translation of the *morale laïque* of the French Third Republic. The term was particularly important for education policy which came into being in the late nineteenth century and sought to replace the monopoly of religion over education. Emile Durkheim was the chief figure who had formulated *morale laïque* in line with his ideas on solidarity, a harmonious social life, and common consciousness—all to keep society united and together.[143] A cross reference of Durkheim's work with those of Sadak, Gökalp, and Atalay (from *İslam Mecmuası*) reveals that the Ottoman intelligentsia translated and adopted Durkheim's theoretical framework in its entirety with the exception of his understanding of society. While for Durkheim the central concept was society, for Turkish nationalists it was the nation.[144] As discussed by Parla, society had primacy over state in Durkheim, whereas in Gökalp, nation had the same primacy.[145]

The aim of national morality according to these authors was to bring about a secular understanding of morality that was compatible with Turkish nationalism. This understanding of morality would shape the basic notion of solidarity in society. Although many scholars have evaluated the emphasis of solidarity for the formation of Turkish nationalism, the role of morality in this formulation remains vague. As a matter of fact, nationalists formulated solidarity as a solution to the so-called "moral crisis." In addition, a broad role is attributed to morality for solving social and individual problems that had increased due to the war. The emergence of the discourse of a "crisis of morality" was a reaction to these problems—an attempt to coalesce all social and individual problems under one heading. *Yeni Mecmua*'s vast interest in morality in the very years of war stemmed from the fact that its prominent writers considered wartime as an opportunity to broaden the sphere of nationalism and hasten the involvement of the state and government in untouched realms such as family. This formulation of social revolution, called *ictimâî inkılab*, not only staked claim to the moral realm and shook its religious foundations but also institutionalized a new morality deemed inherently superior to the religious one. It indeed challenged the existing social and political order.

Yeni Mecmua coined a new concept to label the time through which the Ottoman Empire was passing: the stage of transition (*intikâl devresi*). The authors claimed that the crisis of morality was a natural result of this period and had been observed previously in other developed countries. The transition entailed a transition to the age of social division of labor (*ictimâî iş bölümü devresi*). They argued that this process would soon be completed and finalized during the national period (*millî devir*). However, since the Ottoman society had not established a social morality (*ictimâî ahlâk*), this period had become one of chaos. For Gökalp and Sadak, the old "ascetic morality" that was primarily concerned with the "self" and individual salvation was being shaken worldwide; soon a new collective morality would prevail in every developed country as a condition for a happy life.

For the polemicists in *Yeni Mecmua*, the sources of morality should be national. Instead of superstitions, "useless" traditions, and norms (that had been adopted from foreign cultures) and imitation of Western culture, the new morality should rely on the mores of the "pure nation" and the collective conscience (*ictimâî vicdan*). The reasons for the moral crisis were conflicts that arose between education in Western-style schools and the realities of Ottoman Muslim society. Therefore, the two scholars emphasized the importance of milieu (*muhit*) in the moral development of an individual. This did not mean that the moral values of contemporaneous Muslim society had to be accepted per se; on the contrary, by the end of the transition stage the milieu and new moral values would become compatible.

The new morality was the key to coping with wartime problems, as well. For instance, the only remedy for war profiteering was to establish corporations with the principle of solidarity. The members of these corporations would have a collective understanding of morality and would never allow profiteering to happen. Due to the war, the Turkish people had come to understand the meaning of collectivity; therefore, wartime realities—despite their destructive effects on society—also open the gates for a new society. In the context of war, moral decline, according to the commentators, was revealed especially with respect to the issue of war profiteers because a new morality based on social solidarity had not yet been established in society. To establish such virtues in society and thereby overcome the problem of moral decline, the task of upbringing (*terbiye meselesi*) had to be undertaken in a modern way. Only through education, Sadak and Gökalp emphasized, could moral decline be eliminated.

Most articles on morality were published in the sociology (*ictimaiyyat*) section to emphasize that moral values had to be discussed from a "scientific" perspective. This stemmed from the influence of Durkheim on the development of the discipline sociology among Ottoman intellectuals.[146] In line with this, the authors of *Yeni Mecmua* institutionalized moral decline debate within the confines of sociological approaches. For them, once the reasons for decline were revealed scientifically, it would be easier to solve the problem. For the sake of analysis, I highlight those articles that point to the context of war as important to the shortcomings of current moral values. A new understanding of morality based on a "new life" (*yeni hayat*), on which social life based on solidarity (*tesanüd*), would be the ground for Turkish secularism. Ziya Gökalp called this new understanding of morality national morality (*millî ahlâk*).[147]

The Morale Laïque and the Sociological Analysis of Morality and Moral Decline

The idea of *morale laïque* emerged within the French Third Republic at a time when tensions between revolution and counterrevolution were on the rise. The French Republicans were inspired by Auguste Comte's positivism in their anticipation of the triumph of scientific progress over religion. A sort of "scientific" morality came to be perceived as a progressive force in history that was able to preserve the social order and create harmony in social life. The term was particularly important in the emerging discipline of sociology for use in education policies in France. Durkheim's concepts, solidarity, harmonious social life, and common consciousness were perceived as essential for the creation of "citizens" of the Republic.[148] The concept of *morale laïque* revealed distinctively "European" features that were related to the elimination of the role of the clergy in education and politics.

Debates concerning sociology took root in the Ottoman Empire, having much more resonant repercussions than ever expected. Since Ottoman intellectuals were in search of a way to save the Empire from the severe political, economic, and social crises it was facing, they turned to the discipline of sociology, which many of them admired. Particularly for Turkish nationalists, sociology seemed to offer a cure for all the "social diseases" that constituted barriers to national progress. For the authors in *Yeni Mecmua*, morality was something to be dealt with by the discipline of sociology. Moral decline, in this sense, was a sociological problem with scientific explanations if approached using the methods of sociology. Therefore, the issue fell in the realm of *ictimâîyyat*, a term that Gökalp coined as a translation of sociology.

Morality and its elaboration by the Ottoman intelligentsia stood at the center of issues that concern both nationalism and secularism. Yet, in its journey from the Republic of France to the Ottoman Empire, the *morale laïque* would take on a new form in the hands of Ottoman thinkers. A Republican, European sociological concept took on a new form and was paradoxically Islamicized, Turkified, and reworked in order to make it more appealing to Muslim audiences.

Durkheim was convinced that the moral crisis in French society was derived from changes in social structure that had destroyed the common consciousness by removing the basis for ethics.[149] Some French intellectuals of the Third Republic, including Durkheim, undertook the task of creating an official secular morality as a fundamental precondition for social integration.[150] Education was central to the project of nursing children on the new Republican values. As Morton indicates, "morality in education gradually came to mean a civic religion, with regular readings of the Declaration of Rights, civic chants and patriotic fervor as its main components."[151] Moral renewal was only possible by setting up great collective goals that united individuals around common ideals.[152]

In Durkheim's works, morality was treated as a "social fact" explicable only from the standpoint of sociology.[153] A significant part of his studies was dedicated to developing a *morale laïque* in the service of society that he envisaged would be organized according to the principle of the "division of labor."[154] He introduced the *science des moeurs* (sciences of mores) to sociology to observe the customs of a society in order to study morality.[155] Gökalp adopted this formulation and developed it in his studies of mores (*örf*) in Turkish society. However, his interpretation included Islamic scholarship too; he often referred Islamic jurisprudence (*fıkıh*), studies of mores (*örf*), and Islamic theology (*kelâm*) in his elaborations on secular morality.

On August 23, 1917, Ziya Gökalp published an article titled *"Moral Crisis"* in *Yeni Mecmua*.[156] From his point of view, there were two different moralities: ascetic morality (*zühdî ahlâk*) and social morality (*ictimâî ahlâk*). Ascetic morality was the moral system of primitive societies (*ibtidaî cemiyetler*) established on the concept of mystic "holiness" and the categories of the taboo (*haram*) and the obligatory (*vacib*). Apart from these two, there were licit (*caiz*), permitted (*mübah*), and permissible (*helal*) acts. In monotheistic religions, these categories solidified even more because they had consequences in the afterworld. In this perspective of morality, people who commit sin feel guilty, whereas those who fulfill the obligatory rules feel righteous. Therefore, ascetic morality brought high moral values to individuals and established rules in society, up to a point. However, in Gökalp's opinion, as society advanced, ascetism was transferred from the public to the private sphere, which was an inevitable consequence of the social division of labor. In times of social progress, he asserted, only a few can fulfill the obligations of ascetic morality; social division of labor conflicts with public ascetics and diminishes the number of ascetic people, thus causing a decline in decency and moral quality. At this point, he refers to the context in which the transformation occurred:

> Eventually, in addition to the social division of labor, on one hand, and the excessive admiration that we show towards European civilization, on the other, the spiritual earthquakes that the war caused shook ascetic morality completely, and as a result, souls and consciences tended to be freed from all moral concerns.[157]

For him, once emancipated from the influence of ascetic morality, it was natural and necessary that individual desires would become rampant. And, Gökalp argued,

> that is what we call individualism *(ferdcilik)*; after denouncing principles of old morality, people left moral concerns aside and only ran after personal pleasures, joys, and interests. Today, the immorality movement that harms innocent souls with a tragic fate is nothing but a wretched consequence of the disease of individualism.[158]

As is clear from these lines, he defined "religious morality" as an ascetic morality that—as times changed—would inevitably diminish in society due to three developments: war, the emergence of the division of labor, and admiration for European civilization. "Religious morality" can no longer be adopted, since it belongs to another age: "Both religion and law may establish special codes in society, however; both derive their strength from morality."[159] This idea was the exact opposite of that of the religious morality defenders in *Sebilürreşad*. Gökalp indicated that morality was the source of law and religion, while *Sebilürreşad*'s authors emphasized that religion was the source of both morality and the law. Gökalp took his point further and argued that the conservatives who defended the revival of old morality to overcome crisis of morality were contributing to the current moral decline: their insistence on the old morality made the resistance of individualism to the "domination and tyranny of a diminishing morality" stronger. However, more so than these "old morality defenders," the people most responsible for moral decline were intellectuals who had not worked on codifying and developing a new morality.

Gökalp simplified the definition of "new morality" to a "social morality" that had to be established on sociological methods. He made it explicit that "nobody would respect" principles not based on scientific evaluation "in the age of reason." In order to follow the principles of morality, people had to know how those were established in the course of social advancement and then to define their purposes and benefits from the perspective of the positive sciences, not scholasticism or literary knowledge. He offered two sociological fields to cope with moral and religious decline: moral and religious sociology (*ahlakî ictimâîyyat* and *dinî ictimiâîyyat*). Only these two fields of sociology could save adolescents from the apparent conflict between the positive sciences and religious and moral emotions. This conflict was what created the gap from which individualism was benefiting. Strikingly, he criticized not only the moral understandings of materialism, biological determinism, and spiritualism—none of which were able to establish a positive moral scholarship—but also the moral perspectives of Kant, Comte, and Spencer for being agnostic (*gayr-ı münfehim*). He concluded that "sociology is the only positive science that can help maintain the current religious and moral sentiments that constitute the backbone of real duties for social order... Therefore, we expect the cure for today's moral depression only through the true path that sociology illuminates."[160]

On the topic of individualism and the impacts of modern thought on morality, İsmail Hakkı published an article in *Yeni Mecmua* titled "*Ahlâk Mücahedeleri*" (Moral conflicts).[161] After acknowledging the existence of a moral crisis in society, he analyzed the influence of certain philosophical trends on the decline of morality. According to him, because society was in a period of social dissolution, such trends could easily affect the people, particularly the youth. Among these trends, he considered moral nihilism (*lâ-ahlâkîlik*), biological determinism (*tabiatçılık*), idealism (*fikircilik*), particularism (*infiradcılık*), collectivism (*ictimâîcilik*), conservatism (*muhâfazacılık*), and false idealism (*sûnî mefkûrecilik*). He strictly opposed moral ideas derived from nihilism and Darwinism. Emphasizing the nature of moral codes as social principles, he agreed that "moral Darwinism" was a misinterpretation of Darwin's "survival of the fittest," and he claimed that applying such principles to morality was wrong because it leads to a total rejection of moral judgments. Like Gökalp, he proposed the idea of solidarity to cope with the crisis of morality vis-à-vis philosophical trends stirring up conflict in society.

Returning to Gökalp's sociological analysis of moral decline, we should note that he divided morality into several forms and wrote about each separately. This was in line with his idea of sociological classification to observe "social facts" using a scientific approach. These five moralities were: individual morals, professional morals, sexual morals, family morals (he wrote twelve series of articles on family alone), and, finally, general morals (*şahsî ahlâk, meslekî ahlâk, cinsî ahlâk, aile ahlâkı, umûmî ahlâk*, respectively). Accordingly, during war, "crime against property increases because the nation becomes a single family and thus it stirs the spirit of collectivity, while on the other hand economic poverty accelerates."[162] Consequently, he referred to war profiteering as easily earned wealth shook the economic and moral foundations in society. He contended that if "professional morals and individual morals have been established in the country before the war, profiteering would not have become such a big problem and it would not have been possible to spend that illicit money in an immoral way."[163]

Gökalp considered sexual morality to be the most important part of *şahsî ahlâk*. He asserted that sexual morality deserves particular attention because the sense of crisis in terms of sexuality reached an utmost degree.[164] After giving a long historical, anthropological background of gender segregation, his main idea in overcoming crisis of sexual morality was the necessity of establishing the mutual respect of both sexes as the essence between men and women relationships. Once personality was defined as sacred and the "free will" of both woman and man was recognized, this kind of moral crisis would be eliminated. The first stage in the recognition of this free will was to legally recognize the equality of the sexes. Repeating his claim that this was the age of the division of labor, he strongly argued that old moral codes concerning veils and gender segregation created obstacles to women's participation in the division of labor and had to be eliminated. Conservatives had to accept an understanding of "mental veiling" instead of physical veiling.[165]

Gökalp continued dealing with "the issue of women" in a series of articles titled "Family Morality." One of these articles, titled "The Love for Chevalier and Feminism," had interesting insights on morality, or in Gökalp's terms— "sick morality."[166] After arguing that feminism was misinterpreted in current intellectual circles and was confused with medieval understandings of aristocratic women chevaliers, who were accepted as superior to men, he defended feminism as a democratic movement that demanded the equality of men and women. He attacked the Tanzimat literature, especially the *Servet-i Fünun* genre (except for Tevfik Fikret), that adopted aesthetic judgments of women from French literature, for its role in "sick morality." In this aesthetic view, the beauty of women was reduced to their psychical appearance, whereas in other literary genres, such as those of British literature, the beauty of women stems from not only appearance but also high morals. For him, "the material beauty of woman and her high morals are indivisible from each other," and "the way to unite love with morality is only possible through marriage." Adopting feminism in the social and political spheres also meant educating women in national and professional morality since they heretofore lacked these qualities. On the other hand, women's sexual morality was higher than that of men; according to him, man should take the strength of woman as an example from this point of view. We should note that these arguments are the opposite of *Sebilürreşad*'s that emphasized the weakness of women on the issue of sexual morality. Gökalp, on the other hand, recognized the "will" of women in this sense and accepted women sexuality within this framework. His views on morality imply the fact that he was convinced that morality was socially constructed—in line with the sociological view.

The Concept of "İntikal Devresi," Solidarism, and the Understanding of "National Morality" in Yeni Mecmua

The authors of *Yeni Mecmua* agreed that the Ottoman Empire was undergoing a stage of transition (*intikal devresi*). Accordingly, a sense of moral crisis was a natural outcome of this stage. Used in many different contexts, the stage of transition meant a transformation from ummah to nation, from backwardness to advancement, from feudalism to modernity, and from the extended to the nuclear family. This transition had been marked by social crisis or social dissolution in those countries that had experienced it. Furthermore, the agonies accompanying the transition were evident in every sphere of life; all institutions—including morality, family, marriage, labor, business, bureaucracy, and the military—suffered from turmoil of transition. For instance, Ahmed Midhat's (Metya) article titled "Professional Groups and Moral Life" claimed that even though it had been one and half centuries since the social turmoil of the Industrial and French Revolutions had started, the world was still struggling with moral and legal tensions.[167] As discussed above, Gökalp claimed that there had been a transition from ascetic morality to social morality. Women's participation in the labor force was also a sign of the transition to the modern division of labor that would eventually necessitate legal changes to recognize women's rights in the public sphere.[168] Sadak agreed with him and claimed that it was also "a transition period in the spiritual mindset of the public."[169] He wrote in 1917 that three years of war had brought moral decline in society and argued that the old morality should be replaced with a new one.

All civilizations went through a similar social crisis in the transition stage; however, for Gökalp, the problem was deeper and remained unsolved in the Ottoman Empire due to the lack of "great intellectuals." Recognizing solely Tevfik Fikret as a "great intellectual," he argued that there were no other intellectuals in the spheres of morality, law, and philosophy with Fikret's intellectual caliber. These intellectuals in other countries had guided society from ascetic to moral religiosity and from ascetic to social morality.[170]

Apart from the disadvantage of not having great intellectuals during the stage of transition, the cures for overcoming the shortcomings of this period were to reform existing institutions and establish new ones as necessary according to the principles of the social division of labor. Moral problems discussed with respect to the social division of labor were war profiteering; women's participation in social, economic, and political life; and the education of adolescents. I discuss the first two here and reserve another heading for the education issue because while the first two were "immediate" projects, education was a long-term solution for moral decline, yet with a similar perspective based on the notion of solidarity.

The authors of articles dealing with war profiteering approached the issue as a moral problem. For them, getting rich off the war was the result of an individualist, self-seeking morality. War profiteers only pursued their own interests, not only economically but also socially. Refik Halid (Karay) wrote an article titled "The War Rich" in *Yeni Mecmua* and expressed that there were two major calamities in the country: louse-borne typhus and war profiteers.[171] According to him, the newly rich thought that being wealthy meant wandering around like a turkey with a full stomach and running after females in the streets. Such rich people, for Karay, did no good for their homeland. They ate, drank, had fun, and showed off. Their money, Karay said, did no good for the country; these newly rich never donated to charity. On the contrary, their way of spending money harmed the public good. At the end of his article, he emphasized that these newly rich had emerged within Ottoman society; they were "domestic products."[172]

Such a description of the war profiteering problem indeed had long-lasting echoes, particularly in literary works. Strikingly, the problem was not deemed a consequence of the economic policies of the ruling party. Instead of discussing the failure of the economic policies of the government, intellectuals concentrated on the immorality of businessmen.[173] Therefore, the solution to the war-profiteering problem was to establish corporations and unions—or, as described by Sadak in French, *groupements professionals*. These corporations would be established on the basis of professions as units that would check the work ethics of their members. Even without any "legal" punishment, these corporations would apply "social" punishments such as exclusion from professional circles for "not comply[ing] with the national consciousness."[174] These corporations would be the tools by which individual interests would be attached to the national interest, and each corporation would share "social" duties according to the principles of the social division of labor. In other words, the logic was formulated as: "corporations would find harmony between individual and national interests and instill a national morality in the members of the professional groups."[175] For instance, Sadak said, "If we had had a proper trade [society] before the war, we would never have ended up with profiteering in such an ugly and improper way."[176] For him, people engaged in profiteering because of the lack of "national morality"—that is to say, a moral understanding shaped by solidarity and the institutions that were established on the basis of solidarity. National morality, on the other hand, was the idea of considering the public interest to be superior to individual interests; this was the foundation of the "new life" and the source of all kinds of moral activity.

In the nineteenth century, concerns over children occupied the political and intellectual agendas of societies which considered themselves modern and civilized.[177] Maksudyan shows in her work on orphans and destitute children that the political rivalry for demographic superiority (in terms of both quality and quantity) and making children reliable members of a certain ethnic/religious community in the Ottoman Empire was evident.[178] Füsun Üstel's work emphasizes that the new conception of citizenship that emerged after the Constitutional Revolution of 1908 attributed a great role to the transformative function of "school" and the political agency of "children" in the construction of citizens that would replace the "subjects of the Sultan."[179] Berkes states that education was the "fulcrum" of reformers who assumed the role of liberating individuals from "the yoke of tradition."[180] In this framework, *Yeni Mecmua* had a separate column on the issue of education and upbringing titled "The Problem of Upbringing."

Necmeddin Sadak was the leading figure writing about ideal education in *Yeni Mecmua*. He underlined that some problems in education system had resulted in a crisis of morality in the country. According to him, the initial problem was the conflict between the modern school curriculum and milieu. Sadak asserted in his article titled "The Education of Our Young Girls" that the factor most contributing to "moral decline in the world of women" was the education that young girls received.[181] He contended that the conflict that arose between modern education—particularly the curricula of foreign schools—and the social conditions of society was the actual reason for moral decline. This education had no real basis in the society and created expectations that could never be realized. These girls found salvation by migrating to other countries or places and, in the worse scenario, by committing suicide. In order to cope with this problem, the conflict had to be eliminated; family, the social environment, and schooling had to work in harmony to educate adolescents. Girls had to be educated not only to be wives or mothers but also skilled employees. Morality had to be instilled through this education to convey the "great ideals" of both family and the workplace. In another of his article, he criticized excessive materialism. The article titled "The Danger of Sports" argued that moral progress is superior to bodily progress.[182] The importance of education and the reform of education had become possible thanks to the war. Eventually, national education would be victorious over clerical education.[183] The morality crisis could be eliminated by a "national education" that would give to the young generation "noble causes" and "great ideals."[184] These ideals would attach the youth to their families, society, and the nation with patriotic feelings.

As discussed in this chapter through some representative journals of wartime, morality polemics had wide political, legal, and social implications that would have a divisive impact on the Ottoman political spectra. The complex stories and historical context surrounding discourses of moral decline present a fertile ground to develop a better understanding of the contest over morality: Would morality remain inseparable from religion? Or, would a secular, collective, new morality revive every aspect of life, including religion itself? What would be the basis of new morality, if it were not Islam?

Despite their differences, what united conflicting ideological discourses was an insistence on an authentic morality and their critique of the Tanzimat era. Later on, a critique of materialism added to these points in common. Apart from these two points, their analyses of moral decline differed. In addition to these, the debate about morality had abundant references to Muslim women, their place in society, and the new wave of feminism and the discourse of women emancipation in the empire.[185]

From the perspective of intellectuals involved in morality polemics, discourses on moral decline served to set out ideological differences. While nationalists defended the need for a social reform involving the improvement of the condition of women in the family, political Islamists used the moral decline paradigm to reestablish Islamic moral hegemony over public space. In this respect, a focus on morality was key to wartime political and intellectual discussions when most writers saw an opportunity to shape future society.

3

The Public Morals, Prostitution, and Cultural Perceptions

Military and bureaucratic attempts to protect public morality were mainly concentrated on two interrelated issues. First, in the course of the war, offenses violating public morality became part of growing national security concerns; and second, wartime rivalries among combatant countries manifested itself in the solidification of the so-called cultural oppositions in which moral contestation played a significant role. While the former dimension entailed more practical and administrative concerns, the latter had cultural implications. Keeping these points in mind, this chapter deals with a range of questions: How did Ottoman authorities define acts against public morality and how did they deal with these offenses? Was there a consensus among military and bureaucratic elites on definitions of immorality? To what extent did religion play a role in measures pertaining to public morality? How were discourses on moral decline reflected in politics and legislation? Given that morality occupied an important place in public opinion, how did the Ottoman government respond to moral concerns? What were the limits of state power in this sense?

Indeed, state documents from the Turkish Prime Ministry Ottoman Archives, particularly those from the catalogues of the Ministry of Interior Affairs and the police department, shed light on these questions. Moreover, the minutes of the Ottoman Parliament include debates regarding the morality concerns of ruling circles, while some documents from the Archives of the Turkish General Staff (ATASE) reveal efforts of the military that were crucial for mobilization. Some articles published in Ottoman newspapers also address the "moral battle" of the government. Moving on from the questions above, I address the Ottoman notion of public morality and definitions of offenses against public morality, wartime concerns about national security and its intersection with moral crisis, and prostitution and its containment.

The Ottoman Empire was no exception in increasing public attention to moral behavior among combatant countries. Emphasizing that wartime brought back the "fears of degeneracy" of the late nineteenth century, Grayzel argues, "the behavior of the entire population of belligerent nations was scrutinized during the war, because it became part of the war effort to preserve an idealized society that was worth dying for and to maintain the virility and success of the competing armies."[1] Indeed, during the war, there were many examples illustrating concerns about morality in Britain, Germany, and France, particularly with respect to the moral standards of women and adolescents. For instance, in Britain, the term "khaki fever" was used to describe an "epidemic disease" indicating that young women were behaving immodestly and acting "in dangerous ways" when confronted with the military men.[2] Although, "khaki fever" was observed mostly among young British women between the ages of thirteen to sixteen (the age of consent was sixteen) from poor working-class families, it was believed that the "disease" threatened the middle class, as well, marking "the First World War as a climactic time of concern about young women's social and sexual behavior."[3] This discourse, indeed, paved the way for the establishment of the Women Patrols Committee and Women Police Service by middle-class women to control these young girls in cinemas, dancing halls, and bars and prevent them from having "dangerous" interactions with soldiers.[4] In France, a solidarity campaign that invited French women to become godmothers (*marraines*) of soldiers sparked debates on moral laxity when soldiers started to seek women through such advertisements: "I have no need for socks, but would be very happy to correspond with a young, pretty, affectionate *marraine*."[5] In Germany, Ute Daniel underscores, state policies were especially focused on male adolescents. According to her, this stemmed from the fact that this group was both a resource for the army and a source of labor during the war.[6] Every kind of behavior among adolescents was under police surveillance. "Youth decrees" (*Jugenderlasse*) were issued by municipalities announcing that adolescents were forbidden to smoke in public places, to frequent bars after 9 p.m., and to go to the movies, in addition to an evening curfew.[7] However, the most remarkable measure to control the youth was compulsory saving enforcement, which was announced on March 18, 1916, allowing all male and female juveniles, to spend only eighteen marks from their weekly wages and a third of their remaining earnings until they reach the age of eighteen. Employers deposited the rest in bank accounts to which adolescents and their families had access only if they obtained consent from the aldermen of their place of residence.[8] It was partly true that there was a rise in crime (especially against property) among young workers, but the main concern was how young workers spent their wartime earnings.[9] In other words, morality was instrumentalized in a way to legitimize cuts from the wages of young workers.

Public attention to the behavior of working women constituted another central issue. The First World War was unique in the history of women's employment and presence in public space. The question of whether war work contributed to the emancipation of women remained a heated topic in the war historiography for decades.[10] As harsh economic conditions prevailed in cities, women on the Ottoman home front—like in other belligerent countries in the First World War—were employed in war factories and state institutions as well as in municipalities and marketplaces. Many middle-class women undertook active roles in war aid societies, including the Red Crescent (*Hilâl-i Ahmer*).[11] For the first time in the history of the Empire, women had right to pursue university education following the foundation of the Women's University (*İnas Darülfünunu*). Although small in number, women also served in labor battalions. All these facts contributed to the heated debates about women's place in society and their political and economic rights. The Ottoman feminist movement also contributed to these debates. Starting in the 1890s, the movement demanded the inclusion of women in the public sphere in a society where gender segregation and inequality were justified with reference to Islamic law.[12] However, recent studies on gender relations and war work show that gender roles were maintained in society despite women's participation in war work. Nicole van Os comments on the contemporary war and gender literature: "During the First World War the objective position of women in society indeed changed, but their relative (subjective) position did not."[13] Women workers were under strict moral control in their workplaces through gender segregation. Their ways of spending money, their interaction with males, and their attire in public space constituted focuses of interest. For instance, in Britain a perceived change in women attitudes was the fashion of shorter mid-calf skirts and trousers, and going out without the company of chaperons.[14] In some cases, as Laura Lee Downs shows in her work on gender division in metalworking industries during the war, women workers' behavior—including their political demands and engagements—was attributed to their moral weakness, and policemen assumed that "among women, labor militancy (or any aggressively asserted political stance) sprang from unchecked sexuality."[15] Surveillance of women workers became institutionalized in some cases. In Britain, National Union of Women Workers established the League of Decency and Honor in order to watch women workers' moral behavior.[16]

Fighting against prostitution and venereal disease constituted the major interest of belligerent governments in the realm of morality. Unregistered prostitution was an obstacle to the incorporation and mobilization of the home front. First of all, it eroded the so-called reason for the war as a defense of honor. Second, it risked public health as such diseases were spreading both on the home front and in the army. The new type of clandestine prostitutes was called "amateur girls" in Britain and "secret" or "wild" prostitutes in Germany.[17] As for the Ottoman Empire, Ahmet Rasim called this new kind of prostitution simply "new prostitution" (*fuhş-i cedid*).[18] Belligerent governments cracked down on unregistered and clandestine prostitution. The British government issued many orders to prevent unregulated prostitution, even allowing military authorities to expel prostitutes from specific areas via a regulation called "Defense of the Realm Act." To eliminate the spread of venereal disease among soldiers, prostitutes were kept under surveillance and arbitrarily arrested. The women's supposed ignorance of disease was not an acceptable excuse.[19] In Germany, measures against uncontrolled prostitution—mainly to protect against venereal disease—were strict. Members of the army who were caught carrying a disease had to identify the women who might have transmitted it, and those women were imprisoned. Women who had sex with several men in the span of a month were labeled prostitutes after two warnings, regardless of whether they were paid. The bars in Berlin, where women hostesses were working, were closed. The military doctors were responsible for examining prostitutes for venereal disease.[20]

On the other hand, army-controlled prostitution was tolerated in the areas behind the fronts provided that prostitutes had regular, mandatory medical examinations. French and German military authorities opened and regulated brothels segregated according to military rank along the Western Front. While soldiers among the lower ranks visited cheap houses, officers had access to expensive brothels. The Habsburg military also opened brothels for soldiers. On the other hand, Great Britain, and its dominions, and former colonies forbade such controlled prostitution near the front. While the US army officially barred soldiers from visiting brothels, officers were tolerant of those who did yet required medical examinations.[21]

Immorality or morality would also become part of war propaganda during the First World War. Combatant countries accused enemies of being immoral, thus justifying their own causes based on an argument of moral superiority and inferiority. For instance, in 1916, rumors that Germany and France promoted bigamy or polygamy because of huge losses on the battlefield created "a horrified reaction" among the public.[22] German soldiers who occupied Belgium were

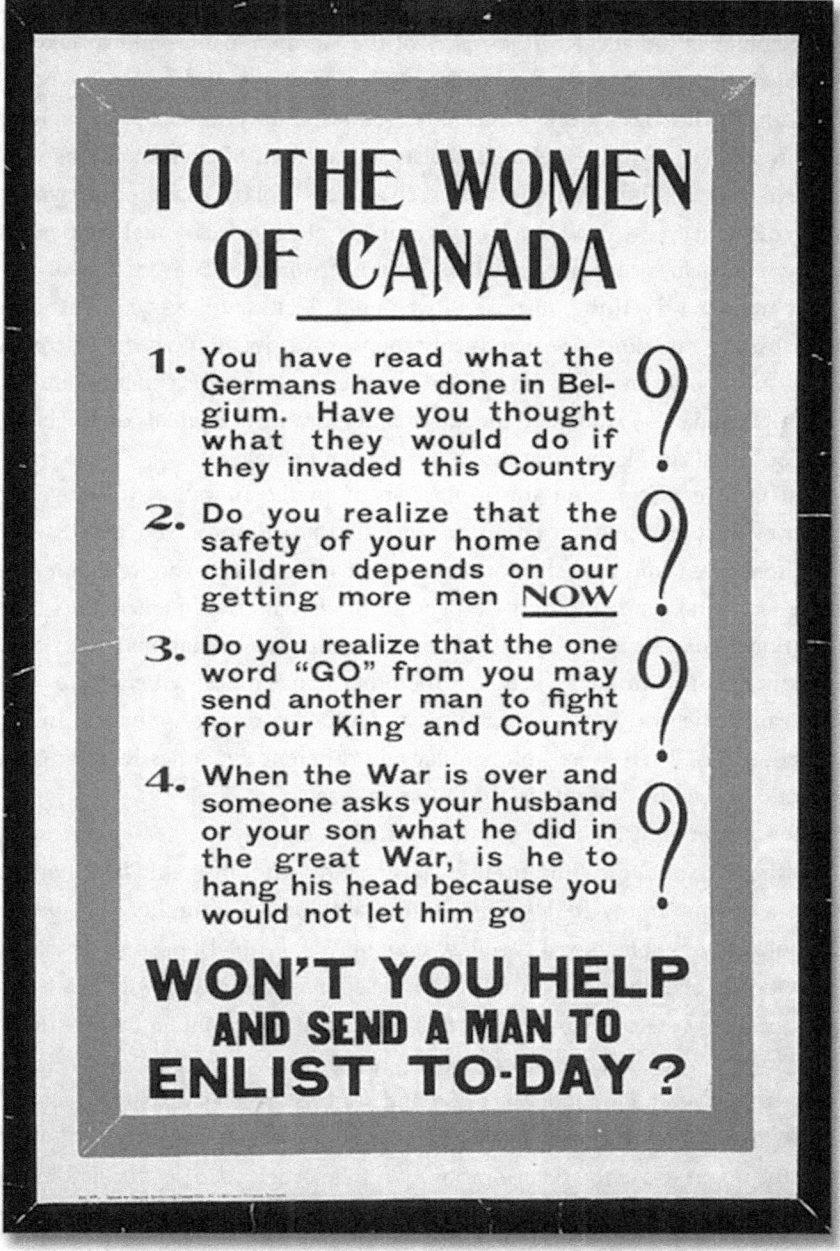

Figure 3.1 Canadian recruitment poster from the First World War. (Archives of Ontario, Online War Poster Collection, Reference Code: C 233-2-4-0-263.)

depicted in the British press as horrible and barbaric: "To remember Belgium is to remember the alleged immorality of the German armies and to take up arms against them."[23] In German propaganda depictions of the enemy were in line with a gendered aspect of morality. While military newspapers depicted Russian soldiers in East Prussia as rapists, the women of enemy nations were portrayed as unfaithful and of immoral character.[24] "Black shame" propaganda in Germany served to create a negative image of French colonial soldiers by portraying black soldiers raping white women.[25] Moreover, the "immorality" of enemy nations served the purpose of waging a "legitimate" war. For instance, the Habsburg invasion of Serbia during the war was justified with a discourse of the "moral inferiority" of the Serbs.[26] In order to demoralize enemy soldiers, war propaganda also addressed the honor and morality of civilians on the home front. Soldiers' families were at the center of such propaganda.

Wartime regulations on the protection of public morality in belligerent countries were mainly focused on uncontrolled prostitution, venereal disease, working women, and the behaviors or habits of adolescents (who were potential future soldiers) and mothers—especially their entertainment habits and educational goals. It is possible to observe an emphasis on national security in the responses to "immoral" acts. On the other hand, morality became part of propaganda rhetoric justifying war aims and underscoring "differences" among rival countries. There were both similar and different dynamics regarding the protection of public morality in the Ottoman case.

The state documents in the Ottoman Archives employed several expressions to define or condemn immorality: acts against morality (*ahlâka mugâyir hareketler*), immorality (*ahlâksızlık*), immorality or bad morality (*sûî ahlâk*), and violation of public morality (*ahlâk-ı umûmîyeye hıyânet*). In some cases, the concept of "violating public morality" was used interchangeably with "violating public order" in state documents. In this regard, we can maintain that Ottoman authorities approached the protection of public morality as part of the wider framework of maintaining public order and security. This was partly because of the fear that public reaction, such as gatherings or protests against violations of morality, might cause the deterioration of public order. Also, as detailed in the following sections, it was believed that moral corruption brought about a chain reaction of criminality, causing further increases in the number of incidents disrupting discipline and order.

Together with public order concerns, the cultural atmosphere of war in which morality became part of international rivalry needs to be taken into account. Given that the Ottoman Empire was the only Muslim-majority country in the war, it is possible that further emphasis on authentic Muslim morality was employed to further mark the differences. Therefore, immorality emerged as a social illness constituting a threat not only to public order but also to the prestige of the Ottoman Empire. Other expressions of immorality in state documents illustrate the latter in a more striking fashion: acts against Islamic manners (*âdâb-ı İslâmiyeye mugâyir*), acts against Islamic principles (*hilâf-ı İslâmiyeye mugâyir*), acts against the principles of Islam and national manners of the Ottomans (*şe'arir-i İslâmiye ve âdâb-ı millîye-yi Osmaniyeye mugâyir olarak*), and acts against the dignity of Islam (*haysiyet-i İslâmiyeye mugâyir*). This emphasis on Islam rather than ethnicity was peculiar to the Ottoman Empire not only because it was the only Muslim-majority country in the war but also because the Ottoman war effort and propaganda relied on Islam and the declaration of jihad. Thus, immorality was associated with acting against Islamic principles—principles that were crucial to efforts to wage "holy war against the infidels." Eventually, the quest for authentic Muslim identity in a country where official political agenda had yet "to catch up with the West" constituted a great tension for morality. Hence, the points that marked the so-called differences between East and West became main issues in morality discussions.

Some political and economic developments in wartime in the Ottoman Empire that contributed, on one hand, to the efforts of the government to take more effective steps to eliminate immorality while at the same time limited those efforts due to the country's financial needs, on the other. The abolishment of capitulations in September 1914 constituted a remarkable moment in the combat of prostitution. Previously, brothels owned by foreigners were subject to the same commercial laws and privileged position as any other foreign enterprise in the empire. This resulted in relative flexibility with respect to the operation of the sex industry within the borders of the empire. At the outbreak of the war, the Ottoman government unilaterally abolished capitulations and thus took control over such houses. The hunt for traffickers of women became part of the Ottoman effort to save the prestige of the empire. Prostitutes and procurers who were foreign passport holders found themselves "enemy aliens" on the Ottoman home front. Furthermore, their requests for Ottoman citizenship would be denied on the basis of their famed "immorality." The proclamation of martial law and suspension of constitutional rights in those areas where martial law was declared were other dynamics contributing to the protection of morality. Expelling prostitutes or "immoral people" from these areas became a widespread practice in the Ottoman Empire during the war. These operations were conducted in the name of national security and public order.

On the other hand, as the next chapter will show, turning to daily realities, the measures against immorality, immoral acts, and things causing moral decay were limited. Particularly with respect to the control of entertainment venues and regulation of alcohol consumption, there was a tension between the country's financial needs—that is, its need to excise taxes—and maintaining high moral standards.

Morality and Public Order under Martial Law

During the First World War, martial law became a tool to protect home front morality within the borders of the Ottoman Empire. People accused of "immorality" were expelled from martial law territories as they constituted internal threats to public order (*asayiş*) and discipline in the homeland (*inzibat-ı memleket*) and were thus to be kept under control for the sake of national security.[27] Although spatial isolation of prostitution and banishment of prostitutes had a long history in the Empire, the emphasis during wartime was different from earlier practices.[28] During the war, the use of national security discourses to fight prostitution constituted the main distinctive point.

Martial law became part of routine administration in the last decades of the Ottoman Empire. Starting in the Russo-Ottoman War (1877–8), martial law proclamations continued during the crises of the constitutional era. Resorting to martial law meant suspending constitutional rights if they conflicted with military measures. Initially to suppress and prevent separatist revolts, especially in the Balkans, martial law became institutionalized as part of mobilization efforts during the First World War.[29]

The Article 113 of the constitution of 1876 defined the conditions for the establishment of military law. Accordingly, in times of upheaval, martial law could be proclaimed in a specific place and articles of the constitution that conflicted with martial law could be suspended. Those who violated the security of the state would be deported or exiled by imperial decree.[30] According to Köksal, the concept of *idare-i örfiyye* originated from the fact that soldiers had been in administrative positions in Ottoman provinces since the classical period. These rulers with a military background were called *ehl-i örf*, meaning "men of customary law," in contrast to the "men of religious law" such as *kadıs*.[31] Eventually, military administration became associated with the term *örfî* and became a single term *idare-i örfiyye*. Moreover, the term *divân-ı harb* was coined in the Military Penal Code of 1870 and referred to courts that dealt with cases concerning soldiers.³² However, with the first proclamation of martial administration, these courts came to be known as *divân-ı harbi örfî* and were distinguished from their predecessor because it had the authority to try civilians. The martial courts could operate only in those places where martial law had been proclaimed.³³ While, under usual circumstances, the constitution precluded the trials in different courts apart from secular (*Nizâmî*) and religious (*Şer'î*) courts, Article 113 became the legal basis for trying civilians in martial courts.³⁴ As Levy-Aksu discusses, the proclamation of martial law was an Ottoman version of the "state of siege" and must be considered in light of encounters between the Islamic legal tradition and contemporaneous European legal developments occurring within the political and social context of the late Ottoman Empire.³⁵

For the first time in the Ottoman history, the parliament proclaimed martial law in Istanbul on May 24, 1877, amid the increasing tensions following the Russian occupation of Ardahan during the Russo-Ottoman War.³⁶ While this event started a tradition of martial law declarations in late Ottoman history, the first institutional framework for military rule followed a few months later, on October 2, 1877, with a decree that constituted the basis for all subsequent martial law declarations. This decree consisted of thirteen articles that ultimately transferred the powers of civil-bureaucratic administration to the administration by the military (*hükûmet-i askeriyye*).³⁷ The text was called the *İdâre-i Örfiyye Kararnâmesi*, meaning Martial Administration Decree. Accordingly, the execution of the decree was under the jurisdiction of *divân-ı harb*, the martial courts. The Article 2 of the decree suspended any articles of the constitution that were not compatible with military law. Terms such as "discipline" and "order" constituted major concerns of the text. For our purposes, the most important part is Article 6 of the decree, which constituted the legal basis for exiling and deportation.

> The military government shall have power to; first, search residences when necessary, day or night; second, deport and exile those who are convicts or suspects and those who are not officially registered residents from martial law areas to some other place; third, confiscate weapons and munitions of the people; fourth, ban newspapers that publish objectionable content and similarly ban such organizations.³⁸

The right to search residences openly violated the principle of the constitution safeguarding private property, yet it allowed the Ottoman police to operate raids. Also, it is important to note that even if the crimes described above have been committed before the proclamation of martial law, the case could be transferred to the martial courts.

On August 2, 1914, the day full mobilization was declared in the empire, an imperial decree proclaimed martial law throughout the country.[39] Indeed, martial law was in effect in Istanbul from 1909 to 24 July 1912 until Gazi Ahmet Muhtar Pasha, the grand vizier, abolished it. When his government shut down parliament amid strong disagreement with Unionist deputies, tensions in Istanbul increased. Consequently, martial law was proclaimed again on 17 September.[40] Yet, the martial law could not be carried out throughout the country in the beginning of the war as a whole at once; therefore, it was imposed gradually in different provinces.[41] I should also add that throughout the war, both the spatial and legal boundaries of martial courts were matters of negotiation and discussion between civilian and military authorities. However, some parts of the country were considered more vulnerable given the circumstances of the mobilization and remained continuously under military administration.

Unregistered prostitutes, procurers, and traffickers of women were often sent away from martial law territories to central Anatolia, where railway connections were limited and the place was far enough from the battle fronts. Their acts were considered an obstacle to mobilization and national security as official correspondence reveals: "prostitutes are violating local morality and consequently leading the violation of security and degeneration of the country."[42] Strikingly, these people were not tried in the courts, yet based on information that local police or authorities provided to the military, they were exiled under the scope of administrative decisions. This situation calls for a careful analysis of understanding of public order in the late Ottoman era, particularly the period in question. As discussed by Deniz Dölek Sever, ensuring public order on the Ottoman home front went beyond concerns about preventing crime with an increasing perception of "internal threat" and legitimized violence with the discourses of maintenance of public order.[43]

Therefore, we can also consider operations against immorality from the perspective of protecting public order. As shown through some example cases, the use of martial law to fight immorality demonstrates the prevalence of national security concerns.

Fighting against prostitution was a major task to protect public morality on the home front. In the Ottoman Empire, neither prostitution nor its regulation was peculiar to the war.[44] The novelty of wartime was unregistered prostitution, which came to be conceived as part of daily life.[45] According to Ahmed Rasim, social circumstances during the First World War paved the way for debauchery in Ottoman society, and prostitution took on new forms to spread among

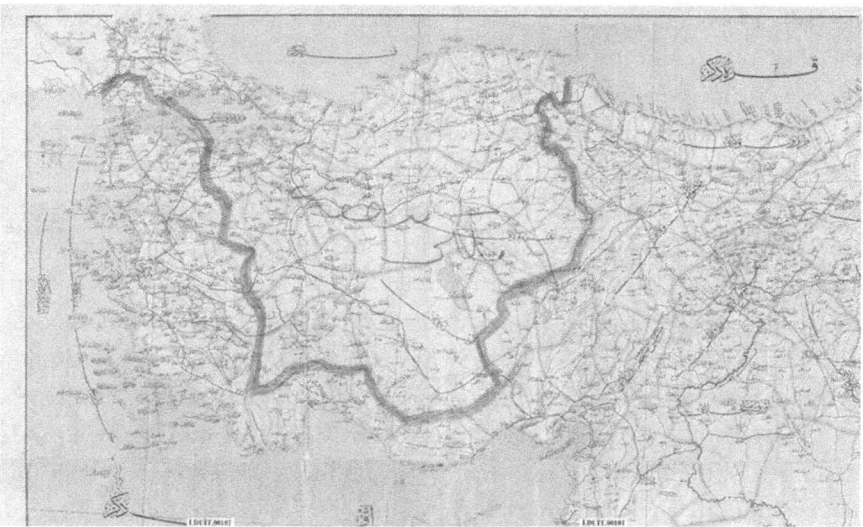

Figure 3.2 Martial law was abolished in the area inside the borders of the thick line drawn with a pencil (except for Istanbul). (BOA, İ.DUİT. 101/101.)

Muslim people.[46] Ahmed Emin asserts that this new form of prostitution was more common among Muslim women in the Ottoman Empire than among non-Muslims.[47] Fears about the spread of this new prostitution were closely related to violations of public morality. Such clandestine prostitution constituted the major reason for the spread of venereal disease among civilians and soldiers.

One remarkable measure of the Ottoman wartime government was the declaration of a new regulation to combat venereal disease. While this regulation showed the extent of the problem, it provided official recognition of the brothels at the same time. In 1915, the government issued a detailed regulation on prostitution called the *Regulation on Preventing of the Spread of Venereal Disease*.[48] Whereas the previous regulation concerning brothels from 1884 was limited to certain areas of Istanbul such as Beyoğlu, the new regulation embraced all of the provinces and defined a legal framework along with detailed directions.[49] As is clear from the title, the purpose was to keep the spread of venereal disease under control. To achieve this task, the regulation subjected brothels to state control, registered prostitutes, and kept them under medical surveillance. A variety of fines and punishments were meted out to those who violated the regulatory measures. However, as Toprak notes, this regulation maintained a liberal approach and mainly targeted controlled prostitution rather than prohibiting it entirely.[50] A considerable number of articles in the regulation concerned only the elimination of venereal disease and sanitary measures. The morality aspect of prostitution was not explicitly mentioned. Yet the regulation established a classification of prostitution that needs further elaboration because the state defined the limits of prostitution through this regulation.

The 1915 regulation begins by defining a prostitute: "In return for an interest or as habit, those who work to gratify the pleasure of others by having intercourse with more than one man are called prostitutes." The places where two or more women visited or resided for the purpose of prostitution were euphemistically called *public* or *common houses*. The regulation contends that pensions or hotels used for the same purposes be called public houses, as well. Properties that are rented or owned for the purposes of prostitution or procuration are called meeting points—like *rendezvous* houses in French. Other categories of prostitution included *sürtükler* (streetwalkers), who were described as those women who wander around for the purposes of engaging in prostitution. They had to reside in brothels and were also to be registered. Furthermore, relationships out of wedlock with a similar nature to prostitution were considered by the regulation. *Mistresses*, described in the regulation as those who had intercourse with only one man, would be registered. If they continued with it as an occupation, they would be subject to the same regulation as prostitutes.

I propose rethinking the regulation of venereal disease from the aforementioned perspective of national security. As mentioned earlier, the war increased anxieties about morality in many combatant countries and triggered a submission to the collective good regarding so-called dangers or threats to social order. Prostitution in general and venereal disease in particular were among such dangers that had the potential to destroy the collective good—that is to say, the public health of a nation.

On war and regulation of prostitution, Judith Smart provides valuable insights in her work on venereal disease regulations in Australia during the First World War. In her study, she presents a multilayered approach toward the regulation of prostitution and venereal disease that shows how such regulations of sexuality came to fall in the scope of national defense measures.

> If defence needs and duties of citizenship made the conscription of young men's bodies possible, the same requirements of total war for involvement by the whole society made the control of young women's bodies seem equally necessary because their unconstrained sexuality was represented as being dangerous to the fighting strength of the armed forces and to the reproducibility of the nation.[51]

She also takes into account the patrolling of public space with regard to such regulations that concerned women's sexuality. Certain categories of prostitution were introduced in these regulations to clarify the "public woman" from the "private" one, distinguishing the "good" from the "bad." In this sense, there are similarities between the Ottoman regulation concerning venereal disease and the Australian one given their common concern with classifying the woman and thereby containing prostitution.

On the other hand, it should be noted that the very existence of venereal disease among soldiers and civilians—whether in great or small number—indeed contributed to the solidification of anxieties about morality. After all, such diseases had a fame of immorality and were regarded as consequences of immorality. Venereal disease stood between moral and medical discourses.[52] In the context of war, as Chapter 2 discusses, the spread of venereal disease became a tool for propaganda opposing Ottoman claims to represent Muslim civilization. Particularly in this political context, as Seçil Yılmaz argues, "syphilis and prostitution became grounds for the political contestation of public morality" for the "national and religious prestige" of the empire.[53] Apart from these, morality discourses were regarded as part of a "mental struggle" against venereal disease due to the lack of adequate medical controls.[54] Although it is often assumed that female sexuality was the main target of social and political control, Yılmaz's study shows that lower-class men both as soldiers and migrant workers were the primary targets of control and surveillance as they were considered "syphilis vectors" carrying the diseases to their families.[55]

On another level, the aims of employment campaigns for women can be evaluated within the broader framework of protecting homefront morality. As discourses on the "promiscuity" of working women began to be voiced aloud, government and semi-governmental organizations explicitly propagandized employment campaigns to protect the honor and morality of Muslim women. For instance, the Society for the Employment of Ottoman Muslim Women explicitly indicated this fact in its mission. "The aim of this society is to find jobs for women and to safeguard them while customizing them to honorable ways of earning money."[56] This organization not only provided jobs but also made marriage by the age of twenty compulsory for women workers. The organization actively took part in arranging marriages, provided a trousseau for prospective brides, and investigated potential grooms with the help of the police department.[57] Moreover, similar institutions encouraged women to become seamstresses or undertake similar activities because these jobs had the advantage of maintaining gender segregation. For instance, in 1914, a garment house called Biçki Yurdu was established to teach poor Muslim women to sew, and Behire Hakkı Hanım, who published sewing books on behalf of this institute, achieved a medal for her efforts.⁵⁸ There was consensus among some women intellectuals as well as government and semi-government organizations that dressmaking was the best job to prevent Muslim women from interacting with foreign men.⁵⁹ Mahir Metinsoy details the social pressure on women in their newly acquired economic and educational life during the war. While many women had to work in complete isolation from the outside world, those hired by the state had to observe strict segregation and veiling rules even inside the workplace. There were instances that the local men were not content with women selling their goods in the marketplaces—the places that were opened by women themselves in the absence of their men.⁶⁰

Instead of focusing on prostitution itself as a wartime phenomenon, discussing how wartime dynamics played a role in the prevention of "immorality" for the sake of the war efforts is significant to grasp a better understanding of the sense of moral crisis and its relation to national security. With reference to correspondences between military and civil authorities and petitions written by persecuted people, below I discuss specific measures against the violation of public morality in martial law areas. Prevention of "immorality" by military measures was a significant phenomenon during the war, contextualizing morality as a national security concern.⁶¹

During the war, "undesirables" who were considered harmful to the war effort and mobilization were dismissed from martial law territories and relocated to other parts of the empire.⁶² The documents indicate that the punishment for morality offenses was usually banishment from martial law territories due to the acts against public morals (*âdâb-ı ahlâk-ı umûmiye mugâyir if'alden dolayı idâre-i örfiye mıntıkası hâricine te'bid*). In the Prime Ministry Ottoman Archives, much correspondence is about banished prostitutes and procurers sent to Anatolian cities such as Kayseri, Konya, and Kütahya. Some of these people were initially sent to Ankara before a final decision about them was made. Many were free to settle wherever they chose except for places close to railways or battle zones.

In most cases, the governor in the martial law territory was responsible for identifying people who violated public morality. These governors informed the Ministry of Interior about people engaged in prostitution or procuring, or that harbored such activities. For instance, the governor of Bursa, Ali Osman, sent a list of such women via encrypted telegram and requested the ministry to obtain martial court orders to banish them to a "proper" place.⁶³ Therefore, the process began with local civil authorities, was then passed to the Ministry of Interior, and lastly approved by the courts martial.

Since finding a means of livelihood for people who had been banished was a prominent problem, archival documents on such cases are abundant. Petitions written by banished people who sought a livelihood enable us to follow their stories. Through these stories, it is also possible to see whether the "ostracism" of immorality went beyond the limits of the military measures and became a social phenomenon. How did these people make a living in exile? How did local authorities approach them?

In most cases exiled people had many difficulties in the places where they were sent. They were living like fugitives, traveling from one place to another, had neither jobs nor the skills to get a job, and carried a stigma of "immorality." Keeping up "bad old habits" was not a wise choice, but in many instances, that was the case. For example, Zeyneb bint-i Ibrahim was a woman residing in Istanbul. Together with her companion, Süreyya, she was banned from the martial law territory upon a decision of the military government (*hükûmet-i askeriyye*) for the offense of operating brothel without a license. The court martial decided to imprison them for twenty-five days for this offense.[64] However, after being released from prison, they kept on "breaking the peace" according to the documents. Eventually, the military government banished them from Istanbul to Ankara on February 22, 1916. A document dated May 17, 1916, indicates that the two women were in Bilecik (a city on the border of Hüdâvendigar province). Local authorities kept them there since they had neither money nor any allowance to continue to Ankara.[65] On March 29, 1917, the local governor of Kütahya sent a letter to the Ministry of Interior, indicating that Zeyneb was sent to Ankara upon a martial court order, but she ran away from Ankara and went to Kütahya.[66] The governor told the ministry that Zeyneb had no relatives, neither money nor someone to send her stipends, and she had a tendency for "inappropriate behavior." He asked if it was possible for the ministry to pay her a daily stipend. However, the Ministry of Interior refused the request and informed the governor that people deported by the martial courts were allowed to travel to other districts (apart from military law territories) to make a living. Therefore, Zeyneb was free to stay in Kütahya. Paying stipends for such people was not possible; the ministry advised that in order to provide her with a living, the district should employ her in a proper job.

In some cases, local governors took the initiative to provide the daily sustenance (some bread) for banished prostitutes. On December 26, 1915, the governor of Konya informed the Ministry of Interior that some sixteen women were "encouraging prostitution among youngsters by engaging in illicit relationships and thus violating the order and discipline in the homeland."[67] The court martial in Konya decided to banish them as a punishment to encourage self-rehabilitation (*ıslah-ı nefs*). Execution of the decision took three months, and these sixteen women were exiled to different parts of the city. Later on, documents in the same folder indicate that six of these women were banished to the town of Bozkır without even sufficient money to buy bread. The local governor of Bozkır said that the municipality had spent 600 *kuruş* to buy daily bread for these women over fifty days. Eventually, the Ministry of Interior Affairs agreed to reimburse this amount from its discretionary fund (*tahsisât-ı mestûre*).

Many prostitutes and procurers were banished from Istanbul to Kayseri by court martial orders. As the battle zones broadened in the course of the war, the scope of the martial law widened accordingly. On March 7, 1917, the local governor of Niğde sent a letter to the Ministry of Interior Affairs expressing his opinions on fighting prostitution and protecting morality which is worth quoting here.

> From Kayseri province and from others, as well, certain prostitutes were banished to Niğde on the basis that they were violating public morality and thus upsetting public order. This practice of banishment will not have a positive effect on the improvement of morality. It is certain that eight-tenths of these women engage in prostitution due to hunger. Therefore, instead of banishing them, they should be provided with employment in workshops for a while until it is obvious that they will avoid such misbehavior. However, without such measures in place, it is enough to notify a policeman to exile these women from one place to another. Who will assure that these women won't break the peace wherever they go? It is obviously more efficient for local authorities to attempt to discipline these women. Especially those with property or any ties to a place should be encouraged to stay there. Another option, if it is not possible to employ women in jobs offered by the municipality or the local administration, is to keep them under the protection of their parents or wardens. Therefore, it is requested that this situation come to an end through the orders of the ministry.[68]

As a matter of fact, officials in the ministry were astonished to hear that a provincial governor had been issuing banishments without the approval of the military. A note by Aziz Bey of the ministry was attached to this letter questioning why civilian authorities undertook such measures without court martial decisions.[69]

The Ministry of Interior contacted the Kayseri governor about this issue. The governor replied that two women who were had been exiled to Kayseri settled near Sivas (which was part of Kayseri province), but the place they settled was in close proximity to the battlefront. The Third Army decided to relocate prostitutes further to Niğde. Another woman who continued living off prostitution was exiled to Niğde upon the approval of the head of the Recruiting Office of Fifteenth Division (*On Beşinci Fırka Ahz-ı Asker Kalemi Reisi*).[70]

Providing a livelihood was even more difficult for foreigners who had no economic means other than procuring or prostitution. According to the General Directorate of Police (*Emniyet-i Umûmiye Müdüriyeti*), two Russian citizens, Fişel [sic] and his wife Anna, were banished from Istanbul since they were "wandering in Istanbul" without property or wealth and were engaging in procuring (*muhabbet dellallığı*). On December 21, 1914, the governor of Ankara wrote to the ministry that these two Russian citizens had been temporarily sent to Ankara to be resettled in a place "far from railways and without administrative difficulties."[71] They had no wealth or skills to find a job. They spoke Russian, German, and a bit of Arabic. The governor said there was neither a position in which to employ them nor a place to which to send them where they could earn a living. Eventually, he asked for a way to provide a livelihood for this couple. Both the directorate and the ministry agreed in their correspondence that the local municipality had to deal with the subsistence of such people. The governor of Ankara replied, indicating with reference to the local municipal assembly reports that the municipality had used up its entire budget allocated for such cases and therefore needed additional funds. Upon this answer, the General Directorate of Police asked the grand vizierate for special permission to provide a stipend for these cases from the war subsidy.[72]

In order to make a living, some deported people asked the police for permission to travel to other districts. Some documents demonstrate that initially local police departments and governors did not allow them to travel to other cities and kept them under strict control. Therefore, a general order was declared indicating that these people were free to travel except in military zones.[73] On March 4, 1916, the General Directorate of Police declared this order, to be applied in all the provinces. In the order, it was indicated that traffickers of women, vagrants, and suspects (*maznu-î sûi*) were banished from Istanbul (a martial law administration area) to other cities. The directorate pointed out that due to constant complaints from these people, it was clear that local authorities were not even allowing them to travel to other parts of the empire where the military law had not been established. The directorate stated that these people were free to travel anywhere to make a living except for martial law areas and especially not Istanbul.[74]

Both deported people and their relatives constantly petitioned for pardons from the Ministry of Interior Affairs. These petitions reveal details about public morality offenses. The case of Marika de Lamiçe [sic] is one of these cases. She was accused of procuring Muslim women. The details of her offense were described in the document as "inviting honorable Muslim women over to her house, making them wear hats, and introducing them to foreigners for the purposes of prostitution."[75] Eventually, Marika was banished from Istanbul to Konya on April 16, 1917. After a year, Marika's relatives wrote a petition to the Ministry of Interior asking for her pardon. They indicated that Marika had written many petitions claiming that she was innocent. Even though she was guilty, they wrote, a year of exile was enough for the mother of two fatherless children: a sixteen-year-old daughter and a twelve-year-old son. Nevertheless, there is no indication in the archives that she received a pardon.

A case from Eskişehir shows that not only courts martial but also local actors took initiatives to combat prostitution in their own cities. The governor, together with other local authorities, arranged marriages for such women and sent some of them to villages to work for the harvest. This story was revealed on account of Ziynet and Aişe, two women from Eskişehir who sent telegrams to the Ministry of Interior Affairs complaining that they have been banished on false accusations of prostitution in July 1917.[76] The General Directorate of Police asked for an investigation report from the local Eskişehir governor to determine whether the banishment was in accordance with the law. The governor corresponded with a long letter revealing how he dealt with the issue of "public morality" in his district. Based on the fact that prostitution was spreading among honorable families due to poverty, he admitted that they were attempting several preventative measures. First, local authorities investigated whether these women had relatives or properties in Eskişehir. Then they took them for medical examination to see if they had caught venereal diseases. The ones who did not have diseases but had relatives in surrounding villages were sent to those villages where the Council of Elders (*Köy Heyet-i İhtiyarisi*) arranged their marriages to village men. If marriage was not an option, prostitutes were banished to other villages of their relatives or parents where they were made to work for the harvest. According to the governor, because men were absent due to the war agriculture relied almost exclusively on the labor of women, and prostitutes could make a contribution. Some prostitutes were even unable to find such employment, and thus, eventually returned to Eskişehir. When soldiers' relatives engaged in prostitution, the governor reported their names to the Military Recruitment Office. The soldiers' families remained in Eskişehir and were neither "punished" by serving in agriculture nor forced to submit to arranged marriages. Eventually, he denied the allegations of Aişe and Ziynet and wrote that the two women were still in Eskişehir contrary to their claim that they had been banished.[77]

Strikingly, even under conditions of war, Ottoman authorities did not stigmatize these people to the extent of leaving them on their own to starve. The scope of banishment measures was limited to keeping these people out of martial law territories. Rather than evaluating this as a sign of tolerance, I believe it stemmed from fear of further moral decline and further deterioration of public order, which could accelerate due to poverty.

As mentioned earlier, although the spatial isolation of prostitution and the banning of immoral people from living in specific places was not a new measure, its implementation during the war was different from previous implementations. It is important to see the new way of dealing with the violation of public morality and unregistered prostitution within the scope of military measures undertaken for the sake of national security. To focus more on the national security and its relation to morality, the issue of foreigners and immorality, which was at the intersection of cultural and political developments regarding public morality and the discourses of moral decline, provides a fruitful ground for inquiry.

"The Immoral Foreigner": The Role of Political and Cultural References in Moral Perceptions

On February 27, 1915, the *New York Times* published an article titled "Curb White Slavery in Constantinople: Ambassador Morgenthau's Efforts Effectively Seconded by Sultan's Police."[78] The correspondent reported that due to the capitulations "the suppression of the white slave traffic was practically impossible" in the Ottoman Empire. Accordingly, traffickers held passports from several countries in order to maintain their commercial privileges. In some cases, some also held Ottoman citizenship in case it became necessary. The Ottoman government abolished capitulations at the outbreak of the war, so "the time for the authorities to attack white slavery in the capital had therefore come." Indeed, while the Ottoman police could take measures against the trafficking in Muslim women, the trafficking in foreign women remained "ambiguous," as Wyers noted.[79] The abolishment of capitulations added another dimension to the public morality debate by giving the Ottoman government the opportunity to increase control over the sex trade. However, the situation was not as simple as keeping prostitution under control.

Prostitution and trafficking in women had different implications with regard to cultural and political contests for moral superiority, particularly during the war.[80] In the Ottoman Empire, non-Muslims and foreign passport holders were considered to be the ones who had dominated the sex trade due to commercial privileges granted to foreign citizens and the relatively lesser surveillance of non-Muslim communities. Indeed, this situation was reflected in the cultural and political realm as "foreigners promote moral degeneration."[81] As discussed in Chapter 2, many polemicists indicated that the adoption of European values was the source of moral decline in the Ottoman Empire. Indeed, this was not a new perception. Syphilis was called *frengi* in the Ottoman Empire, implying the disease had originated in the West. (The Ottomans used to call Europeans "Frenk.") On the other hand, in France the disease was called the "disease of Naples," while Italians called it the "French disease."[82] During the First World War, the increasingly nationalist tone of propaganda contributed to the rise of anti-foreigner sentiments in morality discourses. In Turkish literary works, it is possible to observe that moral degeneration was attributed to foreigners or non-Muslims, especially during the war and the occupation that followed it. Yakup Kadri's *Sodom ve Gomore* is a great example of a work in which Istanbul under occupation is presented as a city "drowned in moral and spiritual corruption" in contrast to "pure and moral" Anatolia and the Anatolian Turks.[83]

Irvin Cemil Schick argues that despite the existence of brothels in Kadıköy and Üsküdar owned by the Muslims and the fact that a wide spectrum of ethnoreligious groups were involved in the sex trade, proponents of Turkish nationalism accused non-Muslim elements of the Ottoman society of being the owners of the sex business.[84] He states that public health was not the real agenda behind attacks on prostitution; rather, it was political and aimed at discrediting cosmopolitanism.[85] Arus Yumul poses a similar argument through the story of the marginalization of the Pera quarter where a real cosmopolitan public sphere had emerged in the late Ottoman era. According to her, the cosmopolitan nature of Pera challenged the nationalist ideology of the Early Turkish Republic from a spatial perspective: It was neither "in" nor "out."[86] Hülya Yıldız also evaluates the reasons why particularly non-Muslim women were depicted in Turkish novels as prostitutes. According to her, this representation served as an aesthetic symbol of the "encounter between Ottoman society and the 'Other' that is both inside and outside its boundaries."[87]

Rifat Bali's work sheds light on the assumed role of foreign Jews in prostitution and trafficking in women.[88] Given the geographic position of Istanbul, the city was a major transit for the trafficking in women between the East and West.[89] Some foreign Jews who fled persecution or military service in Russia, Rumania, and Hungary arrived in Istanbul and established a trafficking network. These traffickers even had their own synagogue, *Or Hadash*, since people engaged in this business were not allowed to enter the main Ashkenazi synagogue. Bertha Pappenheim, a leading feminist figure who combatted the trafficking in women and founded Jewish Association for the Protection of Girls and Women, came to the Ottoman Empire to observe the participation of Jews in prostitutions network and established a foundation to prevent it. She was shocked by the very existence of traffickers' synagogue, and stated her opinions in a letter sent to a friend during her 1911 tour of the Ottoman Jewish enclaves.

> Here among the Jews [there is] a complete lack of ability to understand that this trade in humans as something dishonorable, a moral defect that in any case derives from living together with the Turks, or—what appears to me more probable—a hereditary mindset among the oriental Jews. The "sexuality" here has not given rise to any moral outrage.[90]

We see that the attitude toward the Orient and the association of the Orient with moral laxity was the other side of the coin. In Edward Said's formulation of *Orientalism*, sexuality constituted a major departing point. He drew attention to the persistent association of sexuality with the Orient by European novelists such as Flaubert.[91] Therefore, for both sides, immoral was the "other." For instance, Allied propaganda presented the Orient as the greedy consumer of European females—that is to say, "white women"—and contrasted the Orient with the superior morality of the West.[92] Not surprisingly, this became a propaganda tool against the Ottomans during the First World War.[93] Fuhrmann discusses this point in anti-prostitution campaigns and emphasizes how gender, imperialism, and nationalism played a role in the fight against or tolerance of the trafficking in women. He argues that the issue of controlling sexuality became part of a broader political debate "in the context of colonial and semi-colonial struggles for hegemony."[94] Prostitutes and their nationalities had symbolic meanings that implied the moral and thus political inferiority of the country from which they came. "The subjugation of women's sexuality metaphorically represented the subjugation of their country," writes Fuhrmann on how national profiles of prostitutes and traffickers led generalizations about the immorality of certain nations and jeopardized the political and social interests of those nations.[95]

Indeed, Ottoman authorities were "willing to turn a blind eye or even be protective of traffickers' and pimps' networks in their capital because of their corrosive effects on European supremacy."[96]

To a degree, Ottoman authorities did approach non-Muslim immorality differently than Muslim immorality. Samuel Cohen, for example, illustrated this point in an enquiry made for the Jewish Association for the Protection of Girls and Women in June 1914.

> The Turks do not shrink from making use of the public brothels, although they are very strict about their own women folk not leading immoral lives. The answer generally given by them when asked why the present state of affairs is permitted, is that the matter does not concern them so long as the inmates of the brothels do not belong to the Mohammedan faith. With regard to the prostitutes of other faiths, they do not see why they should interfere. Their argument is that if other nations and other religions permit women to act as prostitutes in their own country, why should they be prohibited from doing so in Turkey.[97]

Assuming that a certain society lacked moral values was part of a political contest that created the "other" to put a distance between a certain identity and the authentic one. This became particularly important in the context of First World War when national rivalries among combatant countries intensified.

Apart from ideological and cultural background that played a role in shaping perspectives on morality and prostitution, it is also true that before the abolition of capitulations, Ottoman authorities could not take control over the brothels and prostitutes for practical reasons. For instance, in 1876 the Ottoman Ministry of Justice loaded two ships with foreign prostitutes for deportation; however, European consuls intervened and forced the Ottoman government to abandon the operation.[98] In several previous confrontations prior to the war, the Great Powers defended the rights of their citizens in order not to risk their commercial privileges for a few sex workers.[99] In March 1914, the Ottoman Ministry of Foreign Affairs sent requests to the French, Russian, Italian, and Austro-Hungarian embassies requesting special permission to conduct sanitary inspections of brothels run by citizens of their countries. The embassies responded positively on the conditions that they are informed of the addresses of these houses and that doctors alone be in charge of the inspections.[100] It was a diplomatic matter to visit non-Ottoman commercial offices or residences. In the same dossier, a document written by the Legal Counselor of the Sublime Porte (*Bâb-ı Âlî Hukuk Müşaviri*) stated that because "most clandestine prostitutes were foreigners who resided in their own residences instead of in brothels," the Ministry of Foreign Affairs needed to ask for the cooperation of foreign embassies to regulate and inspect clandestine prostitution.¹⁰¹ Legal concessions to non-Muslims made them more resistant to the Ottoman law regarding control over the sex industry.¹⁰²

The setting for harsher measures vis-à-vis immorality was multilayered. While the abolishment of capitulations lifted legal restrictions on the control of sex business, the proclamation of martial law suspended constitutional rights, precisely those regarding the protection of private property. Before martial law, local authorities from provinces and Istanbul constantly complained that constitutional rights prevented them from undertaking stricter measures to stop prostitution. As the governor of Hüdavendigâr province put it in 1910, "despite government decrees to prevent prostitution, constitutional rights that prohibit the violation of private property discourages further investigations."¹⁰³

A discourse on human rights accompanied the diplomatic and political rivalries among combatant countries and various actors with respect to eliminating the problem of the trafficking in women. Morality-related arguments, most of which concerned prostitution and the international network that fed it, were of great importance from the standpoint of the national and international prestige of the states concerned. For instance, the American ambassador to the Ottoman Empire, Henry Morgenthau (1856–1946) actively and proudly took part in preventing the trafficking in women in Istanbul during his service. In his memoirs, he indicated that he had advised Bedri Bey, the Ottoman chief of police, to eliminate the white women trade in Istanbul when Bedri Bey had asked "whether he could not do something that would justify me portraying him in a more favourable light" when he heard that Morgenthau was planning to write a book.¹⁰⁴ Accordingly, he used this opportunity as head of a committee established to fight against trafficking in women. In order to save his reputation by becoming the person to save the city from this "disgrace," Bedri Bey, thus, conducted an effective operation: "In a few days every white-slave trader in Constantinople was scurrying for safety; most were arrested, a few made their escape; such as were foreigners, after serving terms in jail, were expelled from the country."¹⁰⁵ Morgenthau subsequently made the *New York Times* to report on the event to honor Bedri Bey for his achievement, and after this he established a good friendship with him.

Archival documents shed light on the banishment and deportation of alleged traffickers of women. A six-page notebook in the archives shows some details about the banishment and deportation of traffickers and prostitutes.¹⁰⁶ The notebook contains a list of 167 people, of which 151 were deported, and 11 were exiled to Sivas, and 5 were sent to Kayseri. This notebook was prepared by the Istanbul Police Directorate for the Ministry of Interior Affairs. It provides names, father's names, citizenships, places of residence, short indications of crimes (all of which were trafficking in white women), and dates of deportation. Among these people were Russian, French, Austrian, Romanian, and Ottoman citizens who mostly resided in Galata. For some, no date of banishment was indicated; instead, it was reported that they were "banished with the first group." In other cases, the dates were January 31, and February 1, 1915. Following these deportations, on February 3, 1915, the Ministry of Interior Affairs introduced a general decree regarding public morality offenses and measures to be taken. Unfortunately, I could not find this decree among the archival documents even though widely referred to in the correspondences.

Owing to petitions written by the alleged traffickers of women, we can follow their time in exile. Madam Yaş Şodaç [sic] and Ernestiya [sic] were sent to Kayseri on February 1, 1915, along with many people who were accused of the same crime. Their names were among those on the six-page list of the first round of deportation. These two women claimed they were victims of a slander. Indicating that there was no rabbi in Kayseri with whom they could perform their religious duties, they asked to go back Istanbul or at least to be resettled in Konya. They added that they were suffering extreme misery and poverty (*sefalet ve perişaninin son noktasındayız*). However, according to the General Directorate of Police, these women violated security and were constantly acting suspiciously (*ahvâl ve harekâtının selb-i emniyet ve dâimi şübhe bulunmağla*) and since they had engaged in an international crime, that is to say, trafficking in women, they could not be pardoned.[107]

Among archival documents regarding banishments, Dina Kalazar's case is the most detailed.[108] Her case is revealed through the correspondence between the General Directorate of Police and the Ministry of Interior Affairs in addition to petitions. She was known as "Sarı Madam" and was famous for owning five brothels in Galata. Apparently, she was a central figure in international trafficking in women. She was banished from Istanbul to Kayseri on January 31, 1915, for the offense of trafficking in white women. Her offense was indicated in the documents as "*ahlâk-ı umûmiyeye hıyânet*," which means violation of public morality. The police department indicated that she had been involved in trafficking for many years together with her husband, Marko. Eventually, Marko was banished to Sivas and Dina was sent to Kayseri. Dina wrote many petitions, some of which were collectively signed by other female companions in Kayseri. They began sending petitions to the Kayseri governor and the ministry as soon as they were settled there. They tried many ways to be relocated elsewhere. First Dina signed a petition complaining her lack of livelihood. Later she signed a collective one claiming that there was no rabbi in Kayseri with whom they could perform their religious duties. And she kept on writing in the end claiming that the climate of Kayseri did not agree with her. Eventually, she received permission to travel to Eskişehir and settle there.

Dina's case also reveals facts related to the banishment process and life in exile. For instance, the local governor of Kayseri indicated in one correspondence that these women made their livings for a while by selling their belongings. Dina, Agtiana Gala Naka [sic], Sultana, and Viktorya wrote a petition on May 25, 1915.

> Your servants it's been a while since [we] opened brothels. We are Ottoman citizens and we belong to the Jewish community. When martial law was proclaimed, they deported us from Istanbul and banished us to Kayseri. We are not men; we have no profession to make a living. We cannot meet even our basic needs in Kayseri. It is known that we never had problems in brothels that we ran. We cannot adapt to the climate in Kayseri, our children are in Dersaadet, and our husbands are in Sivas—all of us are in misery. It has been five months now; only God and we know how we have suffered. If we are not—and never will be—allowed to work in this profession, we are ready to sign documents guaranteeing that we will never run brothels.[109]

Another petition in the same folder was signed by Sultana, Viktorya and Mari İzdaç [sic]. They claimed that one of them had a son and he was a soldier in the Ottoman army. They wrote that they served important households in Istanbul, and they had been punished while the real owners of the brothels were still in Istanbul. Also, Dina's sister Fiska Yenirman [sic] wrote a petition on March 21, 1916, to the General Directorate of Police. After briefly summarizing the events, Fiska asserted that her sister possessed wealth; she would live an honorable life in Dersaadet if she were allowed to return. However, the answer was unfavorable; the directorate emphasized that trafficking in women could not be pardoned.[110]

After two years of banishment, on January 1, 1917, Dina wrote another petition in which she indicated that upon her own request she had moved to Ankara (Eskişehir) from Kayseri with special permission. Her husband (apparently back to Istanbul) had typhoid fever, and she asked for special permission from the province of Eskişehir to return in order to take care of her husband in Istanbul. As soon as she arrived in Istanbul, police took her into custody and sent her back to Kayseri, the place where she was first banished. She asked the ministry to travel back to Eskişehir saying that she could not make a living in Kayseri.

> Two years ago, I was banished to Kayseri due to a trafficking in women offense. However, I could not adapt to the weather there. I asked permission to go to

Ankara, and they allowed me to do so. As soon as I heard that my husband had typhoid fever, I went to Dersaadet with special permission. They said I came without notifying the authorities. They sent me back to Kayseri with my six-year-old child.[111]

Eventually, she received permission to go back to Eskişehir.[112]

It is interesting to note that the General Directorate of Police indicated that Dina's punishment was not based on a decision of the court martial. The directorate commented that it was unnecessary to get a court decision for these cases since trafficking in women was an international crime; moreover, the government had announced a preventive measure that such people be banished even without a conviction.[113] This shows that Dina was banished by the directorate. However, she wrote in one petition that she had been banished due to the proclamation of martial law.[114] The most reasonable explanation is that the Ministry of Interior had established preventive measures at the outbreak of the war and applied them without even referring to the martial order.

Non-Ottoman citizens who were deported or banished due to immorality offenses applied for Ottoman citizenship with the hope of receiving a pardon or guaranteeing their ability to stay within the borders of the empire. However, such applications were declined immediately after reports indicating their "immorality" were sent by the General Directorate of Police to the Ministry of Interior. Even though a person had not been convicted of a "morality" crime, she or he had no chance of receiving Ottoman citizenship due to "immorality fame."

During the First World War, the citizenship status of foreign passport holders in the Ottoman Empire became a matter of interest for several reasons. Especially civilians who held the citizenship of one of the Entente Powers were faced with harsh measures as "enemy aliens."[115] These people had a long history in the empire not only as visitors, businessmen, or workers but also as permanent residents. Evaluating citizenship applications by foreign passport holders who allegedly violated public morality and were subsequently banished or deported demonstrates how morality became a significant impetus at the intersection of multiple dynamics.

In addition to wartime measures, the abolishment of capitulations at the outbreak of the war meant that being a non-Ottoman citizen within the borders of the Empire was no longer a privileged position. The abolition curbed interest in sex trade, and military surveillance of morality resulted in great unrest for non-Ottomans. As archival documents reveal, the dates of citizenship applications suggest this argument. Almost all applications I studied in the scope of this project were submitted in the beginning of 1915, some months after the declaration of mobilization and right after the government's announcement of measures concerning both the situation of non-Ottoman citizens and the protection of morality in martial law areas. These cases show that morality was an important requirement to be granted Ottoman citizenship. Many of the cases considered here are related to prostitution, trafficking in women, or procuring. The fact that none of the applicants managed to receive citizenship shows how moral judgments worked together with national security concerns and how wartime measures enabled the "undesirable" elements in society to be eliminated.

The catalogues of the Ministry of Interior are full of such demands, petitions, and applications of alleged "prostitutes and procurers" to become Ottoman citizens. However, their applications were declined immediately whenever the police department's investigation reports were sent to the Ministry of Interior. Even applicants who had not been convicted or banished due to morality crimes were rejected when their police report indicated that they were immoral (*ahlâksız*). No further investigations were carried for that individual and the application was declined immediately. Furthermore, thanks to the investigation, he or she would get charged as well.

On March 15, 1915, a preliminary law was issued regarding residence and travel regulations for foreign citizens in the empire.[116] According to this preliminary law, provincial and local governors, after informing the Ministry of Interior Affairs, had the right to banish or deport foreigners who violated peace and order within the borders of their towns or cities. Those who were deported could not return to the empire without formal permission. Breaking this law would entail imprisonment of up to six months and/or a fine of up to fifty gold Ottoman coins.[117]

Mişel Salomovic was among traffickers of women deported from the Empire on January 29, 1916.[118] His wife, Madam Bertahlamovic, petitioned the Imperial Secretary (*Mabeyn-i Hümâyun Başkitâbet Dairesi*) and asked for a pardon emphasizing Mişel's old age and that there had been others who had returned to the country whose cases were similar to Mişel's. Upon her petition, several departments held an investigation. Finally, the directorate of police answered the Ministry of Interior as follows:

> Due to trafficking in white women offenses, foreign passport holders were deported from the country while Ottoman citizens were exiled to other Ottoman

cities. Mişel Salomoviç, a Russian citizen, convicted of women trafficking was deported from the country along with others on January 29, 1916. Since his return would violate the seventh article of the foreigner's law, the request has been rejected.[119]

While the abolition of capitulations clearly broke the previous contract between foreign passport holders and Ottoman authorities, the preliminary law on foreigners of 1915 brought about new measures to keep foreign citizens under control and punish them in cases of violations of order. Combined with the mobilization efforts—that is to say martial law—wartime was characterized by the increasing power of civil and military offices over civilians.

There were many shortcomings of being a citizen of an Entente Power in the Ottoman Empire during the First World War. For example, reprisals against civilians became integral to fighting the enemy during the war. Civilians were punished with deportation or banishment in retaliation for bombings targeting Ottoman citizens. For instance, as payback for Entente bombings in Köyceğiz, a person named Ferguson was to be exiled to Kastamonu. However, since he had left the country, the Ottoman police tried to find his father. Unable to find none of them, the police found another foreigner, Robert McGill, to banish in retaliation.[120] Apart from retaliations, non-Ottoman citizens, including Muslim ones, were under the surveillance of Ottoman security forces. They were subject to a special curfew that restricted their movements at night.[121] A general circular by the Ministry of Interior Affairs to the provinces prescribed the banishment of "harmful" (*muzır*) citizens from Allied countries to "non-prohibited zones"— that is, provinces under civil administration.[122] But in Syria, which was under the command of the Fourth Army, all citizens of Allied powers, regardless of whether they were "harmful or not," were banished to Urfa. As a precaution against spying, the harboring of spies, or the conducting anti-government or anti-war propaganda, many were banished to central Anatolia to less-connected regions such as Kastamonu, Sivas, Çorum, Konya, and Kayseri as well as to cities far from military deployment routes. The Black Sea, Aegean, and Marmara coasts were considered especially vulnerable to naval attacks and were considered the places where spies were potentially being harbored.[123]

The act of banishment not only served as punishment for political offenses as mentioned above but was also a mechanism for the preservation of public order. Such public order cases varied from drunkenness to pickpocketing and from prostitution to loose morals. While banishment was generally the result of a court martial decision, some were *idareten sürgün*, meaning an administrative order for banishment.[124]

The "morality requirement" is explicitly observed in official documents regarding citizenship applications. On January 10, 1915, Terzi Povayir [sic], Vitali, and Tesab Arş [sic] applied for Ottoman citizenship through the Citizenship Directorate of Ministry of Foreign Affairs (*Hariciye Nezareti Tâbiiyyet Müdüriyeti*). The ministry sent the cases to the Ministry of Interior Affairs to be investigated by the police department. According to police reports, all three men were residents of Şeftali Street in Galata, and had been previously banished for making a living by encouraging prostitution; thus, their cases did not deserve further investigation and their applications were denied immediately.[125]

In another case, the denied request of a Russian citizen, Eşmil Aron veled-i Birkof Gerson [sic], who was a barber in Şeftali Street Galata, was based on the fact he was involved in trafficking in women. The document reported that his application was denied because "such people do not deserve the honor of receiving Ottoman citizenship," and moreover, he should be charged for this offense.[126] Here, it should be noted that Eşmil Aron had neither been convicted nor banished previously for trafficking in women. He applied for citizenship from his place of residence.

Although the documents did not give further information about how the police had investigated the case and how they reached such conclusions, the records of some cases suggest that personal accounts during the investigation mattered, as well. For example, the case of Rafyan reveals that police relied on personal accounts during the background investigation to evaluate his citizenship application. Rafyan applied for Ottoman citizenship on December 3, 1914. He was a Jew, a citizen of Russia, lived in Karaoğlan Street, Galata, and worked as a street vendor. Six years earlier he had deserted from military service in Russia and settled in Istanbul. Apparently, as he was a fugitive in Istanbul, he had never submitted a document to the Russian Consulate. According to the police report, he had a relationship with a prostitute in one of the Galata brothels, and he made his living from this relationship. The report went on to say that he was known as "immoral Rafyan" among the people.[127] Eventually, his application was denied. A similar case was that of Rolmeş veled-i Volef Karonfelk [sic], who applied for citizenship on December 21, 1914. He was a street vendor and resident of Karaoğlan Street, Galata. His application was denied on the basis that he earned his living from his relationship with a prostitute.[128]

Not only men but also women foreign nationals applied for Ottoman citizenship in order to secure their living and situation in the country during the war. For example, Liza bint-i Mendel, a Russian citizen and resident ten-year resident in Karaoğlan Street, Galata applied for citizenship on December 31, 1914. Since she was operating a brothel, the document reports, "she does not deserve to be registered and accepted as an Ottoman citizen."[129] Another case was Elis from Adana's Taşçıkan neighborhood, who applied for Ottoman citizenship in February 1915 claiming that she was American. However, she could not provide any documentation of her citizenship other than her command of English. The Ministry of Foreign Affairs declined her application foremost because she could not prove her country of origin and second because her immorality was "well known."[130]

There are cases of religious conversions not being accepted, as well, due to immorality accusations. An Armenian woman, Mari, a resident of Kumkapı, and the daughter of Giragos the gardener, applied to the Ministry of Justice and Religious Denominations (*Adliye ve Mezâhib Nezâreti*) to convert Islam on July 6, 1917. After an investigation by the Istanbul Police Department, the Ministry of Interior Affairs concluded that she was earning her living from prostitution. Her application was denied, and she was not allowed to convert to Islam.[131] In another case, local authorities in Istanbul approached the conversion of an English man differently. This case is also interesting since it involved an interreligious relationship between a Muslim woman and a non-Muslim man. Arthur Talin [sic], a British citizen, was banished from Istanbul to the town of Bozkır in 1915 when police discovered his affair with a Muslim woman. After three months in exile he converted to Islam, changed his name to Ahmed Arif, and asked the Ministry of Justice and Religious Denominations to approve his conversion. Having received his application, the ministry found it suspicious and asked for more information about his motives for religious conversion. The Ministry of Interior Affairs reported that Arthur had converted to Islam to marry a Muslim woman. Emphasizing that he had obtained permission to marry from the father of that Muslim woman, his application was accepted, and he was allowed to return to Istanbul.[132]

As these cases demonstrate, the Ottoman government conducted special investigations regarding the moral qualities of citizenship applicants. Given the circumstances that foreigners in the empire experienced as enemy aliens, many applied for Ottoman citizenship in order to secure their residence in the empire. However, Ottoman authorities imposed strict background checks and denied the applications of foreigners in cases of suspected of immorality.

This chapter discussed the protection of public morality from political and social perspectives in the context of the First World War. As shown, anxiety over public morality had ramifications beyond a simple rhetoric of preventing prostitution and controlling sexuality. Particularly on the topic of foreigners and immorality, I propose to consider the setting of the war and rivalry between combatant countries because immorality discourses served political and cultural claims. Despite many similarities between the Ottoman Empire and other belligerents in terms of increasing moral control, the Ottoman case had its own peculiarities deriving from its own dynamics such as gaining its long desired sovereignty over people who lived on its territory. Some developments such as the abolition of capitulations and military measures, including the search of private houses, banishment, and deportation from martial law territories, constituted an opportunity for Ottoman authorities to "clean up" the home front, especially in martial law areas. As some cases illustrate, morality was a concrete requirement—a condition of eligibility to obtain Ottoman citizenship or convert to Islam.

Years later, the Republic of Turkey would take further measures to keep prostitution out of the country. In 1930, the government enacted an abolitionist law on prostitution mandating the deportation of all foreign prostitutes. Nationalist motives were accompanied by critiques that Istanbul was the global center for the trafficking in women.[133] It is possible to argue that the wartime measures mentioned in this study were the early stages of this "clean-up campaign" of the 1920s and 1930s designed to increase the prestige and reputation of the country.

4

Morality between Discourse and Daily Realities

When it comes to the discussion of what is permissible [in Islam] and what is not, the tax imposed on pork and wine too are not permissible. Oh my, these [debates] are outdated.
  –Hacı Şefik Bey, Deputy of Istanbul, MMZC

Although the most powerful discourse on morality manifested itself in the polemics on prostitution and sexual behavior, other topics in the domain of morality were more central to everyday life. Prostitution, indeed, was part of a broader discussion on public morality in which vices, conspicuous consumption, and European cultural penetration into the Muslim community became rallying points. Neither ill-reputed behaviors nor critique of them were peculiar to wartime; however, the obvious context of war contributed to a rise of moral considerations and added new dynamics. Nevertheless, this did not mean that Ottoman authorities, whether bureaucratic or military, achieved absolute authority over public morality.

The recurrent themes in morality polemics revolved around the broad categories of entertainment and leisure as vices causing further moral decadence. Entertainment and leisure activities had become the subject of heated debates due to their alleged role in the penetration of European cultural influence into Muslim societies. As discussed in Chapter 2, advocates of Islamic morality pointed to this influence as the primary reason for moral degeneration in the Ottoman Empire. From the conservative point of view, compliance with or resistance to this influence constituted the grounds for moral standards. Like prostitution, habits such as alcohol consumption and gambling—and to a certain degree frequenting modern entertainment places where European "vices" were on display, such as theaters, cinemas, and taverns—were associated with immorality. During the First World War, an increased hostility toward enemy countries strengthened discourses on "imported immorality."[1] Apart from religious conservatives and authentic morality advocates, other intellectual elites were also among those targeting such entertainment and leisure activities due to their degenerative impact on society. Some popular perceptions regarding morality, or more precisely immorality, were accompanied by fears inspired from biblical stories of calamity. On another level, declaration of jihad added more emphasis to the religious dimension in discourses on morality.

As I discussed in the previous chapter, in the eyes of the state authorities public morality was part of a broader framework of public order. As long as public order was not concerned, individual's "private" lives did not attract particular attention in official documents. What did alarm state authorities was possible social upheaval (*halkın galeyâna gelmesi*) that could be stirred up by the violation of public morality. For instance, conspicuous consumption and excessive entertainment on the home front could attract public reaction and spark protests. Moreover, these might affect the motivation of soldiers on the battlefield.

Despite these concerns, the Ottoman state approached the issue pragmatically and used spending on entertainment to increase its own revenues. Given the context of the war, such revenues obviously became indispensable for the state budget. While semi-government war relief organizations invested in entertainment to collect this revenue, the moral instruction and nationalist propaganda achieved limited success due to the conflict between financial interests and the expectations of spectators. Therefore, in this study, I suggest that entertainment and the vices associated with immorality were part of a moral contest among various actors with various agendas. Also, turning our attention to the daily aspects of morality provides a more complete, complex picture of the vast reach of morality discourses.

The link between public order and public morality can be observed in a regulation issued prior to the First World War, on March 12, 1912. This was a supplementary law added to the Article 99 of the Penal Code stipulating new measures for maintaining discipline and order in the country and preventing the violation of public manners, morality, principles of health.[2] The decree consisted of six articles that prevented ex-convicts from carrying weapons: asked full cooperation of travelers with police requesting them to show their documents; made it compulsory for landlords and hotel owners to inform the police departments of the identities of their tenants and guests within twenty-four hours; prohibited theater plays that might insult or humiliate religions and madhabs recognized by the Ottoman state as well as the ones that violated public manners, morality, or public order; prohibited the opening of brothels in forbidden areas; and lastly, banned any kinds of attempts explicitly stirring up public turmoil and violating manners and the practice of religion in Ottoman lands. Indeed, these were the points that constituted the backbone of the main issues of public order and public morality in the eyes of Ottoman authorities.[3]

An analysis of popular perceptions regarding war and immorality, and of topics such as conspicuous consumption and war profiteering, shows how morality discourses were central to the critique of social inequalities during the war. Official attempts to regulate entertainment venues reveal the government's dilemma concerning financial profit and moral control. The same dilemma can be observed on the issues of gambling and alcohol. Through these points that shed light on the complexity of public morality discourses, I also aim at addressing what can be defined as early versions of current debates on "lifestyle" and its relationship to morality.

Is it possible to list the things deemed a threat to public morality in the course of everyday life? Was there a common discourse or a popular perception on the signs of immorality? If so, how did this discourse intersect with the context of war? Although less documented, it is possible to find some clues about a mentality that assumed a relationship between immorality and calamities throughout Ottoman history.

Prohibition on alcohol consumption, for instance, constituted a result of the assumed link between immorality and calamity. Prohibitive discourses served to reproduce the authority of traditional elites by establishing their moral authority over society. For example, after pestilence and a fire disaster in Istanbul in the seventeenth century, the Ottoman *ulema* started a campaign that blamed practices that deviated from Islam for the disasters. And eventually they achieved their aim to prohibit the sale of wine in the city.[4] According to Kırlı, in the second half of the sixteenth and the first half of the seventeenth centuries, sumptuary laws and the moralizing discourses of ruling elites intensified in the Ottoman Empire as a consequence of challenges by new social forces against the existing order.[5] The moral decline polemicists in the early modern Ottoman Empire thus attempted to preserve their hegemony and extant social hierarchies through sumptuary regulations that emphasize the degeneration of moral order. Kırlı states that this hegemony not only maintained the political position of the ruling classes; it was also an ideological hegemony that explains the prevalence of moral discourses among those of the same opinion about declining moral values even though they were not part of the ruling class.[6] The moral discourses that emerged in the early modern era targeted "urban public spaces" such as coffeehouses, places that "represented the breakdown of social hierarchy and thus served as a metaphor for urban disorder."[7] Sultan Mahmud

II's regime, which coincided with social upheaval and radical reform, strongly emphasized orthodoxy and morality during the abolishment of the Janissary corps. The heterodox Bektashi order (infamous for drinking) was closed, and their properties were handed over to the orthodox Nakshibendi order.

Public spaces such as coffeehouses were also mistrusted because they constituted the locations from which gossip and rumors spread, including political commentaries.[8] In the nineteenth century public attention intensified on "heterogeneous" public spaces such as theaters, cinemas, parks, pubs, and cafés, where "unrelated men and women could mingle."[9] Throughout the nineteenth century, the spatiotemporal organization of urban life attracted the attention of the ruling classes from the standpoint of both modernity and public order. In the previous system, urban order and moral control had been provided within defined spatial units among which the *mahalle* constituted the basic unit. In this system, personal surety (*kefalet*) played an important role in stipulating collective responsibility for maintaining public order and morality.[10] Nighttime, however, offered opportunities to those bent on evading society's existent norms.[11] When the streets began to be illuminated in the nineteenth century, the night became subject to the growing control of state authorities. However, as Nurçin İleri argues, there was a paradox between a more efficient system of surveillance and controlling the night and the "cultivation of nocturnal sociability."[12] The illumination of the night created new spaces for leisure activities that came to be associated with disorder and immorality—and at the same time with modern life and economic progress.[13] The "moral order" defenders, thus, not only targeted the entertainment places but also established parallels between moral decline and European cultural influence based on the fact that such entertainment places were the products of Western civilization.

The initial phase of the late Ottoman version of what I call "the immorality chain" began with the instillation of degenerate values through theater and cinema. This type of entertainment not only brought men and women together at the same stage and thus disregarded gender segregation but also held up the "private" lives of other people and their corrupt values as examples to the youth. Furthermore, alcohol, which is explicitly forbidden in Islam, lowered inhibition and prepared an environment in which illicit sex and prostitution might occur. Since prostitution requires money, men would resort to gambling and risk the income of their families. Eventually, such people were cursed with the stigma of venereal disease. To some extent, this line of thought can be observed not only in conservative circles but also among nationalists with respect to their critiques of immorality. While religious moralists preferred to cite stories of divine punishment, such as the famous story of Sodom and Gomorrah, nationalist narratives focused on social and national destruction as consequences of immorality.[14] In the upheaval of the war and also during the armistice period, the latter narrative of collective destruction gained momentum.

During the First World War, some members of the Ottoman *ulema* used the proclamation of jihad as an opportunity to revive the narrative of immorality and divine punishment. A madrasa teacher from the Temple Mount (*Harem-i Şerif*) wrote a letter to the Ministry of Interior Affairs at the beginning of the war claiming that if the government hoped to succeed in jihad, it had to watch people's morality, in particular that of women's, because "the first rebellion [against God] happened in this world because of women."[15] He proposed steps be taken for the sake of jihad, including:

> The prohibition of all acts that were incompatible with Islam; the closing of taverns and coffeehouses; the prohibition of alcohol and gambling for Muslims; the prohibition of those things causing or encouraging adultery; the obligation of women to behave with perfect manners (*kemâl-i edeb*) in bazaars, theaters, and parks; and the ban of those kinds of women's clothing that were incompatible with Islamic principles.[16]

For him, the theaters in which women were dancing with their "uncovered chests" and provoking illicit love affairs were the places where immorality was spread among Muslims and Muslim youth. He asserted that to tolerate such instances would harm the holy cause and have a negative impact on other Muslim countries. Another madrasa teacher, Abdullah Fevzi Efendi, who joined the army during the First World War, wrote in his memoirs that "the fire from howitzers and planes are just as it was told in Quran: calamities arriving from the sky to the earth" that were God's punishment for sins that Ottoman soldiers had committed.[17]

Ordinary people also shared similar opinions about immorality. "To serve humanity," they sent letters to the Ministry of Interior Affairs asking measures be taken against immorality. These letters presented lists of houses where illicit sex allegedly occurred.[18] A notable man from Kayseri requesting the prohibition of brothels in the city asserted in a letter that calamities such as earthquakes, fires, disasters, shortage of rain, lack of profits, and insufficient harvests were the consequences of a curse brought by immorality.[19] The author of this letter used the same "chain of immorality" to illustrate the links between moral and social disorder.[20]

Despite the bitter tone against violations of public morality, the main motive of authorities was to take measures to protect public order. The approach was relatively flexible, official discourse notwithstanding. Even Abdullah Fevzi Efendi, who cursed Ottoman soldiers for their immorality, wrote in his memoirs that "those who accomplish their duties" need joy and entertainment, and it can be tolerated so long as it was "once in a while" and without public display. These "unwritten rules," indeed, constituted public approbation or toleration of immorality. As long as immoral acts remained secret and occurred only "once in a while," both the public and state authorities would tolerate them. In the case of open violations, punishment could be severe.

Carousal (*işret*) and paying women to dance (*kadın oynatmak*) were among the most documented violations of public morality.[21] It seems that this type of entertainment was especially common among the bureaucratic and military elites in the provincial areas. It came to be documented in archival correspondence when conflicts arose when security forces intervened or local people complained to the police. Again, these events were documented for breaking the peace and public order because they created an uproar among the local community.[22] The military or bureaucratic officers caught drinking and watching women dance were tried in courts martial.[23]

Perhaps, it is worth considering the public impact and imagery of occasions when soldiers and high-ranking military men were involved. İhsan Turjman, a soldier based in Jerusalem, vividly described such representative stories of social as well as military life in 1915 and 1916 in his diary.[24] He often contrasted the misery of ordinary people and low-ranking soldiers with the indulgence of those of high rank. He was disgusted by the "whoring and drinking" parties of high-ranking men taking place at a time when the Ottoman army was fighting in Çanakkale and where thousands of soldiers lost their lives.

> Ahmad Cemal Pasha issued an order today, in celebration of the anniversary of Sultan Mehmet Rashad V's ascension to the throne, to distribute mutton and sweets to members of the armed forces... A big party was being prepared at the Commissariat, to be presided over by the two Cemals [Cemal Pasha and Küçük Cemal] and Ruşen Bey [Commander and Residence Inspector][25] and other senior admirals and officers... A number of Jerusalem prostitutes were also invited to entertain the officers. I was told that at least 50 well-known whores were among the invitees... While this was happening, our brothers were fighting in the Dardanelles... I suddenly became despondent and very sad for our condition.[26]

Obviously, Cemal Pasha was among the three most significant figures of the CUP and had privileges over low ranks. He was notorious among the local population of Greater Syria as he had ordered the deportation and execution of many leading figures on the basis of accusations of spying while the locals were struggling with famine as well as locust attacks. His reputation of immorality added yet another dimension to this story of a type that attracted vast interest among the locals. Turjman's testimony details how such occasions sparked an "identity crisis" that shook the Ottoman collectivity and estranged Arab soldiers from Ottoman identity.[27]

In another context, reputation for immorality played an important role in expressing ethnic discontent. A French Lazarist priest in Syria wrote in 1917 about the Cemal Pasha case. "Apostasies are the order of the day in the cities. How many have given themselves to Muslims, or have given up their honor for a morsel of bread… All of the Turkish officers, Jemal Pasha at their head, can't have enough Christian girls to sacrifice to their perversions."[28]

During the Arab Revolt of 1916 too, the Sharifian propaganda against the Ottoman rule was based on the idea that Sharif Hussein was doing his duty against those who violated the Sharia by introducing secular laws and lifestyles. The Sharif of Mecca targeted not only Cemal Pasha's perversions in his anti-Ottoman propaganda but also his role in employing women in state offices, which for the Sharif signified the fact that Ottomans were not qualified to rule the Muslims.[29] Reputation for immorality played a role in constructing the "other" at the international level and contributed to the contest of practicing "true Islam" and legitimate Islamic governance.

Moral Decline and Conspicuous Consumption, Debauchery, and Wartime Profiteering

A moral discourse often accompanied critiques of war profiteering which almost obscured the political failure of the "national economy program," from which the profiteers benefited. Especially after the Balkan Wars, when the CUP seized full control of the Ottoman government, a new economic policy called the National Economy (*Millî iktisat*) was pursued in order to empower Muslim businessmen. The new economic policy had a simple formula to save the Ottoman Empire: to create a Muslim bourgeoisie as an alternative to the non-Muslim merchants in the empire.[30] In line with this policy, the traditional Ottoman bourgeoisie, comprised mainly of non-Muslims, was eliminated from commercial networks due to their perceived sympathy for foreign powers. The accumulation of wealth was to be left in the hands of the Muslim bourgeoisie. In fact, the war provided many opportunities to actualize this project. The First World War was a massive opportunity for profiteers to bypass previous rules of commerce through political engagement with the CUP. The national economy policy facilitated war profiteering by providing transportation rights, credits, and privileges to Muslim entrepreneurs. Not only large enterprises but also small merchants profiteered, especially on urgently needed goods such as oil, gas, sugar, and flour. Meanwhile, large landowners benefited from the ambitious agricultural policies of the government. New companies were established under state protection and benefited from privileges designed to keep commerce in the hands of Muslim entrepreneurs. Black-marketing of goods in demand made it possible for many to make huge profits during the war.

Istanbul was significantly affected by privation, due to its reliance on imported goods. At the beginning of the war, the city met its consumption needs through existing stocks, but as the war went on, local merchants speculated and stored the resources. This food crisis provided the basis for a transfer of wealth from non-Muslim merchants to the Muslim bourgeoisie. Some organizations, such as the National Defense Society and the Artisans' Society, played significant roles in this transfer.[31]

On May 24, 1917, under the pressure of public opinion, the Ottoman government issued a provisional law to prevent speculation. The courts martial were in charge of executing the penalties from then on. An Anti-profiteering Commission (*Men-i İhtikâr Heyeti*) was established to enforce the law. Although the efforts of the government to end the black market were initially successful, the political agenda of creating a national economy conflicted with these efforts in the chaotic atmosphere of the war.[32] Those who were able to stock goods thanks to transportation rights, credits, and state protection accumulated immense wealth.[33]

Consequently, a new class of war profiteers (*harb zengini*) emerged. War profiteers, a specific group of merchants, became the most resented character in Ottoman public opinion. Their way of living, which was often affiliated with debauchery and corruption, was a major theme in Turkish literature of the postwar period.[34] In most of these narratives, the main character is a formerly pious Muslim man who easily acquired wealth owing to the circumstances cited above. As soon as he becomes rich, he frequents nightlife venues popular among business circles—such as Hotel Tokatlıyan—to meet new acquaintances and display his wealth. To increase his reputation and make his name more presentable in high society, he makes up a family name with the suffix "-zade," meaning "descendant of." Leaving his old traditional *konak* house behind, he moves into an apartment flat and furnishes it in a European bourgeoisie fashion. His moral laxity that allows him to benefit from privation is evident in his new habits, such as hiring a mistress, consuming alcohol, gambling, and partaking of saloon entertainment.[35] In the end, he is a vulgar imitation of the modern bourgeoisie—a parasite of society who made a fortune through political connections in a time of crisis. Therefore, these wealthy men did not hesitate to cooperate with the new political powers that be, the Allies, who occupied Istanbul in the aftermath of the war.[36] The critique targeting the lifestyle of this wealthy class was different from the early criticisms in the Tanzimat era, however. A new narrative of treason and social destruction replaced stories of individual destruction as a result of over-Westernization.[37] According to Akın, war profiteers and their ways of acquiring wealth created a tension that would eventually result in the "loss of legitimacy" of state authority; indeed, public criticism targeting "injustice" curbed the war effort.[38]

Strikingly, as discussed in Chapter 2, most contemporary writers approached the problem of war profiteering as a problem of morality, thus making it part of a discussion of moral decline instead of considering the role of politics in the rise of profiteering. This is further evidence that political and social discontent was translated and melted into the discourse of morality. In fact, a similar tendency was evident in other belligerent countries, as well. For example, Jean-Louis Robert discusses the association of immorality with profiteering in his study of wartime caricatures. He argues that wartime caricature "redefined the internal social order" through contrasting, moralized images.

> In different ways and at different times they arrayed home versus the front; city versus countryside; men versus women; consumers versus merchants; munitions makers versus the rest; the nouveau riche versus the ordinary man; as well as the time honoured opposition of capital and labour. Most of these images focus on the question of consumption, and the shortages of basic commodities which affected different groups in different ways. This is not surprising, since it is precisely what the readership experienced. But if this evidence reinforces our sense of material grievance, it also provides good grounds for concluding that the Great War crystallized a set of moral codes, which can be seen in the popular press.[39]

The immoral imagery of Ottoman war profiteers can be evaluated within this framework. During the war, a moralizing rhetoric was often employed as a way to express social inequalities. Novels and popular works displaying such

Figure 4.1 "The World of the Nouveau Riche" as depicted in Sedad Simavi's cartoon album. (Yeni Zenginler/Les Néo-Riches, Istanbul, 1918 (rep. Adam Yayıncılık, ed. Turgut Çeviker, 1993)).

a moral dichotomy dominated Turkish literature for decades after the war, a fact demonstrating that the collective memory of the war was shaped by this moralized imagery of wartime inequalities. The profiteers were represented in the collective memory as being morally lax and having degenerate values.

A closer look at the regulation of entertainment venues (*lubiyyat mahalleri*) during the First World War presents a complex story in which several factors played a role. Besides religiously motivated objections, entertainment venues were subject to concerns over urban control and social order as these venues posed a potential threat to the political and cultural order.[40] On the other hand, the approach of the Ottoman state regarding these venues was pragmatic, as they constituted a significant source of revenue for the treasury. The war added new dynamics to this ambivalent approach toward entertainment venues.[41]

While war profiteers were enjoying their time in the Pera Palace Hotel or in the Hotel Tokatlıyan, cinemas and theaters constituted the main locations of mass entertainment for the lower classes during the war. As discussed earlier, the means of entertainment in these venues attracted criticism with respect to their role in moral decline. During the war, a new critique emerged from nationalist sensibilities that such places distracted people's attention from the war and contributed to a lack of interest in the future of the nation. Therefore, a formulation combining moral and financial interests emerged during the war by which private entrepreneurs were levied with heavy taxes and semi-government war relief organizations were encouraged to collect revenues through nationalist shows. Also, owing to the abolition of capitulations, venues formerly belonging to foreign companies became subject to Ottoman law, and thus taxes could be imposed on them.[42] However, as shown in the following sections, regulated content and nationalist shows did not bring in the anticipated income due to lack of public interest. The ideal of creating "respectable popular leisure activities"[43] thus conflicted with financial interests.

The semi-government war relief organizations, namely the Society for National Defense (*Müdâfaa-i Millîye Cemiyeti*), the Naval Society (*Donanma Cemiyeti*), and the Red Crescent (*Hilâl-i Ahmer*), considered entertainment as a source of income in addition to being a tool to make war propaganda. As Özbek argues, these aid organizations constituted a "political public sphere" that emerged from an attempt of the CUP government "to direct civic activity and public enthusiasm towards the nationalist and militarist policy concerns of the party."[44] The first pamphlet of the Naval Society advertising coming theater shows clearly indicated this political agenda underlying the entertainment: "We found a new way for people who want to help the Naval Society... Thanks to this initiative [of establishing a theater], the Society will not only receive financial support. This initiative will also contribute our people in social and national aspects [and]—with due respect—perhaps teach them great lessons."[45] While these institutions were exempt from special taxes, other entertainment companies were subject to a 10 percent tax transferred to the budget for the Poorhouse (*Darülaceze*).[46] During the war, in order to guarantee this important source of revenue, the police were charged with monitoring tickets sales and issuing bans if the venues refuse to pay the taxes for the Poorhouse.[47] In addition to the Poorhouse tax, all the tickets were subject to a stamp duty for Hedjaz Railways (*Hicaz Demiryolları*) with a value of twenty *para*.[48] Through the end of the war, new taxes were introduced for the tickets of cinemas, theaters, concerts, proms, horse races, and similar activities as the state expenses increased due to the war.[49] As indicated in an archival document, the Ottoman government undertook similar financial measures as other belligerent countries and collected taxes on pleasure and joy (*zevk-ü keyf*) rather than vital needs (*ihtiyacât-ı hakikiyye*). While small enterprises were hit by heavy taxation, war relief institutions enjoyed the opportunity to offer "legitimate" entertainment.[50]

Entertainment venues became subject to morality debates in two respects: first, moral instruction and war propaganda through entertainment, and second, the elimination of content that violated public morality and sparked public protest. War relief entertainment, however, did not appeal to public taste. The masses did not frequent the highly intellectual moral instruction shows. Initially, these organizations sought to save the entertainment industry from vulgar shows by replacing them with moral and educational shows; however, they soon realized that they had to win popular approval to make profit. To increase revenues, it became apparent that the shows had to appeal to a broad audience, which meant compromising enlightening ideals and moral instruction through entertainment.

When the Ottoman Fine Arts School (*Dârülbedâyi*) was established in 1914, there was a great enthusiasm among intellectuals who hoped to educate masses through entertainment. Abdullah Cevdet celebrated the arrival of André Antoine, who came to Istanbul to establish Dârülbedâyi's theater organization saying: "Our friends told us that this country needs many things before theaters. [Yet] We can't prohibit entertainment in society, but we can save our people from dirty, ugly, and vulgar entertainment venues and take them to the foot of the theater stage which teaches high ideals."[51] The first play staged in Dârülbedâyi was Emile Fabre's *La Maison d'Argile* (*Çürük Temel*), a family drama allegorically referring to the dissolving empire. All the revenues of the shows were transferred to the Women's Society for Soldiers' Families (*Asker Ailelerine Yardımcı Hanımlar Cemiyeti*). However, after being staged a few times, the hall remained empty because spectators were not interested. Instead, improvisational plays (*tulûat kumpanyası*) and comedies were attracting spectators.[52] Therefore, organizers of war relief entertainment found a middle road by performing comedies immediately after national and historical dramas.[53]

The quality of shows staged in these institutions attracted intellectual criticism due to their lack of moral instruction. Muhsin Ertuğrul, who was among the leading theater and cinema figures in the late Ottoman and early Republican era, had to leave his job in Dârülbedâyi as a consequence of the conflict between profitable and educational plays. In 1918, he wrote in *Temaşa* journal—a journal that was published by intellectuals who opposed the vulgar war relief entertainment—and asserted that moral and social plays are not popular in society; therefore, these plays are not profitable.[54] He commented that theaters should help increase morality and educate society, and he complained that in order to a make profit, plays served only the purpose of attracting popular attention, thus decreasing the quality of the art.

In addition to intellectual reflections on the impact of entertainment on morality, there were also bureaucratic and military perspectives that focused on regulation from the viewpoint of protecting public morality. The foremost issue that deserves attention is censorship. At the beginning of the war, the Ottoman High Command (*Başkumandanlık Vekâleti*) published Instruction on Censorship (*Sansür Tâlimâtnâmesi*) consisting of sixty-one articles that brought about heavy censorship of the press and personal mail, as well as theater plays and cinema films.⁵⁵ Accordingly, censorship centers were established in all the important cities and these places would be responsible for the elimination of "harmful" content, particularly curbing war efforts and affecting the morale of the Ottoman people.⁵⁶ However, censorship of theater plays was the subject of several debates. On February 23, 1915, the Ottoman High Command sent a general decree to all provinces announcing that the police would be in charge of censoring theater plays instead of the military.⁵⁷ This decision was taken upon an incident that was considered as a "negligent" act of the Beyoğlu Military Censorship Commission (*Beyoğlu Askerî Sansür Heyeti*) who approved a play titled *Great Vartan* in Armenian in which the battles of ancient Armenia were staged. The decree announced that due to the heavy workload of military censorship offices, and given the extraordinary circumstances of war, for the sake of public morals, security, and the safety of the state, theater plays (especially non-Turkish ones) were to be investigated by the police.⁵⁸

After charging the police with censorship, the Chief Police Department started preparations to regulate entertainment venues. In 1916, the Ministry of Interior Affairs issued a detailed "Regulation of Theatres, Cinemas, Café Chantants and Outdoor Performances."⁵⁹ Among the sixty articles of regulation, there were also the ones dealing with the issue of public morality. The regulation stipulated the ban of theater plays that could offend the religions or ethnicities of the Ottoman people, as that could harm national values and public morality. In the third part—on Café Chantants, musical coffee houses, and concert cafés—it was stated that women singers and actresses were not allowed to show up or dance in the presence of customers. Adolescents younger than eighteen and students in uniform were not allowed to enter these places. Other types of entertainment, such as horse and tightrope acrobatic shows, circuses, storytelling shows, and puppet theaters, were required to obtain a license from the police. Street performances and tent theaters were only allowed if the venues were sufficiently close to a fire station and police department. However, to my knowledge, this regulation did not get implemented during the war, at least not officially. Corroborating this assumption, the last document I came across, dated March 24, 1918, was a correspondence by the Ministry of Interior to the Council of State asserting the urgency of the approval of the regulation "for the sake of discipline and order."⁶⁰

The regulation prepared by the Ministry of Interior Affairs was the result of a long process during which local police quarters were interviewed and measures that were being implemented in other European countries were reviewed.⁶¹ In contrast to this meticulous preparation, orders directly issued by Enver Pasha, the Minister of War, attempted to bring harsh and more immediate measures. On February 5, 1918, Enver Pasha sent an order to the Ministry of Interior Affairs regarding excessive advertisement of entertainment in the Ottoman press and on street posters.

> In order not to break our soldiers' endurance to withstand the difficulties of war, from now on the Ottoman press is neither allowed to publish any advertisement in newspapers or for distribution on the streets that promotes pleasure, extravagancy, and luxury; nor any advertisement for entertainment, theaters, cinemas, concerts, songs or feasts except for ones sponsored by war institutions and for war relief. These kinds of advertisements can only be displayed inside the entertainment venues. Secondly, those who do not comply with this order shall be prosecuted by the military courts.⁶²

The General Police Department replied and asserted that to prosecute the people for opposing this order, first, the Council of Ministers had to approve the decision; and second, it was impossible to ban all luxury advertisements. Enver Pasha answered this with another letter agreeing about the procedure yet urging the police to realize the measure: "Therefore, I ask the Police Department to investigate these cases [to be transferred to the Council]. Advertisements of items that are not among vital and natural needs, such as those published by costume houses and beauty rooms (*tuvalet ve zarâfethâneler*) to attract customers, can be counted among luxuries."⁶³ Eventually, on March 4, 1918, the military ordered all cinemas and photography shops in and near Istanbul to obtain a license from the intelligence division of Military Headquarters in Istanbul (*Karargâh-ı Umûmî İstihbârat Şûbesi*).⁶⁴ This case demonstrates that leading figures of the Ottoman military were aware that during a war, violations of public morality in the sense of excessive entertainment and consumption shattered the spirit of collectivity.

As shown, regulating entertainment venues during the First World War had several purposes besides protecting public morality, such as making propaganda and collecting revenue. A remarkable point at the intersection of these aims was bureaucratic, and military approaches to content that violated public morality were closely associated with concerns for public order and national unity. While the government was able to take more effective measures to regulate entertainment venues owing to the abolition of capitulations and by resorting to military measures, other factors—mainly the generation of income through entertainment—conflicted with the project of refinement the content of mass entertainment.

Gambling and Drinking: The Mother of All Vices and Taxes

The dilemma between regulatory measures and financial interests was revealed in debates over alcohol and gambling, as well. Starting in the seventeenth century and continuing throughout Ottoman history, there were many attempts to ban alcohol or limit its sale. Such measures specifically targeted Muslim drinkers, because as Georgeon states, "a drinking Muslim," after all, would find himself in places where non-Muslim communities socialized, thus constituted a threat to Ottoman order founded on the separation of ethno-religious communities.[65] According to Kırlı, "taverns were entrapped by a vicious circle." "While they were closed down on the basis of 'deteriorating public morality,' they were reopened since state finances could not bear the burden of being deprived of the tax revenue generated from alcoholic beverages."[66]

A brief history of attempts to regulate alcohol consumption in the nineteenth century confirms the argument regarding the association of public order with public morality. For instance, the 1858 Ottoman Penal Code and the 1858 Streets Regulations stipulated that drinking was to be punished only when it caused serious disturbances to public peace, morality, and security.[67] In several other regulations, similar anxieties associating public morality and public order are evident. In 1862, a new regulation was issued titled "Regulations on Alcoholic Beverages" (*Müskirât Nizamnâmesi*) and concentrated on the spatial organization of alcohol-selling businesses.[68] In 1878, new taxes were introduced on coffeehouses, casinos, and alcohol-selling places. In his attempt to emphasize his reign's Islamic nature and respect for Islamic principles, Abdülhamid II limited the amount that shops or places serving alcohol could sell.[69] In 1912, a new regulation was issued regarding the opening hours of places selling alcohol.[70] Taxes from such establishments greatly contributed to municipal budgets, as well. As Hanssen states, over a quarter of the annual income for the municipal budget of Beirut in 1913 came from taxes on petrol, alcohol, and gambling.[71]

A closer look at prohibitive measures shows that they were far from effective. Along with financial interests, the factor of "resistance of drinkers" contributed to the failure of prohibitive projects.[72] Although alcohol was strictly prohibited by Islam and labeled as the "mother of all vices," the Ottoman Muslims enjoyed alcoholic spirits quite in a liberal fashion. As Matthee indicates, alcohol consumption paradoxically "always played a surprisingly important role in male elite circles in the Middle East."[73] Until the nineteenth century, this habit was "hidden" from the public. Starting in the second half of the nineteenth century, alcohol consumption was embraced by the Ottoman Muslim elite as "an indicator of the modern lifestyle."[74] This allowed religious critics to label alcohol consumption the result of "over-Westernization" and to identify it with the decline of Muslim morality. This moralistic discourse was later reinforced by the rise of a medical discourse against alcohol.[75]

Starting in the nineteenth century, both prohibitive and liberal discourses regarding alcohol had political and cultural implications. Embracing such habits or rejecting them constituted the basis for discussions about perceptions of European civilization. In religiously motivated circles, prohibitive discourses on alcohol served the purpose of establishing moral authority. In this respect, the morality discourse went hand in hand with the contest over the public space.

Critiques of alcohol consumption in the early modern Ottoman Empire used the "calamity" argument to ban alcohol in the Empire. During the Tanzimat era, consuming alcohol became affiliated with being civilized and culturally open to progress, though by the end of the nineteenth century, a strong medical argument accompanied the religious objections. Following the war, when Istanbul was occupied in 1920, Allied military authorities used "chaotic and unruly nature of Istanbul at night" and the "protection of public morality" to justify their interventions in the city.[76] The Ankara government prohibited alcohol in 1920 as a consequence of "an unanticipated union of traditional populists (and Islamists) from the *İkinci Grup* (who advocated prohibition on religious and moral grounds) and medical and public health officials (equipped with medical and social science)."[77] Later on, in Kemalist Turkey, alcohol consumption reemerged "as an even more prominent marker of Turkey's status as a Western and modern nation-state."[78]

On the issue of the war and alcohol, Ahmed Emin held up the gradual increase in *rakı* production—which doubled from 1914 to 1917—as an indicator of moral decline.[79] On the other hand, the government also benefited (or attempted to benefit) from the consumption of alcohol, particularly during the war. On July 8, 1915, the Ottoman government introduced a tax tariff to be imposed on mail and telegrams as well as on tobacco and alcohol in order to fund the establishment of scientific and industrial institutions for the education of children of martyrs (*evlâd-ı şühedâ*).[80] Whether a dispute over the moral dilemma of using alcohol taxes to support the children of martyrs' would have broken out in the parliament is unclear because it was not convening when the government passed this law.

In the Ottoman parliament, the imposing of taxes on playing cards, for instance, had led to a discussion on whether the priority of the government should be to protect public morality or to collect regular but small tax amounts on such items to benefit the budget. On December 17, 1917, draft legislation on the taxation of playing cards was discussed among Ottoman parliamentarians.[81] The proposed draft stipulated a five *kuruş* tax on each pack of cards. Ahmet Ağaoğlu, the deputy from Karahisarı Sahib, argued that the state should not rely on such revenues; otherwise, "public morality would be under a serious threat."[82] He proposed that the government should adopt a "prohibitive" approach regarding gambling and increase the tax to 50 kuruş in order to fight against what, according to him, had become an "epidemic disease" in the country.[83] After him, Şeyh Saffet Efendi, the deputy from Urfa, took the floor and proposed to increase the tax to 100 kuruş because, "according to the Ottoman Constitution, the religion of the state is Islam." Thus above this constitution there was a "holy constitution"—that is, the Quran—which explicitly prohibits Muslims from gambling. As his title indicates, he was a cleric. For him, the Ottoman Empire was the land of "the Great Caliphate of Islam," so the government had to respect divine orders and take steps to correct public morality. He argued that the draft was not intended to discourage gambling; instead, the draft aimed to benefit from gambling by imposing taxes on it. Following these words, other deputies took the floor and delivered excited speeches regarding the protection of public morality, while other deputies showed sympathy and chanted "Bravo!" In this enthusiastic atmosphere, some deputies proposed increasing the amount of the tax to 500 kuruş per pack of cards. On the other hand, some deputies called on the others "to dismiss the religious discussion of permissible and impermissible (*haram-helal*)," noting that "taxes are also imposed on pork and wine," and they also received support from some deputies.[84] Finally, Minister of Finance Mehmet Cavit Bey took the floor and gave a speech on the dilemma of the government between the sake of morality (*menfâ'at-i ahlâkiyye*) and the sake of economy (*menfâ'at-i mâliye*), particularly with respect to topics related to pleasures (*mükeyyifat*). He argued that prohibitive approaches would pave the way for a black market, thus eventually violating yet another ethical rule. After his speech, the deputies agreed on the amount of five kuruş for the tax.[85] Indeed, his words explicitly illustrated the moral dilemma of the Ottoman government.

Ahmed Emin asserts that during the First World War, the Ottoman government passed an anti-gambling law but only enforced it rigidly for a few days.[86] However, as indicated in the newspaper *Tanin*, the Ministry of Interior Affairs did not issue a new anti-gambling law. Instead, the office merely recirculated what was already stipulated in the Ottoman Penal Code regarding gambling and ordered that these cases be taken to the courts.[87] Strikingly, despite some public expectations regarding prohibitive measures on gambling, the Ottoman government kept relying on the discretion of the courts to punish gambling.

The anxiety over public morality had ramifications beyond a simple rhetoric of preventing prostitution and controlling sexuality. As this chapter attempted to show, a close look at the topics that fell under the domain of public morality in the daily life shows the fault lines in contemporaneous discussions on the link between lifestyle and morality. Although these moral encounters emerged in the vast context of the nineteenth century, the war constituted a peak and a condition of intermingling of the national and cultural anxieties. Moral encounters in daily life became the markers of the differences between the rich and the poor and the combatant and the noncombatant. However, attempts to protect public morality remained limited due to the financial interests of the government vis-à-vis expenditures on pleasure.

At the end of the war, polemics of moral decline carried yet another political implication. The dichotomy was not Muslim morality versus European morality but Anatolian versus Istanbulite. For instance, the wartime image of immoral Muslim women disappeared and made way for the image of heroic Turkish women. The category of "immoral women" was reduced to just those women of the Istanbul elite who collaborated with Allied forces. This sharp image that established itself through morality deserves further attention, but the topic is beyond the scope of this book.

5

Family at the Center of Moral Decline: Legislation Targeting the Regeneration and Protection of Ottoman Muslim Families

If you further investigate the reasons for immorality [in society], you will finally end up in family and bewail what you witness there.
    –Tüccarzade İbrahim Hilmi, Avrupalılaşmak Felâketlerimizin Esbâbı

During a visit to my hometown, Sivas, a man whom I met coincidentally, asked what I was studying. I told him the First World War and added: "Specifically the home front." He immediately replied excitedly and said, "I know a lot about that!" He continued, "when the war broke out and the people heard about the mobilization, men said 'shoot [kill] all the crippled and one-handed men.'" Not able to follow him at first, I asked the reason, and he said, "Because, only crippled men would remain in the town and the fellows did not want to leave the women to them!"

"Hunger and love are what moves the world."[1] With mass mobilization in the Empire reaching almost 3 million men, a population of mainly women, children, and elders remained on the home front.[2] They suffered not only from the absence of their breadwinners but also from the lack of protection in patriarchal sense. The family as an institution was heavily affected by wartime conditions. The formidable problem of manpower was accompanied by heavy taxation on agricultural products in towns and villages. Amid economic deprivations, the Ottoman countryside witnessed a chaotic situation regarding the protection of soldiers' families from being sexually exploited. In addition, the absence of the male members of households brought about concerns regarding the involvement of soldiers' female relatives in extramarital sexual activities. As discussed in the following sections, this "uncontrolled" environment was referred to as "the form of moral decline in rural areas" in the writings of Ottoman intellectuals and state elites. The scope of this moral decline surpassed the capacity of civilian authorities to cope, and the Ottoman government (and military authorities) found new ways to deal with the problem.

I begin my analysis with an overview of the impact of the war on the family, contextualizing how family life was affected by wartime circumstances and presenting the background for changing perceptions toward the family as an institution. I then turn to the forms of state intervention in family affairs in terms of taking control over sexual relationships that potentially threatened the family as an institution. I demonstrate how the wartime legislation that targeted the family was driven by moral concerns. Examining gender-related aspects of war contributes to the understanding of political developments, particularly those related to "civic order."[3] I contend that the turmoil of the wartime tested and revealed the vulnerability of once solid, traditional norms and values. As the foundations of the old order were shaken, several legislative attempts were made, paving the way for a new understanding of the family in which state intervention is legitimate.

The next part examines a heretofore unexplored legislative attempt, the Adultery Bill of 1916, and the debates surrounding it. The Adultery Bill was proposed by the Ministry of War to authorize the military to police the sexual conduct of "unfaithful" wives. Although this draft was not put into force, the endeavor shows the extent of moral considerations and the approach of military authorities to the problem of moral decline. I examine how the draft law instigated debates on the understanding of morality crimes, the nature of law, and limits of public and private law.

As a distinctive feature of this study, I consider morality discourses and moral concerns as the common point behind several legislative attempts that aimed at families. These legislation attempts, which so far in the historiography have been elaborated separately, are thus evaluated together in a wider framework. First, I focus on the forms of sexual assault targeting the female members of soldiers' families. Given that such cases explicitly contradicted official war propaganda based on the protection of honor and family, the state enacted a provisional law authorizing courts martial to handle sexual assaults on soldiers' families. Indeed, this legislation marked the beginning of a state intervention in the family. However, instead of evaluating this intervention as the natural outcome of increasing sexual assault cases, I point out the role of individuals—both men and women—in shaping the reciprocal relationship between citizens and the state. By holding the state accountable for a lack of protection from sexual violence, victims of and witnesses to these crimes explicitly asked for further state involvement so that the perpetrators be punished in a more effective way.

Finally, I evaluate the Ottoman Family Rights Decree of 1917 as part of the growing intervention of the state in the family. Here, my aim is not to rewrite the narratives on the widely discussed Family Decree but to establish links between references to norms, values, and morality and the justification for the law. I argue that discourses on morality and national regeneration played an important role in shaping the body of the law. In a way, discourses on the need for social reform went hand in hand with arguments about how outdated and degenerate were the values that encompassed the family. This helped break the taboos regarding the privacy of the family and paved the way for the introduction of family reform.

Specialized studies have enhanced our understanding on the impacts of the First World War on the family as an institution and long-lasting change as in the perceptions of family, women, and children in many combatant countries. Among these perceptions, I believe we should also consider moral values surrounding family formation and dissolution as well as factors that are a menace to family order. In the Ottoman case, the First World War served to attach new meanings to the family in terms of defining its function within society. The impact of total war also manifested itself in patriarchal norms and traditional gender roles in a manner that redefined the relationship between individuals and the state.

The families of soldiers received attention from military and bureaucratic authorities in combatant countries. More than anything else, this attention derived from the fact that war propaganda during the First World War highlighted the protection of women and children more than any other reasons for waging war against the enemy. Paradoxically, the absence of men in pursuit of the very same cause left women and children defenseless against several forms of violence on the home front. The gendered aspect of war propaganda added to these concerns. As Susan Grayzel put it, "in part because the war was justified as a defense of women and children, and thus implicitly of traditional gender roles, there was a good deal of concern about how wartime circumstances might alter these."[4]

The initial policies regarding the family were driven by the motive of compensation in the absence of breadwinners. In many combatant countries, special "family aid" measures were introduced in order to support families.[5] Obviously, the issue of leaving money to the discretion of the women went hand in hand with a form of moral control over consumption, putting women and adolescents under the microscope of social and political control. Women and adolescents from conscripted soldiers' families were constantly under public surveillance with regard to their sexuality, their socialization, and their communication with the soldiers in the battlefield. Their way of spending Family Aid was subject to a debate among the press, police, and several bureaucratic offices. In Germany, some municipalities announced that women who spend money for cinema-going would not be eligible to receive Family Aid anymore. In Britain, restrictions were put on alcohol consumption, which was allegedly spreading among women in reaction to the uncertainties and hardships of wartime.[6]

During the Balkan Wars, the Ottoman government introduced a provisional law providing family allowance (*muinsiz aile maaşı*) for the families whose sole breadwinners had been conscripted into the army. Aid became central to the new Provisional Law on Military Service issued in May 1914 and affected more families due to the large-scale mobilization during the First World War.[7] By means of this aid program, the government financially compensated families for the absence of breadwinners, thus establishing a tacit contract with soldiers pertaining to their sacrifice. Mehmet Beşikçi explains this tacit contract between conscripted men and the state as follows:

> 1) His and his family's basic needs were provided by the state in return for his service; 2) his collaboration with the state increased his social status; 3) he was to be assured that the war effort was worth sacrificing himself for; 4) the duration and conditions of his military service remained unchanged from his initial mobilization. Failure to maintain this tacit contract could produce various forms of resistance to the mobilization effort.[8]

In practice, the allowance was ineffective due to the irregularity of payments, as well as bad or unfair treatment of women by provisioning officers (*iaşe memurları*), including the abuses of corrupt officers who took advantage of their position to sexually exploit women in need.[9] Both in the countryside and in cities there was a sense of increasing prostitution as such. When the news about desperate situation of women on the home front arrived to soldiers at the battlefront, desertion appeared as an inevitable consequence. In 1917, during the war, the Ministry of War mandated the death penalty for officers who caused such incidents for facilitating desertion.[10] Enver Pasha wrote to the Ministry of Interior Affairs that despite all kinds of strict measures and severe punishments, it was impossible to halt desertion.[11] After investigating the situation, he came to the conclusion that the reason behind increasing desertion was the negligence of state employees who were in charge of distributing the aid and destituteness of women as a result. Ahmed Emin describes the situation on the home front as follows: "As the waves of debauchery behind the front caused heads of families to grow apprehensive for the safety of their homes and to desert the front line, special courts-martial were set up to handle the task of safeguarding public morals."[12]

The need for women's collaboration with the state to continue waging the war had significant effects, especially with respect to morale on the front. As many scholars agree, this era was marked by a new concept of a relationship between women and the state. This relationship was more direct than before, without husbands or male relatives as intermediaries. According to Grayzel, "what made this war such a compelling moment in women history is that it provides an opportunity for many women to forge a new relationship with their nation-states."[13] In the Ottoman case, Akın argues, attempts of the government to relieve the financial burden of families and to protect them from various forms of violence resulted in the transformation of women's identities vis-à-vis the state and paved the way for a new direct relationship between the state and women in the absence of men.[14] Toprak addresses this changing relationship vis-à-vis the formation of the nation-state. According to Toprak, the war radically changed the perception of women's role in the society due to the need for a female workforce, and this contributed to the promotion of the nuclear family as the main component of a national state.[15] During the war years, Ottoman society witnessed radical transformation particularly in the urban context triggered both by the intellectual environment of the Young Turk family ideology and Ottoman feminism and by wartime social and demographic changes.[16]

The interest in the family in many belligerent countries derived from the idea that the family as an institution was on the verge of losing its main functions. These functions, according to Daniel, can be defined under two headings: (1) physical, psychological, and societal reproduction of people including the raising and socialization of children and the reproduction of adults in terms of their psychological and physical components, material support, psychological stabilization, and sexuality; and (2) production and consumption of food.[17] Accordingly, during the war, the reproductive function of the family decreased, but the consumption and production of goods increased. When the balance between reproduction and production was broken by wartime circumstances, the sole function of the family remained an economic one. Eventually, the aspects that previously concerned only family started to be part of public interest.[18]

These assumptions are indeed in line with the sense of crisis that was observed by contemporary commentators on family, morality, and culture. However, in the Ottoman Empire interest in the family had wider implications transcending discussions on the basic functions of the family. Owing to strict moral codes along with religious approbation, all forms of man-woman encounters in both the private and the public sphere were scrutinized within a larger perspective of the family institution.

In the aftermath of the Constitutional Revolution of 1908, family became a major point of interest in the Ottoman press.[19] Debates on family included references to a so-called family crisis (*aile buhranı*), which also encompassed morality discourses. Cem Behar and Alan Duben consider the family crisis spoken of by Ottoman intellectuals as a "cultural crisis" following the emergence of the nuclear family.[20] According to them, even though domestic gender roles were not radically changed, traditional elites in society and their distinctive way of living (*konak* life) were undermined by the formation of a new wealthy class—that is, war profiteers.[21] Başak Tuğ argues that the point of departure for the family crisis debate among Ottoman intellectuals was not the transformation from large to nuclear families but instead was the individualistic, loose family ties in Ottoman society.[22] Toprak's studies show that the main agenda of reformist nationalist intellectuals such as Ziya Gökalp was to promote the nuclear family model among Ottoman Muslim families. They attributed a great role to morality in their vision of the national family (*millî aile*) model.[23]

In a way, the concerns over family in the context of the war had wider implications for the maintenance of the collective effort dedicated to mobilization. These implications extended to a broader framework of sexuality transcending the borders of the family as an institution per se. To illuminate this point further, I should note that the concept of "soldiers' family" refers not to family as an institution but to women of the family.[24] Kutluata, who studied Ottoman women's wartime petitions, indicates that women were always defined by the state in relation to their familial ties to men. In the case of widows, the petitions were often signed by a man such as the local headman.[25] Based on her archival research, Mahir Metinsoy also underlines the fact that in state documents women were catalogued as "the family" of men.[26] Therefore, by family I mean women, and the central issue about morality was their sexuality and sexual encounters on the home front.

Contextualizing State Intervention in Sexual Violence, Rape, and Assaults in the Ottoman Empire

According to Islamic Law, relationships out of wedlock are considered acts of adultery (*zina*, or in Ottoman Turkish *fi'il-i şen'i*). Adultery aside, the punishment for rape and similar acts is not defined clearly among the *hadd* which are crimes "against the rights of God."[27] Accordingly, rape (*ırza geçme* or *hetk-i ırz*) was considered under the heading of adultery, yet courts had discretionary power (*ta'zir*) to determine a suitable punishment.[28] There were three types of punishment for adultery: 100 lashes, banishment, and stoning to death.[29] In the Ottoman Empire, the *kanunname*s (Sultanic Codes) of Sultans Mehmed II, Beyazıd II, Süleyman I, and Selim I supplemented Islamic Law with respect to rape crimes and issued different punishments for the act.[30] For instance, a case study from the town of Balıkesir in the seventeenth century shows that adultery was generally punished with banishment.[31] Semerdjian also demonstrates that violation of sexual norms was not punished with draconian punishments as commanded in Islamic juridical writings and banishment was a common practice.[32] Peirce's work evaluates that local knowledge, power relations, and an equilibrium between justice and order played important roles in the punishment of sexual crimes.[33]

Only in the 1858 Ottoman Penal Code, which was the first penal code in the modern sense, were crimes of adultery subject to standardized punishments.[34] This code differed from the *kanunname*s since the law applied to everyone, while the previous codes defined punishments based on whether the crime was committed by Muslims or non-Muslims, slaves or free people.[35] Articles 197–200 of the 1858 Penal Code were reserved for the gender violence cases, rape, and crimes against morality.[36] The punishment of the crime of rape was hard labor. If the victim was a virgin, the perpetrator had to pay recompense in addition to doing hard labor sentence. The severity of the punishment increased if the victim was a minor or if the perpetrator was among family members who were supposedly legal guardians of the victim. If the perpetrator was a state officer, he was fired from his position immediately. If the crime of rape was committed together with other crimes such as homicide, banditry, or theft, the punishment became more severe: a lifelong sentence of hard labor or the death penalty.[37] In the course of the nineteenth century, several supplementary articles were appended to this part of the Penal Code.

The Ottoman Penal Code of 1858 was inspired by the French Code of 1810. It is possible to argue that as a general principle of lawmaking throughout the nineteenth century, state intervention in private affairs and family relationships was considered "unnecessary" because it was perceived that such interventions would further deteriorate family order and peace.[38] Moral instruction and society's moral codes would suffice; every crime is an invention of law and no one shall add more. This principle explains the reason for the limited number of articles devoted to sexual violence, violating morality, and family-related crimes in the penal code.

From the second half of the eighteenth century to the First World War, a reaction toward documenting social code in a written form in a way to penetrate individual morality realm prevailed and a strong reaction against the intervention of law in the sphere of individual morality developed. Law and morality remained as two different spaces. As a consequence, the list of morality crimes remained limited in the penal codes of the time since most were considered crimes without victims or harmless to the state. Even though strict legislation stipulated punishments for immorality in Britain and its colonies, the individualist mentality was particularly evident in the French Penal Code of 1810. Only acts violating the freedom of another individual or those openly inciting public morality were punished.

The First World War marked the beginning of a new understanding for the punishment of morality crimes and crimes against family.[39] Especially crimes against the family constituted an essential part of several penal codes after the war. While some, such as the Italian Penal Code of 1931, greatly stressed such acts, more liberal codes such as that of the Swiss kept the list of morality crimes limited. The redefinition of crimes against morality and family derived from the wartime developments because of which the previous approaches toward the limits of private sphere were transformed. Also, new offenses were added to the penal code such as abandonment of family. According to Dönmezer, this was due to intense migration in the aftermath of the First World War that resulted in the separation of many spouses. He added that the war opened a path to the return of patriarchy, leading to further state intervention to the family.[40] "Saving the family" by establishing severe penalties became a matter for the state (especially for Fascist governments) as a result of the war.

What transpired during the First World War was that both the code and its application vis-à-vis gender violence were insufficient in a time of turmoil. The war shook the foundation of what had been considered private up to then. Not only in the Ottoman Empire and republican Turkey but also in many other countries, the First World War opened a new page on the punishment of acts against public morality and crimes against family. Specifically, crimes against family constituted an essential part of several penal codes after the war due to the concern about population decline.[41] I suggest reconsidering the Ottoman state's and military's intervention in this private sphere during the First World War from this perspective. For the first time in the history of the Ottoman Empire, crimes against morality and family during the First World War were tried in military courts. This intervention created a discussion of the limits of the public and private spheres. There was a specific moment that this situation triggered an important discussion among bureaucrats: the Ministry of War's proposal of the Adultery Bill in 1916, which is discussed at length in the following sections.

Archival documents suggest that sexual assault cases against members of soldiers' families were common even prior to the First World War. An overview of similar cases during the Balkan Wars reveals that female members of soldiers' families were faced with several forms of sexual assault. However, during those years the judicial process worked differently; charges brought up and trials for such cases were under the authority of the civilian bureaucracy, unlike during the First World War. In many cases, soldiers themselves petitioned the Ministry of War regarding their families' situation. The Ministry of War brought cases to the attention of civilian authorities such as the Ministry of Justice and the Ministry of Interior Affairs. Sometimes in a bitter tone in the correspondence, the Ministry of War urged civilian authorities that the government's initial duty was to protect soldiers' female relatives. For instance, Mehmed Ali bin Mehmed Ali, a soldier stationed at Anadolu Kavağı (a district along the Bosporus), wrote a petition on May 3, 1913, to the Ministry of War claiming that his wife had been abducted and raped by some of his fellow townsmen from Kastamonu. The Ministry of War passed the complaint on to the Ministry of Interior Affairs and added that "needless to say, the first responsibility of the government is to protect the women in soldiers' families from attack or assault."[42] As this case illustrates, the process was initiated by the Ministry of War, and the Ministry of Interior Affairs then started an investigation through the provincial governor. In addition to petitions written by soldiers, wives who were attacked or assaulted also sent complaints to the Ministry of War. For example, Fatma from Adana petitioned the ministry complaining that she had been assaulted and robbed by fifteen men on her way to the city center. During her journey to Adana for the purposes of work, the perpetrators stopped her, stole her money and earrings, and assaulted her sexually. She sent a telegram to the Ministry of War and signed it "a soldier's wife, Fatma." The Ministry of War passed her petition along to both the Ministry of Interior Affairs and the Ministry of Justice on October 4, 1913.[43] The Ministry of Interior Affairs forwarded the complaint to the provincial governor of Adana requesting an investigation.

Another case shows that complaints by soldiers regarding the protection of their families were more effective than those by civilian members of the family. For instance, Arif bin Emin, a soldier, petitioned the Ministry of War complaining that local authorities in his hometown of Ürgüb had not heeded his sister Fatma's case.[44] Fatma had been attacked and raped by a certain Çir [sic] Ali and his companions. They cut Fatma's husband's fingers while he defended

Fatma against the attackers. Fatma's four-month-old child died during the incident. The family had applied to local authorities, but no investigation had been initiated. Arif bin Emin, as a member of the military, submitted the case to the Ministry of War demanding justice for his sister. The Ministry of War passed the case on to the Ministries of Justice and Interior Affairs on October 30, 1913, asserting that such incidents have a negative impact on the morale of both the soldier whose family was involved and the battalion of which that soldier was a member.[45] Before the First World War, the Ministry of War passed these cases along to civilian authorities urging them to conduct investigations. Due to the bureaucratic exchanges involved in the process, investigations could last a long time. As the number of conscripted men increased during the First World War, leaving many women on the home front without protection, the Ministry of War initiated more straightforward solutions to bypass such bureaucracy.

Needless to say, the burden of the Balkan Wars on Anatolian cities was at its height when the Empire mobilized its sources for what had been expected to be a short but happened to be a four-year war. Hundreds of thousands Muslim refugees poured into Anatolia and their livelihood was on the village communities.[46] As we will see, some cases refer to refugees both as victims and as perpetrators of sexual abuse during wartime.

As discussed in Chapter 3, the war brought about the expansion of military power throughout the country owing to the declaration of the martial law. At the beginning of the war, on January 3, 1915, the Ministry of Interior Affairs issued a general order to all provinces which read:

> We are informed that in some places, the families of those soldiers—our soldiers who are ready to die to protect the faith, honor, and homeland—are being attacked and assaulted in their hometowns. As it is not desirable to hear of such cases, the protection of soldiers' families is of great importance. Thus, such attacks should be prevented and those who dare to act to the contrary shall be arrested and summoned before the courts martial and condemned to severe penalties.[47]

This general circular was issued even before the proclamation of the provisional law authorizing courts martial to handle sexual assault cases involving soldiers' families. This means the courts martial operated under *idârî karar* (*administrative* measure) until the proclamation of the provisional law. On September 8, 1915, the Council of Ministers approved the official provisional law mandating that sexual assaults of members of soldiers' families be taken to courts martial. The text in *Düstur* (the Ottoman Code Book) provides a brief description of the provisional law. The law stipulated that in times of mobilization—during the proclamation and continuation of martial law—rapes and assaults against wives, children, or any female relatives of soldiers be tried by martial courts and punished according to Article 206 of the Penal Code.[48] The bill was not in accordance with usual procedure for such cases. Under usual circumstances, the punishment of civilians who assaulted soldiers' families was not under the jurisdiction of military authorities. Correspondence written by the Ministry of Interior Affairs reads: "As a matter of fact, rape cases involving soldiers' wives or family members are not among military offenses. Nevertheless, it became necessary in the course of the war to investigate and punish those crimes in the military courts."[49]

Military as well as civilian authorities might have thought that trials in courts martial would be more effective given that there was no supreme court above the military courts to reinvestigate the case. Their decisions were immediately applied. Thus, Ottoman authorities (especially the Ministry of War) attempted to prevent rape and violence targeting soldiers' families by authorizing the courts martial and executing sentences more effectively. At this point, it is important to underline the role of individuals calling on the state to take measures against such cases and to point out the bilateral relationship behind the state's measures. The social background of wartime legislation and policies, in which moral considerations played an important role, allows us to see transformed perspectives on the limits of the private and public spheres with regard to family.

Let me now examine the exchanges between soldiers' families and state authorities with respect to sexual assault. First, I present the voices of women through the petitions they submitted to legal authorities. Second, I discuss the petitions of soldiers addressed to the Ministry of War or to the Ottoman Parliament regarding sexual assaults that their families had suffered. Third, I consider complaints filed by locals, *muhtars*, and village elders. Finally, I mention reports written by local military officers such as those of Recruiting Office Chiefs (*Ahz-ı Asker Riyaseti*) and Gendarmerie Commanders (*Jandarma Alay Kumandanlığı*).

Throughout the war, many women communicated with the government by submitting individual or collective petitions. Recently, new studies pointed out the importance of petitions and women's petitions in particular for the study of Ottoman home front. Petitions are useful sources through which one can get an idea on people's demands from the government, their hardships, the way they communicate with the state, their perception of war measures, and impacts of war on daily lives. Many women submitted petitions to complain about privations, hunger, poverty, unpaid or inadequate payments, provisioning officers' misconduct, confiscation of their grain for military needs, and other problems on the home front. Kutluata considers women's petition writing as a manifest of "practicing citizenship" during the war.[50] Akın considers women's petitions in the context of an increasing direct relationship between women and state as a novel wartime development and an act of negotiation for welfare.[51] Widespread collective petitioning in this regard is considered as a sign of collective action indicating an emerging political identity for women. Mahir Metinsoy shows how aspects of "private lives" of women turned into political matters for the state as more women forced the government to take their demands into serious thorough petitioning or if the petitions remained unanswered engaging in illegal activities.[52]

From an historical point of view, petitioning in cases of sexual crimes was not unique to the First World War period. Başak Tuğ demonstrates in her study on sexual crimes in the eighteenth-century Anatolia that petitioning was an efficient tool in communicating such assaults to the center of the state.[53] Petitioners often used discursive strategies that associated sexual violence and lack of protection of honor with the disorder and banditry in the cities as a consequence of absent central authority. For the state, establishing moral order through the direct punishment of sexual crimes became an important element to fulfil its legitimacy vis-à-vis local elites.

In this study, I consider petitions as sources through which the extent of sexual violence as part of home front dynamics can be ascertained. Women as well as soldiers used petitioning as an instrument to remind the state of its duty to protect *namus* (honor) and *şeref* (dignity). They explicitly held the state accountable for rapes, abductions, assaults, and threats, thus inviting the government to take severe measures against the perpetrators of such offenses. As a result, the state gradually began intervening in the realm of the family. Considering a demand from below in this sense, I argue that this intervention was "invited" by people on the home front. Yet, I should add that it would be misleading to ignore the agency of military authorities to take strict measures as such problems at soldiers' households affected morale and thus curbed the war effort.

The most common phrase in women's complaints regarding sexual assault is, in Ottoman Turkish, "*ırzımızı paymal ettiler*," meaning "they trampled our honor." Two women, Emine and her sister Havva from Akkilise, a village near the city of Konya, sent a telegram on November 24, 1915, directly to Talat Pasha, the Minister of Interior Affairs.[54] They accused Captain Osman Ağa and his companions as rapists and aggressors who had trampled their honor. Emine and Havva said, "our husbands are fighting for the faith and the state, but here,

Captain Osman Ağa's gangsters are raping us. We are sisters. They beat us and abducted us from our village." The statement "fighting for the faith and the state" is a phrase commonly found in these petitions. Emine and Havva added something interesting at the end of their telegram: "For God's sake, please save us from these Muscovites." By this, they equated an Ottoman military captain to those of the enemy nation. The second item of correspondence in this file was from the governor of Konya. The governor said that an investigation had been conducted about this case. He claimed that Captain Osman had been appointed to track bandits and that these petitions were meant to prevent him from doing so. Eventually, the martial court found him not guilty.

Another case exemplifies solidarity between families of soldiers with respect to a sexual assault that involved a war widow. Three women from İnegöl, Bursa, wrote a petition on December 25, 1914, to the president of Ottoman parliament addressing him as "father of our nation."[55] They informed him that a municipal council member from Bursa, Hacı Ahmed, had abducted a war widow, Ayşe, and taken her to his farm. These three women emphasized crucial points in their attempt to attract the attention of parliament. They employed key concepts of war propaganda such as protection of the faith, the nation, justice, and honor in their letter. Moreover, they wisely articulated the wartime circumstances with which soldiers' families were faced on the home front. The letter begins: "We are at war with the enemies of Islam and faith. Our sons are being martyred. Their women are the honor of faith and fatherland." These expressions equated their own situation with the honor of religion and the state and were among common phrases that can be found in such letters. They continued as follows:

> They took the widow of a martyr from İnegöl to Bursa promising to pay her a salary [family allowance]. They kept her at municipal council member Hacı Ahmed's farm. They raped her. They made her a whore. Hacı Ahmed has syphilis. Now this soldier's desperate widow has syphilis, too. She is still at Hacı Ahmed's place as a concubine.

It is interesting how they used notions of honor, faith, and nation to defend Ayşe against a municipal official. The mention of venereal disease could also be a conscious means of stigmatizing Hacı Ahmed. In the next part of their letter, the women reminded the government of its promises at the beginning of the mobilization, and they finished their letter with a demand for justice.

> The honor of a soldier, honor of the faith and state have been destroyed. How can this happen? How does your dignity accept this? Will the homeland embrace the syphilitic man who took a Muslim woman as his concubine? For the love

of God, please, avenge the honor of a Muslim martyr. We beg your mercy. In the newspapers we see the promises that our national assembly has made. God forgive you. Investigate the cruelty of infidels who destroy honor. We want justice, dear sir.

They signed the letter with reference to their own belonging to soldiers' families: wife of soldier, Ayşe; a soldier's mother-in-law, Fatma; and the widow of a martyr Medri [sic]. I should also add that despite a general assumption on the fact that the petitions were written by *arzuhalcis* (professional scribes) in the Ottoman Empire due to high level of illiteracy, the use of dialect in this letter and expressions such as "they made her a whore" do not seem to be the work of a professional scribe. It is possible to assume that either one of these women was literate or they found someone literate and dictated their letter.

We can interpret this solidarity letter as a signifier of the demand for justice for all soldiers' families which stemmed from fear that in the absence of their men, others in the town—officials, wealthy townsmen, or local military commanders—would be encouraged to attack soldiers' families if their vulnerability was exposed as such. By establishing relations between different connotations and notions, such as the reasons for the war as propagandized by the government itself—"protecting the state and faith"—and the state's promises to soldiers and their families, they sought justice for a widow, emphasizing her Muslim identity. Upon receiving this letter, the Ministry of Interior Affairs sent it to the province of Hüdavendigar (Bursa) and asked for an investigation. The governor wrote a detailed answer, which is worth quoting here.

> It was notified to our office that Ayşe bint-i Meryem was abducted and taken to the farm of a member of the municipal council, Hacı Ahmed, as a concubine. The aforementioned woman's husband did not return from the Balkan Wars and she was not welcomed into her mother-in-law's place. Therefore, she was drifted around, and at one point she went to Ankara and then to İnegöl, where she was accused of immorality together with another woman called Meryem. Thus, she was taken to Bursa again and was suspected of having a criminal [prostitution] background according to police and gendarmerie reports. Eventually, she began working for Hacı Ahmed Efendi as a servant where she is taken care of just like an adopted child. Since Hacı Ahmed Efendi discouraged her from prostitution, in our opinion it is better for her to stay there instead of wandering around vagrantly. Thus, our police department decided there is no need to take Hacı Ahmed's case to court.[56]

Obviously, we cannot know which story is true, but it is unlikely that these three women who wrote to parliament had anything to gain by giving false or misleading information. Most probably they knew Ayşe from their town. The women considered each other's situations to be alike in the sense that they were all soldiers' families. They might have thought that once rumors emerged that widows, mothers, or any other relatives of soldiers were not under the protection of the government—and even worse, that the government turned a blind eye to abductions, rapes, and assaults—nothing would stop other men from taking advantage of this. In Ayşe's case, the government apparently turned a blind eye by leaving Ayşe at Hacı Ahmed's place instead of paying her an allowance.

Among the archival documents there are similar complaints filed by soldiers themselves. Apparently, their families informed them about such instances in letters asking for help. The soldiers deliberately reported these cases to the Ministry of War or to the Ottoman parliament. One interesting case involved a soldier's sister. Mustafa from the village of Kemer near the town of Salihli in Aydın province was a member of Second Army stationed in Edirne. Mustafa wrote a petition on January 9, 1915, to the Ministry of Justice to be conveyed to the president of the Ottoman parliament. In his letter he said that fifteen days earlier, townsmen raided his sister's house and attacked her. The perpetrators threatened her continuously after the event. He wrote that he had informed local authorities in Edirne and asked the office to inform the Ministry of Justice of the case. After a few days, he received another telegram from his sister saying that she was again attacked in the middle of the night and that other women in the neighborhood had rescued her. Mustafa wrote to the Edirne prosecutor once again and was told that because of the lack of gendarmerie forces in that village, the attackers had not been arrested. After detailing the negligence of local authorities, he continued his letter, reminding the Ottoman government and parliament of its promises at the beginning of the war regarding the protection of soldiers' families.

> Your honor, the declarations of the Deputies and the Notables Chamber addressing the military were read to our units on December 24, 1914. Here, I would like to write down those words as far as I remember. "The day of revenge that the whole nation, from elders to the young and from martyrs to the living, has been awaiting has come at last. You, together with our allies, are fighting against the Muscovites again, the biggest enemy of the Ottomans and the Muslims. Take revenge for those houses they burned, the wounds they opened, and the martyrs they stepped on. Do not ever think about the families you left behind. They are entrusted to us by God." Your honor! I expect only the protection of my sister's rights and the punishment for the perpetrators by our constitutional government of the Ottoman State.[57]

Indeed, the government released an official statement addressing soldiers to praise their bravery and quell their worries about families.[58] Mustafa almost quoted the declaration by the government that had been read in military units in its entirety with special emphasis on the protection of families. This implied the contract between the government and the soldier in which they were united on the idea of "protecting honor." Finally, Mustafa asked not only for the perpetrators to be punished but also for the police officers in his town to be punished for their negligence. He continued, "[I ask you to punish them] because I am soldier. I cannot leave here and go there to follow up on this case. I can only entrust my family to the great conscience and justice of our government of the Constitutional Ottoman State with my best thoughts for the victory of our nation, army, and navy." These lines indicate the basic contract between soldiers and the state regarding the protection of their families. Also, the way that he signed his letter in which he emphasized his Turkish identity is related to the same concern: "From the Second Army unit, yours, ready to renounce his life for the nation, son of Turk, soldier of the Turks."

In contrast to his bitter tone throughout, he added a desperate postscript to his letter:

> As telegrams arrive [from my sister], I crave to commit suicide. I can't talk about this to any of my companions and will never do so… My sister filed a complaint, as well, yet it seems that the police prosecutors did not pay attention to it. I present this case to your conscience and kiss your hands your honor, sir.

Finally, the Ministry of Interior Affairs sent a notice to the province of Aydın asking them to investigate the events. The province replied that the perpetrators were arrested but not taken to the court martial since the event occurred before the general order authorizing the court martial to protect soldiers' families.[59]

In some cases, Recruitment Offices attempted to initiate investigations regarding assaults of soldiers' families with no official complaint from women or soldiers. For instance, on January 18, 1917, the Third Army Command (*Üçüncü Ordu Kumandanlığı*) reported that the office had carried out an investigation following gossip in the city that a certain Salih Beyzade Mehmed, a notable of from Tokat, had been seducing desperate women with the help of his own wife.[60] The commander stated that Salih "a man of dubious morals" sat behind curtains and doors and secretly watched the women who visited his wife at home. With the help of his wife and, the commander wrote, owing to the "women's weakness and factors of necessity" (*zaifiyet-i nisvan ve saike-yi zaruret*), he seduced those whom he fancied. Recently, the letter read, gossip had arrived to the commander that Salih had seduced the daughters of Osman Bey (who was a deceased colonel of the gendarmerie) in the same way. The commander sent his report to the Ministry of War urging it to take action against those insulting the morality and honor of soldiers' families. He added that soldiers should be spared any worries regarding the honor of their families in order to stay focused on their military duties in battle. The commander requested the banishment of Salih as an administrative measure because current law did not apply to his case.

However, gossip was not reason enough to enforce the law in Salih's case. The office of the governor of Sivas (the province of which Tokat was an administrative district) indicated this fact in correspondence addressed to Enver Pasha. The office concluded that despite the gossip regarding Salih's relationship with the daughters of Osman Bey, authorities were unable to prove it and no official complaints had been filed by the women. Eventually, trial or administrative measure was taken against him. However, cases like this prompted discussions among civil and military officials about how to react to illicit relationships if no complaints of sexual assault were filed or if the relationship was established on a voluntary basis. Could or should military or civilian authorities intervene in such cases? This topic will be discussed under the heading of Adultery Bill in the following section.

Another source through which sexual assaults were revealed is the weekly reports by local military authorities, especially gendarmerie forces, to the governors of their districts. For instance, the commander of gendarmerie regiment (*jandarma alay kumandanı*) in Hüdavendigar province reported four criminal cases in the districts (*liva*s) of Söğüt and Ertuğrul on December 30, 1915.[61] Two of the four were sexual assaults and the other two were cases of theft. One concerned an attack of five women, among whom was a soldier's wife, while they were on their way to Eskişehir together with the local headman (*muhtar*) of their village, Hasan Ağa, to go shopping. Some other armed villagers stopped them along the way, stabbed the *muhtar*, and raped the women. The attackers were arrested and summoned before the courts martial. Another case concerned Captain Süleyman, the head of the Subsistence Office (*İaşe Memurluğu*), who was caught raping Ali Osman. (It was not indicated whether Ali Osman was a minor.) The document says Ali Osman was rescued; moreover, the captain had been previously caught having an affair with a woman. The subsistence offices were the main points from which food was distributed during the First World War. Apparently, Captain Süleyman used his position to abuse men (or boys) and women who were in need. There is plenty of evidence in the archives similar to the case of Captain Süleyman in which military officers themselves were accused of sexual assault.[62]

Another vivid account on hardships on home front that I would like to consider here is a letter from the local head of Committee of Union of Progress branch in Giresun addressing the central bureau of the party.[63] His reason for writing the letter was that the situation had arrived at a *tahammülfersâ* (unbearable) level despite all the sacrifices of soldiers. The government guaranteed the safety and welfare of soldiers' families, yet refugees and the locals alike were suffering tremendously because of *hıyânet memurları* (employees of treason). While some employees confiscated some amount over the monthly allowance of women, the bakeries left them unfed for days begging for bread. They left the profiteers go unpunished, and "to satisfy these employees' bestial sexual desires" many honorable lives were destroyed and were "still being destroyed." He continued his letter with describing the terrible conditions of orphans deprived of food and he accused drunkard employees who were supposed to take care of them.

Although we do not have exact numbers, abundance of archival documents suggests that the Ottoman Anatolian countryside was in complete disorder due to the number of rapes, abductions, and assaults against women in soldiers' families. The old codes of moral principles—the "collective guardianship" of morality—were shaken by the wartime circumstances, and apart from severe punishment, no mechanism remained to protect soldiers' families from sexual exploitation. This situation contributed to the perception of moral degeneration and social crisis (*ictimai buhran*) during and after the war. On the other hand, victims of such crimes called for action and held the state accountable for their vulnerability. Eventually, this contributed to the widening of the scope of state intervention in the sphere of family issues.

It is easier to find the final decisions of sexual assault trials than the initial complaints or petitions that would more fully complete the story. As discussed earlier, starting in early 1915, the courts martial began trying sexual assault cases involving members of soldiers' families. Some exemplars in the archives demonstrate a pattern in the punishments of such offenses as well as the procedures of the military tribunals. The military courts tried rape and sex crimes according to the Ottoman Penal Code and forwarded their decisions to the Ministry of War. In most cases, Articles 206 and 198 were applied. While the former stipulated the punishment for rapes involving victims of fifteen years old or younger, the latter applied to rape cases that included abduction. Minister of War Enver Pasha approved the decisions to be issued as an imperial order (*irade-i seniyye*), generally on his own initiative. Once the decision was approved by imperial order, the Ministry of War executed it. The punishment for a rape crime involving a soldier's female relative (usually his daughter or wife) was three years of hard labor. The offender faced harsher penalties if he had resorted to violence, caused damage (either physical o mental), or committed the rape together with another offense such as theft or breaking into private property. In such cases the punishment could increase to up to seven years of hard labor accompanied by the loss of one's civil rights (*hukûk-u medeniyyeden ıskat*) in addition to paying all the expenses of the witnesses and the court. As a general rule, court martial decisions included the public disclosure of the offender (*teşhir*) as part of the punishment. In some cases, soldiers themselves were the perpetrators of such crimes and were punished according to the Ottoman Penal Code as well as the Military Penal Code. The cases below illustrate the decisions in such tribunals.

The case of Menevişe [sic], a soldier's wife from the village of Çakıl near the town of Harput, was brought before the martial court in Elaziz. A certain Hacı Ibrahim was accused of breaking into her house and raping her. The court sentenced him to three years of hard labor based on Article 198 of the penal code. The decision was approved by an imperial order on May 20, 1916. The Ministry of War was the executor of the order.[64] In another case, the Konya court martial tried a certain Hacı Hüseyin for the abduction and defloration of Feride, the sister of the soldier Mehmed. Hacı Hüseyin was sentenced in absentia to death—moreover, the confiscation of his property was ordered—according to the Article 206 of the penal code. The court decision arrived at the grand vizierate signed by Enver Pasha. The vizierate approved the court decision but decided to retry Hacı Hüseyin upon his arrest.[65] In another case, Dimitri was sentenced to three years of hard labor after he was accused of raping a fourteen-year-old daughter of a soldier.[66] In another case, a Circassian refugee named Hasan broke into a soldier's wife's house in the night and raped her. The court martial of Izmir sentenced him to seven years of hard labor based on the Article 198 of the Penal Code, relieved him of his civil rights, and charged him court expenses together with the expenses of witnesses (amounting to 249 piasters).[67] In another case, a certain İbrahim abducted a soldier's wife and raped her.[68] He was sentenced to the same punishment as Hasan. In a case of abduction and rape, the court martial of Ankara sentenced a perpetrator to five years of hard labor.[69] The court martial of Ankara sentenced two townsmen accused of raping Azime, a soldier's wife, to three years of hard labor.[70] However, if rape was not accompanied by abduction or breaking and entering, the standard punishment was three years of hard labor.

In a case before the Izmir martial court, the perpetrator was a soldier while the victim was the wife of another soldier. A labor battalion sergeant named İsmail had raped Cemile, the wife of the soldier Veli, and the court sentenced him to five years of hard labor according to Article 198 of the penal code, demoted his military rank, and relieved him of his civil rights.[71] There are many cases in which soldiers were the perpetrators of rapes ranging from statutory rape to forced intercourse with fellow townswomen. They were sentenced to heavy penalties such as the confiscation of their property, dismissal from duty (in the case of homosexuality), and the standard penalty of hard labor.[72]

For an example of an adultery case—intercourse with the consent of both parties—Hatice's trial in the Ankara martial court can be examined. A soldier's wife, Hatice, was involved in consensual intercourse with Osman, a fellow townsman from her village of Kuruçay. She became pregnant, and in order to not let that be revealed, she committed feticide. The martial court in Ankara sentenced Hatice to fifteen years of hard labor on June 22, 1917, based on Article 174 of the penal code.[73]

These cases are abundant in the Prime Ministry Ottoman Archives. The main duty of the martial courts was to ensure that the current Ottoman Penal Code was thoroughly applied; it was not to introduce new law on the punishment of sexual assault. The involvement of the Ministry of War indeed served this purpose as it was actively involved in the trial processes.

So far, my cases have dealt with Ottoman Muslim women and Muslim families. However, it would be misleading to consider that it was only Muslim women and families who were the victims of sexual assaults on the Ottoman home front. After the deportation, Armenian young women and widows whose male family members were deported were to be married off and they were to be settled in places where Armenians and foreigners were not present.[74] Orphans were distributed to the Muslim families.[75] During the deportation, Armenian women were exposed to "gender-specific abuse," abduction and rape, and eventually murder in several places during their marches.[76] Obviously, such cases are not documented among the petitions. Kutluata argues on her study on the petitions of the period that most petitions arrived from Muslim peasant women and Armenian women.[77] She located seventy petitions between 1915 and 1918 concerning the matters of requests about exemption from deportation because the petitioner was a soldier's family member, conversion to Islam (as a way to be saved from deportation), expression of innocence (especially Armenian mothers' petitions for their children), and loyalty.[78] Kutluata's comparison is significant in terms of understanding Armenian and Muslim women's communication with the state. While Armenian women's main concern was to prove that they were "loyal citizens" and the petitions were to be the tools to recover citizenship ties with their states, Muslim women were confident about their status vis-à-vis the state and more direct about asking their citizenship rights.[79]

Punishing "Unfaithful" Wives: The Adultery Bill of 1916

Infidelity of soldiers' wives was a major concern not only in the Ottoman Empire but also in other combatant countries. Although these cases were treated as crimes, infidelity and adultery are mutually established relationships, and thus there is no victim. As Lisa M. Todd states in her article on German women and sexual infidelity during war, women's "entering affairs of their own free will" without the concern of economic needs troubled German authorities the most.[80] The imagery of wives on the home front who were "enjoying their lives" openly contradicted the "service" that was expected from them.

During the First World War, a remarkable measure by combatant countries to protect morality was to segregate women on the home front from prisoners of war (POWs) and from soldiers that arrived from the colonies. In Germany, radical measures were taken to prevent the interaction of women with POWs working in industry or agriculture, such as declaring the names of "immoral" women in newspapers and taking legal measures beyond public sanctions.[81] Based on the Prussian Siege Law of 1851, German authorities introduced measures to prevent contact between POWs and civilians. Todd states that thousands of German women were arrested as a result of relationships with POWs.[82] Furthermore, on the local level, the names of these "promiscuous" women were posted on the church doors as public humiliation. German authorities, similar to the Ottomans, identified these cases as part of the "moral decline" in German society associated with "national decline." Such adultery cases not only affected the country's reputation abroad but also damaged future plans for a "successful postwar nation."[83]

In another context, the war was characterized by fear of the "mixture of races" due to the mobilization of men in the colonies. Black troops in the United States and the French colonial army were considered threats to the preservation of morality on the home front. Nonwhite troops were isolated from white ones even in their place of work. Especially in France, Senegalese troops were both praised for their skill as warriors, but at the same time these "savage qualities made them a potential sexual and moral threat to the French civilians."[84] A similar attitude was present in the British army vis-à-vis Indian troops. It was feared that the war would eliminate established inequalities between white women and Indian men.[85] Not only men but also the women of colonized regions were a danger. An Australian government minister declared that "Cairo will do infinitely more harm to Australia than all the Turks will do in Gallipoli."[86] Race and nation appeared as further standards for moral control.

In the Ottoman Empire, the connotations of adultery were similar to those in other major combatant countries with respect to moral decline. However, the concerns did not result from interaction among foreign nationals or POWs with Ottoman women. Mostly it was due to the consensual relationships of soldiers' wives. In this regard, I evaluate a legislative attempt by the Ottoman Ministry of War that indicates the growing concern for preventing adultery among the female relatives of soldiers, particularly their wives. I believe that this attempt has remained unexplored because the bill was not enacted. However, this detail does not change the fact that such an attempt by itself importantly reveals the extent of the "problem" and the willingness of the military to intervene in sexuality in the name of protecting family.

Almost a year after the martial courts were authorized to try sexual assault cases involving soldiers' families, a new debate started concerning the authorization of Military Chiefs of the Recruitment Offices (*ahz-ı asker şube-yi reisleri*) and high-ranking commanders to litigate in adultery (*fi'il-i şen'i*) cases—that is to say, whether military men should be able to file complaints and initiate a legal process on behalf of soldiers against their unfaithful wives. On April 26, 1916, the Ministry of War presented a draft of a new provisional law that supplements the earlier one regarding the protection of soldiers' families. The draft read:

> according to Article 201 of the Penal Code, adultery charges can be brought only by the husband, or by parents (legal guardians) in the husband's absence. If no complaints are filed by these parties, the martial courts cannot undertake an investigation. The fact that soldiers fighting on the battlefront or taken as prisoners of war have no means to file complaints raises the issue of the morale of soldiers. And because allowing soldiers' female relatives who commit adultery to go unpunished would provoke protests in the public opinion, a bill appears to be vital that would substitute the complaints of husbands or parents with those of the highest ranking military commanders and the Chiefs of Recruitment Offices in order to protect the honor of soldiers.[87]

Although the bill was not enacted, debate over the bill strikingly relates to the morality concerns. On the one hand, initiatives taken by the Ministry of War enlarged the purview of public realm, bringing private cases under the jurisdiction of martial courts. On the other, once this distinction between public and private was blurred, the notion within Ottoman law on family affairs—which strictly defined the boundaries of private and public matters—was invalidated. From this point of view, morality, honor, and family cases stood in the center between public and private law.

Again, the context of war is crucial for making sense of military intervention in such a delicate issue. The possible grounds for this intervention can be summarized as follows: First, many women seeking financial help or a means of protection engaged in extramarital relationships, or else they were encouraged to have such relationships as a fate better than prostitution. Second, rumors of unfaithful wives deeply affected the morale of soldiers and in many cases resulted in their desertion. Third, the lack of protection for soldiers' families, especially for women, discredited the propaganda of the Ottoman government during the First World War. For example, leaflets dropped by British planes provoked soldiers by mentioning unfaithful wives and hungry children on the home front.[88] Of course, not all extramarital relationships were the result of wartime hardship; there were consensual relationships in the absence of dominant males. The draft law on adultery was aimed at preventing such voluntary relationships by charging the military with the policing morality.

The draft required approval of the Council of State to be enacted. The Council of State consulted with the Ministry of Justice on the feasibility of such a regulation. Eventually, the Ministry of Justice prepared a detailed inquiry into the possible consequences of the bill and concluded that it was not proper to issue it as a law. The statement of the Ministry of Justice argued that adultery offenses belong to the realm of private law, but the bill prepared by the Ministry of War would bring the issue into the purview of criminal law. This point was central to the issue of the legal and social status of soldiers' female relatives. Is the promise to protecting families valid in cases where the woman was in a voluntary relationship with other man? If so, whose rights should be protected: those of the women or those of the soldiers?

The Ministry of Justice listed two main arguments against the bill. The first issue concerned the elimination of the agency of husbands. Accordingly, if local military officials could be litigants, this would result in ignoring the rights of the husband to claim or disclaim charges made on his behalf. Second, the statement emphasized the "nature of adultery" with reference to "moral degeneration." It was asserted that moral degeneration does not appear suddenly; therefore, it needs to be observed over time. According to the statement, only the close relatives of a woman can ascertain moral degeneration and take action accordingly. The only person to decide whether to file a complaint and consider it thoroughly is the husband, because he is the only one who knows the bitter consequences of accusing his wife of adultery. Thus, the husband was expected to behave meticulous enough to bring the case to the court. The statement bitterly criticized the adultery bill in the sense that it substituted litigators (husband or parents) with military authorities, thus forcing prosecution offices to try women who had allegedly committed adultery. Under usual conditions, if someone other than the husband or parents informed prosecutors of adultery cases, their claims would remain as an act of informing (*ihbar*). However, if the draft were accepted and military authorities gained the right to open cases on behalf of husbands or parents, prosecution offices would have to charge the woman immediately. The military was seeking the right to be the sole authority over the control of extramarital relationships, as if it were a party to—that is, "victim of"—the crime. Accordingly, transferring adultery cases from private to criminal law would result in conflicts. The Ministry of Justice clearly noted that while private cases can be dropped by the decision of the litigator, public cases remain open until a final decision is made. The statement also referred to the elimination of the power of civilian authorities. While a mechanism of denunciation was in effect for adultery cases in which prosecutors had discretionary power to decide whether a case should be taken to court, the draft law proposed that the complaints—*şikayet*—of military officials were equivalent to those of husband or parents. Therefore, the discretionary power of civilian authorities would be eliminated. Another point of objection was that the bill would apply only to a certain social group in specific cases and thus contradicted the principle of "unity of law." For these reasons, the Ministry of Justice opposed the adultery bill. The Council of Ministers, deferring to the reports of the Ministry of Justice and the Council of State, rejected the draft law proposed by the Ministry of War.[89] The draft shows the willingness of military authorities to regulate male-female relationships based on concerns about protecting morality so that these relationships would not harm mobilization efforts.

My contention is that the authorization of military courts to try sexual assaults of soldiers' female relatives was the beginning of subsequent interventions into the family during the First World War. It was followed by unsuccessful legislation—the Adultery Bill—and continued with a more deliberate step: the Family Decree of 1917. The objections of the Ministry of Justice summarized above would partly be eliminated in the legislation on family formation and dissolution.

The Ottoman Rights of Family Decree of 1917

The Ottoman Rights of Family Decree of 1917 (*Hukûk-u Aile Kararnâmesi*) is among the most controversial legislations of the war. First, its content and particularly its articles regarding women's right to divorce constitute an ongoing debate in the literature.[90] Second, the timing of the introduction of family reform raises an important question: why did Ottoman governments bypass family reform in the age of the Tanzimat and introduce it only during the turmoil of the First World War?[91] The literature on the Family Decree has emphasized two dynamics in answer to this question: one, the ruling party benefited from wartime conditions and issued a family law that had long been on its agenda, and two—less emphasized in the literature—wartime conditions necessitated the profound change in state intervention in the realm of the family. To present a balanced view, it is possible to claim both are true.

The family issue and reform had been on the agenda of intellectuals since the mid-nineteenth century, but the social conditions that war brought about constituted the foundation for family reform. The war affected many families, caused great disturbances in the formation and dissolution of families, and diminished the basic functions of the family. A recent study by Nihan Altınbaş argues that social conditions were central to legislation on the family.[92] She considers the modernist motives of the ruling party in addition to the expectations of Muslim middle-class women, including the construction of the nuclear family, among the reasons for the introduction of a family law. She also mentions that the new family law allowed remarriage for lower-class women who had lost their husbands, by which they could make a living, constituting another reason for the introduction of the family law.[93] İlber Ortaylı's article evaluates the Family Decree within the context of legal developments and the adoption of a modern legal system throughout the nineteenth century.[94] He considers the Family Decree to be part of the attempts at standardization by the Ottoman government (since the decree embraced all subjects of the Ottoman Empire regardless of religious affiliation) starting from the time of Mahmud II.[95] He emphasizes the role of modernist ideology in such institutional changes. "Changes in such institutions as marriage, divorce and inheritance oftentimes were surprisingly far-reaching. The essential importance of these changes lies in the presence behind them of a modernist ideology and of a debate supporting that ideology."[96] Accordingly, the Family Decree was a "natural outgrowth" of other financial and administrative reforms as well as social and legal changes initiated by the Tanzimat bureaucracy, which brought about a new perspective on the family as a financial unit to be controlled and inspected by the state.⁹⁷ On the other hand, other scholars emphasize the religious nature of the decree—the articles were adapted from the four main Sunni schools—and claim that due to the religious underpinning of the legislation, it is misleading to evaluate it within the context of attempts at modernization. Fındıkoğlu argues against this line of thought and presents the abolishment of the decree in 1919 upon the opposition of both Muslims and non-Muslim religious scholars as proof that the decree was neither welcomed nor accepted as a "religious" text.⁹⁸ The religious underpinning of the legislation, according to him, as well as to other scholars, was just a means of eliminating religious opposition and legitimizing the legislation.⁹⁹

Instead of dealing with these questions, I direct my attention to aspects that situate family reform in the wider context of discourses of moral decline. To this end, the following pages answer two questions: How did critiques of dominant social values and norms play a role in the introduction of family reform? How were moral concerns and the idea of regenerating the family reflected in the legislation? To address the latter, I use the justificatory text (*esbâb-ı mucibe lâyihası*) together with the body of the legislation, while to answer the former, I present critical voices in the late Ottoman intelligentsia that paved the way for fruitful debate on the limits of Islamic Law and the role of social norms in Ottoman Muslim family formation.

The discourse on moral decline was associated with a so-called family crisis in the late Ottoman context. A close look at the works of late Ottoman intellectuals reveals narratives mostly centered on family and the relationships between men and women. The themes of the emancipation of women, family tragedy, critique of over-Westernization along with critique of backwardness were endemic to Ottoman literary works.¹⁰⁰ The destructive effect of war was reflected in themes calling for urgent discussion of national revival. A national revival was only possible by modernizing the family; however, the social values and superstitions of the society stood in the way. The main point of this theme is as follows: The ways of forming families (segregating women and men until marriage is realized) weakens the foundations of the family, resulting in an unhappy marriage. Spouses remain bound to each other because divorce is not welcomed in the society. Because of this unhappy environment, these couple's children keep reproducing the same unhappiness in their own lives. The values of such families have no rational basis; roles and responsibilities of family members are not defined. The children are not sufficiently educated within the family (due to the early marriage or simple ignorance of the parents), and they reproduce the same problems in their own families.¹⁰¹

The crisis of family came to be associated with the crisis of morality because the foundations of the family as an institution are integral to the values of a given society. For instance, what prevented women and men from getting to know each other before marriage? The answer is the moral codes of the society. What prevented women from taking an active role in Ottoman public space? Why did Muslim women not work outside their homes in the cities? These questions are multiple, but the answer is more or less the same. Eventually, norms had to change in order to regenerate the Ottoman family and strengthen the idea of family reform.

The Family Decree is a result of these concerns attempting to change the perception of morality, recognize the "will" of women, and define duties and rights – the latter two are strongly related to morality. The First World War revealed hideous realities and functioned as an engine for legal and perceptional change in the realm of the family. But how does one change the norms that constitute the basis of lawmaking? Islamic Law had claimed the realm of the family for hundreds of years; how could secular powers intervene in this sphere without provoking an enormous reaction? I believe two factors played important roles: first, new interpretations of lawmaking in Islam, and second, the discourse of the salvation of the nation. While the former enabled the possibility of reform in the family, the latter strengthened it by emphasizing wartime circumstances and linking the well-being of the family with that of the nation. The persistence idea was that the degeneration of Muslim families—and thus the foundation of Muslim society—had occurred to an extent that family reform was inevitable.

Without intellectual debates challenging traditional sources of law, family reform was impossible. The advocates of family reform, most of whom were Turkish nationalists, agreed on the superiority of Islamic Law and spoke within a theological framework. They took mores (*örf*) that had prevailed in old Turkish communities as significant inputs for lawmaking. This, indeed, increased the tension between the Islamists and nationalists. Both the Islamists and nationalists shared the assumption that Muslim civilization was in decline. Both agreed on the need for reforms to overcome this problem. However, the problem was to identify the points of departure for reform.

Ziya Gökalp, the chief theorist of the nationalists and a well-known advocate of family reform, formulated his thoughts on the idea that mores (*örf*) have an important place in the codification of Islamic Law.[102] By giving examples from the history of the Islam (including its early years) as well as from the golden age of the Ottoman Empire, he emphasized the major role of mores upon which the rulers relied. Contrary to Islamists' arguments on the need for a "pure" adaptation of Islamic Law, he reserved a space for mores in lawmaking in order to realize family reform. He claimed that mores should be regarded as equally important as classical sources of Islamic Law in order that the law be widely accepted in society. By attaching importance to the "words of the rulers," he sought to eliminate the "divine" interpretation upon which Islamic scholars relied. Emphasizing the need for change, he stated the importance of new values for shaping the new codification. Inevitably, these values needed to be compatible with the modern world and the social realities of Ottoman society. Mansurizade Said, who was a professor of jurisprudence, strengthened the thesis of Gökalp regarding the authority of legislators over the sanction or prohibition of polygamy in Islam.[103] It is possible to argue that this debate over the sources of law, the authority of legislators, and the compatibility of the law with modern times paved the way for the Family Decree. As the old moral order was in decline, progressive norms and values in the shape of mores acted as principles of lawmaking.

On the other hand, discourses on the relationship between the regeneration of family and that of the nation constituted another point of departure in the justification of family reform. Similar assertions were made during the Balkan Wars in the Ottoman press. Eyal Ginio's work on the Ottoman culture of defeat in the aftermath of the Balkan Wars presents how feelings of revenge and loss of honor were combined with discourses on national awakening and the renewal of the nation. "Awakening and renewal" were the notions that served the purposes of formulating a new "regenerated" community.[104]

In this "literature of defeat," the regeneration of the nation was not independent of that of the family and of women.[105] For commentators, social reform was necessary for political success. A contemporary woman writer, Mükerrem Belkıs, explicitly argued that remaining ambivalent about demolishing old customs—particularly insisting on the segregation of the sexes until marriage—amounted to treason.[106] The discourses on "saving the nation" during both the Balkan Wars and the First World War were a pretext to demand state intervention in the family sphere. Serpil Çakır shows that contemporary women writers correlated defeat on the battlefield with desperation at home—that is, with the environment in which the soldiers grew up.[107] In this line of thought, happiness in the family was key to success in battle. One of the major arguments Ziya Gökalp made in his series of articles on the family morality was that the principle of equality in politics could only be realized if equality in the family is established.[108] According to him, the Family Decree was an outcome of this concern.

The war tested the vulnerability of Ottoman Muslim families to the burdens of war. Especially in the countryside, complaints about adultery, abduction, and rape cases strengthened this view. A close look at the articles of the Family Decree as well as its justificatory text (*esbâb-ı mucibe lâyihası*) allows us to interpret the rationale behind the decree and to establish links between discourses of moral decline and the need for family reform. First, a serious problem in the countryside regarding the formation of families was marriages made under coercion that were generally followed by abductions (particularly of minor girls). Tüccarzade addressed this problem, which for him signified moral decline in the provincial areas. "We are aware of the conditions in the big cities. It is also not good what is happening in even the small towns of Anatolia. There, most cases [of moral decline] manifest themselves in the shape of abductions of girls and adultery."[109] Article 57 of the Family Decree attempted to prevent such marriages by invalidating marriage contracts signed under coercion. The justificatory memorandum (*esbab-ı mucibe layihası*) gives clues about how this article came to be introduced.

> Many Muslim women have been abducted and forced violently to marry unworthy people, and the attempts of families to save these girls have failed, thus resulting in huge disasters. On the other hand, the doctrine of İmam Şafii opposes such marriages; therefore, [it] was adopted in Article 57 to prevent such misconduct.[110]

Previously, the Hanefi school accepted even marriages contracted under coercion.[111]

Second, the Family Decree addressed the problem of adolescent education in the family. As the *esbâb-ı mûcibe layihası* puts it, early marriage was one main reason for the "degeneration of the Muslim community" (*İslam unsurunun tedennîsi*) in Ottoman society. "Less-educated" adolescents make a family and establish a lifestyle without being capable of controlling it. Strikingly, the *esbâb-ı mâcibe lâyihası* underscored wartime as the moment of breakdown when family formation and family life in Ottoman society became unsustainable.

> Although the authorities of Islamic law endorsed the marriages of children arranged by their tutors and such marriage contracts were conducted up to now, given the changing conditions in our era, a different attitude is deemed necessary. That is to say, in every era, and above all in this era in which the struggle to survive has become extreme, the first duty of parents to their

children should be to educate them and raise them to be strong in this world of battles and to form a proper family, but our parents keep neglecting education and the instruction of their children, either to see them marry or—that they gain inheritance rights—to arrange marriage contracts when the kids are in the cradle. Eventually, these poor children who are ignorant of the world are married and their catastrophic future is determined in marriage ceremonies. These children who never attended a school, cannot read or write in their native language, do not know the principles of religion, are establishing families that are born to die, condemned to decompose in the first months of the marriage. This is one of the reasons why families in our country are not established on strong foundations.

The *esbab-ı mucibe layihası* emphasized concerns for the marriage of minor girls in particular.

The wife and husband, in constituting a family and managing it, shall act together. While boys are allowed to spend time playing in the streets, girls of the same age are overwhelmed by the greatest burden in human society: being a mother and the manager of a family. These poor girls, whose physical constitution is not yet sufficiently complete to be a mother, live in misery all their lives and suffer anxiety. The children to which they give birth are vulnerable and nervous, causing the gradual degeneration of the Muslim community.

For the first time in the history of the Ottoman Empire, the decree recognized adolescents as new category. Previously, Sharia law acknowledged only two categories: childhood and adulthood. The law forbade the marriage of children under a certain age irrespective of the consent of their families. This age limit was twelve for boys and nine for girls, and the age for independent marriages without consent of the families was seventeen for women and eighteen for men. In this way, not only were child marriages prevented but an intended change in family norms was triggered. The family had to educate children and prepare them for the future. This was the formulation that was believed would improve the standards of Muslim families and thus of the Ottoman nation.

The problem of remarriage was another issue that related the Family Decree to discourses on morality. Since marriages were not registered in Islam and were maintained only as a verbal promise, the only proof of marriage was the testimony of witnesses. In their absence, women or their families might claim that she was not married. The *esbâb-ı mûcibe lâyihası* particularly emphasized the situation of women who remarried while she already had a husband. Women or their families might take advantage of the absence of husbands due to the war and establish (or in some cases be forced to establish) new marriage contracts for various reasons. By means of the decree, the government sought to control marriage contracts by charging courts with the task of announcing the marriage before judges and finalizing the marriage contract in the absence of objections. So far, scholars have interpreted this point in the legislation as an attempt to standardize marriage and control over population. However, as can be seen in the *esbâb-ı mûcibe lâyihası*, the real reason behind this measure was to prevent remarriages, which had become widespread especially in the countryside: "Many frauds have occurred due to the lack of a proper way of making such an important contract, thus resulting in the remarriages of women despite the Sharia's orders. Therefore, the Article 37 is being introduced."

Such remarriages binding women to another man in the absence of her husband were arranged by village elders or relatives.[112] As far as I could find in the archives, letters arrived to various offices from soldiers as well as their wives claiming that married women were forced to marry again (or sometimes willingly did so) in the absence of their husband during the Balkan Wars.[113] Already during the Balkan Wars, the Ministry of Interior Affairs was concerned with the issue of rapid announcement of a soldier's death to his family so that his widow or fiancée could remarry. Some soldiers, again during the Balkan Wars, also abused their positions to prevent women (due to personal reasons, jealousy or hostility) to get married or engaged with others claiming that woman had already been engaged or married to him. In order to prevent such problems registration of marriages and engagements were made compulsory.[114]

In order to address all these problems, marriages had to be registered so that the rights of the husband as well as those of the wife could be preserved in the circumstances of war. The registry would also include information about the *mehr*, the amount to be paid to the woman in case of divorce in order to guarantee her livelihood. Moreover, another article was introduced to allow the remarriage of those women who had lost their husbands at war or whose husbands had gone missing in the course of the war. Accordingly, if a husband is lost during the war, the wife will be considered out of wedlock after the combatant countries sign the armistice and one year passes after the prisoners of war on both sides go back to their homeland.[115] If a woman married without following this rule and her first husband reappeared, her second marriage was invalidated. If she did follow the rule and the husband, who was considered to have died during the war, appeared later on, the second marriage would still be invalidated. Those who married or witnessed the marriage of already married women would be sentenced to imprisonment of up to three years. Medical control before marriage became compulsory also to address the problem of the spread of venereal diseases. Article 122 stipulated that if the husband had venereal diseases, the wife had the right to ask for divorce. In case of possible treatment, the judge could grant a waiting period of one year.

Another issue signifying the relationship between morality concerns and the Family Decree was the prevention of temporary marriages. Article 55 of Family Decree strictly banned temporary marriage contracts (*nikâh-ı mut'a or nikâh-ı muvakkat*). This practice was particularly common among Muslims. It was believed that if couples entered into a temporary marriage contract (in a religious vein) before having sexual intercourse, sex would not be considered a sin or as adultery. A madrasa teacher from Konya, Abdullah Fevzi Efendi, who had joined the army during the First World War and also served as an imam in the army, claimed that these contracts were quite common among the military ranks. In his memoirs, which he wrote in Arabic, he titled one chapter "Morality in the Army" and started it with this sentence: "Damn the amorality of the members of the Islamic army and soldiers in this century."[116] He claims that he witnessed many temporary marriages of military officers in Iraq: "In Hüseyinabad, a village near Hemedan, moral corruption and instances of temporary marriage (*mut'a*) increased further."[117] He stated that official orders were introduced to prevent such cases, and military commanders issued penalties to imams who took part in temporary marriages. These marriages, according to him, caused moral decay as well as the spread of venereal disease in the military.[118] Article 55 of the decree might be related to concern about the practice of temporary marriages, which had especially increased with the mass mobilization of the army.[119]

Finally, enabling women to divorce under particular conditions (which had to be indicated by the women in the marriage contract) can also be evaluated within the framework of regenerating the family. A woman's right to divorce, adopted from the Maliki school, was a distinctive point of the decree. In cases of disagreement, women gained the right to divorce with the consent of a "family council" appointed by the court. Women could also demand divorce on account of illness (including venereal disease), feeblemindedness, and impotency, but only after a one-year period of recovery. This, I believe, was designed to dissolve those families that had lost their function for society—such as "reproduction"—and to enable the reformation of new families by empowering women to do so.

Among the articles on marriage, that on polygamy was the most debated. Although not forbidden, woman had the right to indicate whether she accepted polygamy. If she did not and the man insisted, she had the right to divorce. The Hanbeli school was taken as a basis for this article. Many Islamists opposed this point and claimed that at the end of the war, there would be more women than men, so polygamy would be a social necessity.[120] However, for lawmakers the important thing was the regeneration of family, not the distribution of men and women according to the population ratio. In order to regenerate family, women first had to be empowered within marriage.

Can legislation change norms in society? Or does law reflect norms that already exist in that society? We tend to think lawmaking is the result of structural change, not the converse. However, it seems that Ottoman intellectuals and reformers approached legislation as a way to introduce new family values and thus a new understanding of morality. This point, in fact, was in line with Durkheimian sociology, Durkheim's analysis of norms, and his pragmatic approach to science through which a prescription for the future is possible. According to this approach, an individual or a group of people can solve the disparity between the rules of morality and the actual state of society.[121]

Morality and family reform were related in the sense that the problems of Ottoman family formation and dissolution were associated with moral decay. The advocates of family reform linked the well-being of adolescents, women, and men to those of the nation in order to legitimize the need for reform. On the other hand, that the Family Decree was inspired by these insights and concern about moral decline can be ascertained from its articles.

This chapter addressed the relation of moral decline discourses and discourses on the Ottoman Muslim family in the context of the First World War. By linking the circumstances faced by Ottoman Muslim families during the war and the discourses of moral decline on the Ottoman home front, I argue that state intervention in family had reflected concerns about moral decline. In cases of rape, sexual assault, and abduction, the victims asked for active state protection in return for their contribution to the war effort. I consider the Adultery Bill of 1916 as a further instance of state intervention into the family in order to protect home front morality. Although the legislation was unsuccessful, the content of the bill caused intense debate on the extent of state's role in regulating sexual relationships. The Family Decree of 1917 was a part of the many attempts of the Ottoman government to protect families during the war.

By establishing a close link between the well-being of the nation and that of the family, Ottoman intellectuals and reformers attributed great importance to moral values for the formation, dissolution, and function of families. As Salim Tamari asserted, we tend to see the destructive effects of the war, but there was an "unanticipated emancipatory impact" of the war "that opened up new social horizons," as well.[122] Perhaps, the Family Decree of 1917 can be considered part of this side of the war.

6

Conclusions and A Discussion on Moral Crisis from Past to Present

Morality was instrumental in discourses regarding the preservation of social and political order throughout the history of the Ottoman Empire. Political and social crises were often translated into concerns over morality, making it the ultimate touchstone of whether the state was doing its duty. Morality came to be considered part of the principles of religion, and the role of the Ottoman *ulema* in maintaining moral order meant that their moral authority was established in legislation as well as in jurisdiction. In the course of the nineteenth century, with a shift in the perception of state power, public order, and the formation of a broad intellectual and public space, morality became a contested realm among several actors.

This study analyzes the preconditions that led to the emergence of moral crisis debates in society in the context of the First World War. It focuses on how morality became instrumental for polemics on several issues around political, cultural, and social developments. Throughout this book, I argue that debates over morality had political, social, and cultural implications closely associated with the circumstances of war.

Opinionated articles on morality in the Ottoman press lead one to assume that prostitution and venereal disease should dominate a study on morality as these were considered and perceived as major threats to public morality. However, as demonstrated in this work, both morality and moral decline had wider definitions and implications in the period in question. The sense of moral decline was triggered not only as a result of war-induced anxieties but also due to domestic and external developments. In their quest to save the state and form a new society, the Ottoman Muslim intelligentsia directed its attention to morality, which was the priority among realms to be reformed. It was crucial for the progress, regeneration, and revival of the nation. The problem of morality reveals a common anxiety regarding the national regeneration. As the First

World War was a watershed event for envisaging the future nation, debates on morality became urgent in discussions of the social and intellectual structure on which the nation should rely. From the standpoint of morality polemicists, the system of values and social norms constituted obstacles to the advancement of the Ottoman Muslim society and contributed to the decline of the empire.

Similar to contemporary debates about morality, the issue of women was central to morality discussions. The war created a common anxiety about the consequences of the broader participation of women in social and economic life vis-à-vis the future of the patriarchal order. As most women had to fend for themselves during the war, concerns about the degradation of norms surrounding the patriarchal family dominated morality debates. A common anxiety was evident in debates on what should replace the old moral order. In the highly politicized atmosphere of the war, nationalism met morality, marking a moment of transformation between the old moral order and a new one.

This study explores four major realms for the study of wartime morality, namely ideologies defended by the intelligentsia, official measures and policies implemented by political and military elites, daily realities, and state interventions into the family and female sexuality. Undoubtedly, these areas of inquiry are not mutually exclusive. As shown throughout, these layers continuously feed one another. For the sake of the simplicity of presentation, I presented them under separate headings. The concept of moral crisis specifically addressed the Muslim population of the Empire, their demographic quality and ideal citizenship roles. Unfortunately, the literature written in Arabic remained outside this study due to linguistic limits.

Intellectual discussions about moral decline show how morality was politicized in the context of the war. The rise of materialism, the declaration of jihad, ideological contests over political and public space, critiques of previous reforms, the search for a new life, the war-induced social problem of profiteering, and women's labor and political rights constituted the major topics of polemics of moral crisis. Moral crisis debates offered several prominent intellectual figures an opportunity to discuss and question extant daily and social practices in their quest for social reform and a new spirit. Once an obstacle to progress, morality became an ideal starting point to penetrate in previously untouched institutions. This study deliberately puts the discussion in its historical political and social context in order to understand the increased emphasis on morality.

In a second layer of analysis, by drawing attention to wartime regulations regarding the protection of public morality in combatant countries, I argue that moral anxieties created a common discourse intermingled with concern about both the practical and the political implications of moral decline. In the course of the war, violations of public morality became part of the growing concern for national security; meanwhile, the wartime rivalry among combatant countries constituted the backbone of a cultural opposition in which moral contestation played a significant role. The Ottoman Empire prioritized moral considerations over other concerns, as evidenced by official propaganda underscoring the superiority of Muslim identity. By exploring wartime developments such as the court martial orders regarding immorality and the role of the abolishment of capitulations in the fight against prostitution and the trafficking in women, I argue that there was an increasing emphasis on national security in response to "immoral" behavior. These findings underpin the initial claim of this study that morality reflects political and social change instead of being an independent set of cultural norms.

Foreigners' applications for citizenship were denied on the basis of moral quality of the applicant, corroborating the assertion that moral judgments corresponded to national security concerns and wartime measures to rid society of "undesirable" elements. The nationality of foreigners was important for identifying the "other" in the atmosphere of the war and labeling them as "immoral." The basis of their exclusion was legitimized by using the etiquettes of morality.

In quotidian life, which I evaluate in Chapter 4, the protection of public morality was vital for maintaining public order. However, this did not mean that Ottoman authorities, whether bureaucratic or military, established absolute authority over public morality. Entertainment, leisure activities, and "vices" such as alcohol and gambling constituted a source of revenue for the state. Therefore, the government had a pragmatic approach toward such expenses. Among the conservative public, such vices signified moral corruption as they symbolized the immorality of Western civilization. On the other hand, a second, new critique emerged out of nationalist sentiment that such places distract people's attention from the war. In an effort to sublimate moral and financial interests, semi-governmental war relief organizations became dominant in the organization of entertainment. Eventually, moral instruction and war propaganda conflicted with the need to increase revenue as the public showed little interest in regulated entertainment.

A common trend was that many social, economic, and political problems were translated into the discourse of moral decline in the popular perception of morality. This was particularly valid for the problem of war profiteering, demonstrating that the collective memory of the war was shaped by the moralistic imagery of wartime inequality between the rich and the poor. The literary products of the postwar era explicitly reflect this tension through the representation of wealthy profiteers. The stories of debauchery of such characters attracted wider audiences than political critiques.

When the object of analysis is morality in traditional societies, family is an inevitable subject. Ottoman society was no exception in this regard. Therefore, widespread concern about morality, values, traditions, and norms vis-à-vis the wartime family is one of the major topics of this study. As detailed in Chapter 5, there was evident concern about family and women in many combatant countries, but the Ottoman case had its own peculiarities. In the Ottoman case, attention was directed not only toward the family per se but to all forms of encounter between men and women. I consider the family in this wider context of gender, sexuality, and patriarchy. The relations between men and women were surrounded by a set of norms interwoven with Islamic law and customs regulating sexual conduct.

Legislations on family during the First World War sought to regenerate Muslim families while controlling sexual relationships on the home front. I demonstrate how wartime legislation that targeted the family was driven by moral concerns, and I argue that morality discourses reveal the interaction of social and political conditions with ideas about the establishment of a new civic order. The latter was established on the basis of changing perceptions of the family, sexuality, and morality.

This study is as much about the social circumstances in which Ottoman people lived as it is about intellectual discussions. Contrary to widespread contentions among researchers that prioritize the ideological motive of state elites to modernize the family, I analyzed the demands of the women and soldiers' who asked for protection from the state, reminding it of the government's duties and promises. The sources I use reflect the wide scope of morality debates. Their variety also demonstrates how morality was incorporated into politics, lawmaking, daily life, and intellectual debates. Despite censorship of certain topics, it is possible to say that the morality issue was discussed at great length in the Ottoman press.

Morality and moral decline debates have been the subject of a few studies of the Ottoman Empire, albeit on a limited scale. In the scope of this study, I mainly focus on the central notion of *ahlâk* in the particular context of the First World War. However, further research covering the periods between the Tanzimat era and early republican Turkey will reveal the changing discourses of morality more comprehensively. Since morality is at the intersection of topics such as education, family, law, education, and social life, I believe further studies on morality from a historical perspective will contribute to the historiography of the Ottoman Empire in several other contexts and shed a new light on topics that have been studied previously.

Morality still has a distinct place in debates over secularism, gender, and modernity reflected in different views on lifestyle, school education, male and female relationships, public order, and institutionalization of power. Debates that took place over a hundred years ago are important for understanding the contemporary ideological and political atmosphere of the Republic of Turkey. To better understand this, I would like to discuss some connections between the past and today in the rest of this part. In addition, I shall present a framework to the question of why the Armenians remained outside the debate in moral crisis arguments in an attempt to further locate the moral world that I have discussed in this book.

Through the end of the war, *Tanin*, the mouthpiece of the government, published two editorials on issues of morality.[1] The articles argued that moral crisis manifests itself in three ways: first, prostitution and public manners (social conduct); second, war profiteering; and, third, the misuse of official services. Indeed, almost all the commentators I discuss in this study would share the idea that the general condition of moral crisis was about pursuing self-interest at the expense of the public good. As a critical political and social development that took place during the war which has repercussions echoing today, one important issue, namely the forced deportation of Ottoman Armenians starting from 1915, had remained unseen in the debates on moral crisis and moral problems of the time. Why did Armenian deportations, massacres, and confiscation of their properties remain outside the debates of morality? Was Muslim intellectuals' moral universe limited only to the Muslim community and Muslims' individual responsibility to each other?

Despite the fact that what happened to the Armenians was not considered as part of the moral crisis, many people, including the ones giving the orders of deportation, recognized the immorality of those acts. Talat Pasha, the leading figure behind deportations, revealed his thoughts while discussing the issue with Halide Edib: "Look here, Halide Hanum. I have a heart *as good as yours*, and it keeps me awake at night to think of the human suffering. But that is a *personal thing* and I am here on this earth to think of my people and not of my sensibilities [emphasis mine]."[2] Referring to the massacres targeting Muslims during the Balkan Wars and silence on the side of the rest of the world during those events, he continued: "I have the conviction that as long as a nation does the best for its interests, and succeeds, the world admires it and thinks it *moral*. I am ready to die for what I have done, and I know that I shall die for it [emphasis mine]."[3] Other decision takers too, such as Cemal Pasha, always referred to the "interest of the nation" and avoided self-responsibility when it came to the Armenian deportations. The autobiographies written by the leading names of the time carry the same line of thought—displaying "a lack of agency" and discoursing on extraordinary measures in times of a "national emergency," a strategy that they all took refuge behind.[4]

The narrative that was developed by the CUP members who were actively involved in deportations is still echoing in Turkey's official position when it comes to the genocide. The guilt was first on the European powers' policy of intervention in Ottoman domestic affairs with the pretext of protecting Christians, and second on the Armenians' answering seditious calls of Russia and massacring the Turks in Eastern provinces. During the court martial trials after the war where the CUP members were tried, one can see a similar approach in the responses to the questions concerning the crimes during deportations. Through same reasoning, the decision of deportation was right because the Armenians (civilians and soldiers deserting the Ottoman army alike) in Eastern Anatolia were collaborating with the enemy (the Russian army) and leaving the Ottoman army under cross fire. The deportation was intended to be a "measure" that was brought forward under extraordinary conditions, but things went downhill in the hands of people who applied the decision.[5]

After a victorious War of Independence, the nationalist movement argued that the perpetrators had already been punished (some were hanged) during the trials. From their point of view, the trials also became a political tool in the hands of Allied powers for revenge. Most of the CUP members were exiled to Malta by the British to be exchanged later with the British prisoners of war captured by the nationalist movement. Enver, Talat, and Cemal Pashas had already fled the country immediately after the defeat and were condemned to death in absentia during the trials. Talat and Cemal Pashas were killed by Armenian assassins, while Enver Pasha died in June 1922, when he was fighting the Red Army with Turkic guerrillas near the Afghan border. Many CUP members who took part in deportations joined the nationalist movement and later they emerged in political positions as Republican leaders.[6] Early Turkish Republic also denied the mass return of the Armenians and prevented them from restoring their properties by stripping them off citizenship. The coalition of power which led the success of War of Independence and later that of the establishment of a new regime was based on a silent settlement among local Muslim landowners, the newly emerging Muslim merchant bourgeoisie, and the military, intellectual elites on the suppression of all claims on the side of Armenians.

After the war and occupations, the nationalist press stirred the ideas of revenge against the occupiers and their collaborators. The authors of *Yeni Mecmua* continued their efforts to develop the National Literature genre in which non-Muslim characters usually appeared as deceitful characters in their works throughout the Early Republican Era. *Sebilürreşad* authors increased their criticism toward the nationalists, blaming them for the collapse of the empire by stirring other nationalisms. In their version of events, if the empire had continued the Islamic way of ruling with respect to the administration of non-Muslim communities, there would not be any problems from the start. But no one could claim that Armenians were innocent too, because they had answered the calls of European states and revolted against the Ottomans, and thus acted disloyally, a factor that broke the traditional Islamic understanding of protection of non-Muslim subjects. Armenians also murdered Muslims and prepared this end for themselves.[7] This was also put forward in the defense of the grand vizier and an author of *Sebilürreşad* Said Halim Pasha (who was later killed by an Armenian assassin) during the trials.

In the postwar period under occupation, Armenian women criticized middle- and upper-class Turkish women for their discrimination against Armenian poor, families, and orphans both during and after the war. Using a discourse of civilization to warn the Allied officers who befriended Turkish women at the time, Kohar Mazlımyan wrote in *Hay Gin*, one of the most important and long published Armenian woman journals, that the true face of "philanthropist" and "civilized" Turkish women was indeed as discriminatory and immoral as the male CUP members.[8] These women only helped Muslim and Turkish soldiers' families with all their charities since the last five years. They never opposed the male Unionists—their husbands and friends—to stop the persecution of Armenians and they kept being completely indifferent to the tragedy of Armenian orphans at the time. Indeed, only Halide Edib confronted the Unionists against the Armenian deportations, and later she also changed her position to a more "massacres happened on both sides" discourse.[9]

The distrust and discrimination against the non-Muslims is observable in the evaluation of their moral qualities, as I also discussed in Chapter 3. This narrative survived to date. Accordingly, the initial element of immorality was their close relationships with the West, which was followed by adopting protégé status or acquiring citizenships from European states that allowed them to benefit from the capitulations. The Armenians, Greeks, and Jews in the empire thus gained an immense wealth at the expense of destroying Ottoman economy. Non-Muslim women were guilty of corrupting Muslim morality with prostitution or simply by constituting bad examples for the youth with their moral laxity.[10] It is possible to see in Lerna Ekmekçioğlu's study how this imagery concerned the Armenian community that remained in Istanbul in the postwar Republican era. The editor of Armenian feminist publication *Hay Gin*, Hayganush Mark, and other authors of the journal "knew that as Christians, Armenian women in urban Istanbul had long been branded in the popular mind as Westernized or Europeanized, and therefore potentially immoral and impure."[11] Therefore, they paid extra attention not to attract public criticism in terms of Armenian women's attire and social conduct so that they could blend in Turkish society by adopting its social norms.

There were "righteous" and "conscientious" people too, especially among the locals and local governors, who openly confronted the deportation orders and resisted the executers of this policy despite severe punishments, including death penalty, announced for the ones helping the Armenians.[12] Ahmed Rıza, a member of Ottoman senate, was among the few who openly brought up the massacres and property confiscations in the senate as moral problems as early as December 1915.[13] Obviously, in Istanbul, where the press and many intellectuals were stationed, the scale of Anatolian massacres was less known due to the censorship. Even though they knew what was happening, probably they would not be able to publish their opinion. However, after the war they had the opportunity to do so and they did not.

According to Göçek, the collective violence in Turkish history, its normalization and denial, in addition to the fact that the perpetrators had remained unpunished, "corrupted and undermined public ethics" in society.[14] She states that coming to terms with the past and condemning those who were responsible for violence will contribute to the formation of a more just society, guarantee a better future for everyone, and offer peaceful solutions to the current ethnic conflicts.[15]

In a similar vein, framing sociopolitical crises of the last century within moral crisis had implications beyond its time. The debates, contestations, and negotiations of the era were deeply imprinted into the political culture of the young Republic and they continue to shape the political discourse today. Despite the fact that past atrocities and their ethical legacy rarely appear to be the main point, Turkey keeps discussing the existence of a moral crisis in society today. Current debates on morality that I will outline now will surely remind the reader of the 100-year-old debates that are discussed in this book.

In the world of 2010s, the existence of a moral crisis in Turkish society is still a hot topic that is being discussed by various circles. In the contemporary version of these debates, one can find similar arguments and conditions to the ones in the past. Political polarization and division in society certainly constitutes one of the common grounds between the old and new debates. The antagonism between secular morality and Islamic morality may have never been so sharp in Turkish history. The moral crisis today serves to the purposes of setting out ideological differences once again, but this time lifestyles appear to be discussed more than the ideologies themselves, probably as a result of a common perception of considering lifestyles as a realm of ideological assertion. Today, for the ruling hegemonic political power the idea of moral crisis is a pretext for social and institutional reorganization of society and instillation of Islamic values. On the other hand, for the opposition the moral crisis is a way to express political criticism and expose moral hypocrisy of what is being regarded moral in Islamist politics as well as in society. The continuity of moral crisis reference in the debates past and today is intriguing. My contention is that we owe this to two factors: first is the current political tension in Turkey and second the recirculation of the late Ottoman literary works under state sponsorship as well as private publication houses.

On September 12, 1980, Turkey woke up to a bloody coup d'état that would change the course of its history. The official aim of the coup was to suppress the war between the left- and right-wing groups that had been taking place all throughout the 1970s and to bring an order to the Turkish politics. But on the agenda of the military elite there was also the idea of redesigning society along more conservative lines in addition to a swift transition to neoliberal economy from the state-planned model. The military government promoted anti-communism as an ideological basis for neoliberal politics. The new ideology, the military elites were convinced, had to embrace and synthesize Turkish nationalism and Islamism, an ideology today known as the "Turkish-Islamist Synthesis."[16] A course titled *Din Kültürü ve Ahlak Bilgisi* (religious culture and moral knowledge) became compulsory in schools in 1982. The name and content of the course indicate the unification and equalization of religiosity with being moral superiority. In this environment, nationalist and Islamist publications of the past gained a new value.

While conducting my research, I saw that most of the articles that were published in journals such as *Sebilürreşad*, *Yeni Mecmua*, and *İslam Mecmuası* were transliterated, simplified, decontextualized, and republished with the sponsorship of state institutions, particularly that of the Ministry of Culture, in the 1980s. I was also struck by how familiar the stories that were published in *Yeni Mecmua* a hundred years ago sounded to me—I studied these texts when I was a school kid in the early 1990s.

I believe that the reproduction of nationalist and Islamist works of the late Ottoman era was part of a project to underpin legitimacy to the new regime from the Ottoman past. Works of Ottoman intelligentsia were considered useful for feeding the new ideology of "Turkish-Islamist Synthesis." Although nationalism and Islamism appeared as two competing and conflicting ideologies in the late Ottoman Empire, the 1980s reproduction effort reconciled the two by taking the texts out of their contexts. Later, in the 1990s, right-wing publishing houses and newspapers such as *Tercüman* and *Dergah Publishing* published these works in a similar fashion. In 2010 the Justice and Development Party (JDP) added "values education" courses to the school curricula. Today, a government's mouthpiece, Ensar Foundation, is republishing some of these works through a foundation called the *Değerler Eğitimi Merkezi* (Values Education Center) for instruction in new school courses.[17] Recently, the JDP party's Bağcılar Municipality undertook a twenty-five-volume transcription of all of *Sırat-ı Müstakim* and *Sebilürreşad's* issues into the Latin alphabet under the editorship of Ertuğrul Düzdağ.[18] In the recirculated versions, the Ottoman intelligentsia's statements are treated as ahistorical—timeless guides to life, politics, society, and religion both by the publishers and editors.

Under Recep Tayyip Erdoğan's Justice and Development Party (*Adalet ve Kalkınma Partisi*, AKP, in Turkish), the political Islamist writers of the past gained a fresh new recognition in Turkey. The new mosque of Diyanet İşleri was named after Ahmed Hamdi Akseki, a prominent writer in *Sebilürreşad*, in 2013. The Ministry of Cultural Affairs announced 2011 as the "Year of Mehmed Akif," with many events including symposia, exhibitions, and gatherings. Mehmed Akif's famous conceptualization of youth as "the generation of Asım" in the personality of a certain Asım who could preserve his Islamic values despite Western education is highly praised by AKP circles. In 2015, Erdoğan gave a speech in an event titled "A grandmaster from Asım's generation: Recep Tayyip Erdoğan," where he said that for the last thirteen years his party struggled to raise and revive a generation of Asım.[19] In the same speech, he juxtaposed the character of "geziciler" referring to the protestors in 2013 of Gezi Park with that of Asım, further adding an emphasis on the difference between these two not only from a political point of view but also from a moral one.

As a matter of fact, the Gezi Protests was a landmark event in the moral-political criticism both on the side of the opposition and the supporters of the ruling AKP party. In 2013, the Turkish riot police cleared Gezi Park of a group of activists who opposed the demolition of the park for new construction projects including revival of the old Ottoman barrack, a mosque and shopping mall. The police violence in the park added to the growing senses of opposition toward the ruling party's authoritarian and repressive policies and finally the protests grew to include millions of people filling the streets in Turkey for almost three months.[20] Almost all the points of a classical morality debate were voiced out by the AKP during this time accusing the Gezi protestors of alcohol consumption, sex out of wedlock, homosexuality, pursuing Western lifestyles and interests, and violating property. Erdoğan claimed that the Gezi protestors drank beers in mosques when the protestors had found shelter in Dolmabahçe Mosque to escape from heavy pepper gas clouds that the riot police threw at them. The muezzin of the mosque stated that the protestors did not drink alcohol in the mosque that night—and his place of duty was changed after his statement contradicted with Erdoğan's. Throughout the protests, some Gezi protestors used raising a glass of drink while chanting "salute Tayyip" as a form of protest against his prohibitive measures to alcohol.

There are some turning points that contributed to what I call "moral polarization" in the post-Gezi period. One is the 17–25 December corruption scandal of 2013 that revealed AKP government's, Erdoğan's family members and government-sided businessmen's, involvement in bribery, fraud, bid-rigging, money laundering, and gold smuggling cases.[21] The audio recordings of phone calls between these circles were leaked to the public with a series of YouTube videos. The audios demonstrated that millions of dollars were kept in houses (some inside shoeboxes) and the way public money was circulated and used in the service of government's businessmen. Erdoğan, the then prime minister, refused all allegations against himself, announced that the tapes between him and his son where he asked his son to urgently get rid of tens of millions of dollars at home were a montage, and blamed the Gülen movement (the Islamic brotherhood once a close ally of the government) with forming a "parallel state." Thousands of people filled the streets to protest money fraud, demand justice against corruption, and ask Erdoğan and government to resign. Only four ministers who were closely engaged in corruption resigned, but they did not stand trial before the Supreme Council thanks to AKP votes in the parliament. As much as the scale of the scandal and amount of money, it is shocking how the case was handled and covered up. Some months after the scandal, Erdoğan got the 52 percent of the votes in Presidential Elections in August 2014. Yılmaz and Sözer argue that this success owed much to Erdoğan's discourse campaign on national security that brought many people closer to him against a so-called "greater conspiracy."[22] This success is interpreted by the opposition as part of a widespread behavior on the side of the AKP and its followers, which is summarized with the slogan "they steal but they work." Accordingly, many people pursue only their self interest, vote AKP pragmatically, and turn a blind eye on the moral side of the story.

The second turning point is the case of Berkin Elvan. Berkin, a fifteen-year-old boy from working class mostly Alewi-inhabited Okmeydanı district of Istanbul was hit by a police teargas canister during Gezi protests when he left home to buy bread. Gezi protestors followed his condition closely as his case became the symbol of heavy-handed police violence in June 2013. After nine months of coma, he died at the hospital. Based on Erdoğan's celebration of the police forces for their "heroic" actions during Gezi protests and his declaration that it was him "who gave the orders to the police" for the use of tear gas in June 2013, Gülsüm Elvan, Berkin's mother, stated that it was Erdoğan who killed her boy. Thousands of people attended Berkin's funeral and clashes between police and protestors continued during the funeral. Some days after the funeral, during his propaganda speech for March 2014 local elections, Erdoğan accused Berkin of "terror links," claiming that he had steel marbles in his pockets and a slingshot and was in the street with a covered face.[23] He said it was a lie that Berkin was out to buy bread. He made the AKP crowd protest Berkin's mother, who accused him of killing her boy. And finally, he brought forward another case to justify his side. The night of the funeral, the radical leftist group in Okmeydanı (DHKP-C) declared that they burned down the AKP's election bureaus as an act of revenge and entered in an armed conflict with AKP supporters. The twenty-two-year-old Burak Can Karamanoğlu was killed in these clashes. Erdoğan put it in his speech as two stories to be compared: one is innocent the other is terrorist, and thus he separated "our case" and "their case" and declared Karamanoğlu a martyr. Years after Berkin's death, the crime went unpunished and the police officer who shot him is still free.

Another case that divided public opinion and surfaced moral criticisms is the collective sexual abuse case in the Islamic endowment, Ensar Foundation. In March 2016, Serbay Mansuroğlu, a journalist from the oppositional stance BirGün newspaper, reported that forty-five boys in the ages of nine and ten were raped, exposed to violence, and forced to watch sexual content including animal abuse in Ensar foundation's premises in the Anatolian town of Karaman.[24] The news created an outrage in the public and people protested widely for the closure of the foundation. The minister of family affairs then, Sema Ramazanoğlu, announced the case could not be used to close the Ensar Foundation and embraced the foundation as "an organization that serves the government's stated aim of bringing up a pious generation." The bill to further investigate child abuse was rejected with the votes of AKP's parliament members. Later, it was exposed that most government elites, business circles, and other religious foundations were all involved in the foundation as members and contributors and the case could reveal the complex network of money circulation and land allocations between the politicians and religious foundations.[25] The supporters of Ensar, mostly religious conservatives, opened a Twitter thread, "we are all Ensar," and the opposition indeed pointed that it was true that they were all Ensar in protecting abusers. Today, the foundation is responsible for preparing materials for government initiated "values education" courses for the instruction of Islamic ethics.

Here, I have highlighted only these three points as some of the symbolic moments in recent political history where one can observe how morality discourse is instrumentalized in an authoritarian setting. The members of the Islamist ruling political party have sparked heated debates on several occasions by making comments about the "amoral" behavior of women, such as laughing in public, consuming alcohol, or wearing miniskirts. The moral dichotomy continues to be discussed today within the context of differences between secular and Islamic lifestyles. While the ruling party and its supporters hang onto their Islamic piousness in claiming moral superiority, the articles appearing on the side of opposition blame them for bringing the country in the throes of moral crisis.[26] Highly criticized issues include the moral relativism that comes into play in the narratives of AKP and its supporters, fixation on sexual morality and sexual relationships with women's role and family-centered politics being in the forefront, forced imposition of Islamic morality into society for a united front against "internal" and "external" enemies, and defending all immoral practices in the name of a political cause for the "greater ideals" of political Islam.

Allow me to pursue some more threads connecting past and present. Gökalp defended sociological method as a way to bring forward a secular, civic morality and to solve problems that emerged in the course of modernization process. Now, sociology is being used as a tool to reach out society's disadvantaged and vulnerable groups (in hospitals, prisons, and public student dormitories) through a newly established institution of "Islamic spiritual counseling" (*Manevî Rehberlik*).[27] Today, many imams and alumni of theology departments are able to receive a certificate of spiritual counselor after a few weeks of training.[28] The materials of the training are prepared by Ensar Foundation and *Diyanet İşleri*

Başkanlığı. The latter, once formulated by the secular Ottoman intelligentsia to limit and control the role of *ulema* in politics while making the *ulema* useful in serving the masses for religious advice, now became the principal agent of Islamic morality indoctrination in society with a huge budget leaving eight ministries' budgets behind in 2020.[29] The alcohol issue, just like it was in the past, remains within the framework of usual pragmatism—use moralistic discourse and extract more taxes. In the last eighteen years, the tax over Turkish *rakı* has risen to 1800 percent.[30] The taxation over alcohol and tobacco products in 2020 is above 70 percent and the state treasury expects to receive almost 13 billion dollars in a year.[31]

Turkey's moral crisis is discussed extensively on social media as well. The popular entry platform Ekşi Sözlük (Sour Dictionary) has a title of "morality problem's being the biggest problem in Turkey" which includes more than sixty entries. In one of these, the writer wrote, "an artisan for example, if he performs his prayers, follows all Friday prayers, fasts; the religion ends for him there. I mean there is no thing like being a good person, he would overcharge a customer even though he was fasting at the moment or he would disturb a young girl passing in the street with his leering."[32] Now let us think this statement together with the one in Chapter 2, where I quoted Ahmed Besim complaining that people "feel sorrow if they wash their nose with their left hand [by mistake] during ablution but feel nothing when destroying the lives of orphans' or accepting bribes." In order not to go beyond the scope of this book, I shall leave this interesting topic for future work.

Morality keeps playing an important political and social role in today's Turkish society. Consolidation of power through moral superiority discourses continues to add to the country's political polarization. Centuries-old debates on morality and moral crisis are still echoing in popular, intellectual, and political platforms. This book may be a help to understand better one of the most important yet neglected topics in Ottoman-Turkish history and shed light on the reasons of why morality remains a contested space.

Notes

Chapter 1

1. Yalman, *Turkey in the World War* (New Haven: Yale University Press, 1930), 239.
2. See Mustafa Çağrıcı, *Anahatlarıyla İslam Ahlâkı* (Istanbul: Ensar Neşriyat, 2000); Umut Kaya, *Tanzimat'tan Cumhuriyet'e Osmanlı'da Ahlâk Eğitimi* (Istanbul: Değerler Eğitim Merkezi Yayınları, 2013); Hüsameddin Erdem, *Son Devir Osmanlı Düşüncesinde Ahlâk: Tanzimattan Cumhuriyete Kadar* (Istanbul: Dem Yayınları, 2006).
3. "Morality," *Oxford Dictionaries* (Accessed May 12, 2017). https://en.oxforddictionaries.com/definition/morality.
4. "… insanın yaradılışda haiz olduğu veya terbiye ile istihsal ettiği ahvâl-i ruhiye ve kalbiye." Şemseddin Sami, *Kâmûs-i Türkî* (Dersaadet: Ikdam Matbaası, 1886), 82.
5. Rifa'at Ali Abou-El-Haj, *Formation of the Modern State: The Ottoman Empire, Sixteenth to Eighteenth Centuries* (Syracuse: Syracuse University Press, 2005), 23; Abou-El-Haj, "The Ottoman Nasihatname as a Discourse over 'Morality,'" in *Mélanges Professeur Robert Mantran*, ed. Abdeljelil Temimi (Zaghouan: Cermondi, 1988), 18.
6. Ibid., 19–20.
7. Abou-El-Haj, *Formation of the Modern State*, 40–1.
8. Baki Tezcan, "Ethics as a Domain to Discuss the Political: Kınalızâde Ali Efendi's Ahlâk-ı Alâî," in *International Congress on Learning and Education in the Ottoman World: Istanbul, 12–15 April 1999*, ed. Ali Çaksu (Istanbul: IRCICA, 2001), 112–14.
9. Leslie Peirce, *Morality Tales: Law and Gender in the Ottoman Court of Aintab* (Berkeley: University of California Press, 2003), 6. Peirce, however, emphasizes that nonelite members of the community challenged the claim that they were morally weaker than the elites.
10. Donald Quataert, "Clothing Laws, State, and Society in the Ottoman Empire, 1720–1829," *International Journal of Middle East Studies* 29, no. 3 (August 1997): 409.
11. Ibid., 411.
12. Kırlı, "The Struggle over Space, Coffeehouses of Ottoman Istanbul, 1780–1845" (PhD diss., Binghamton University, Binghamton, 2000), 38–49.

13 Alp Eren Topal, "From Decline to Progress: Ottoman Concepts of Reform 1600–1876" (PhD diss. Bilkent University, Ankara, 2017), 88–9.
14 Ibid., 156–7.
15 Ahmet Mithad, *Felâtun Bey Ile Râkım Efendi* (İstanbul: Kırk Anbar Matbaası, 1875). Beside many transliterated versions in Turkish, a translation of the novel also appeared in English; see Ahmet Mithad Efendi, *Felâtun Bey and Râkim Efendi: An Ottoman Novel*, trans. Melih Levi and Monica M. Ringer (Syracuse: Syracuse University Press, 2016).
16 See M. Alper Yalçınkaya, *Learned Patriots: Debating Science, State, and Society in the Nineteenth-Century Ottoman Empire* (Chicago: University of Chicago Press, 2015).
17 Ibid., 54–5.
18 For the history of the penetration of capitalism in the Ottoman Empire, see Şevket Pamuk, *Osmanlı Ekonomisinde Bağımlılık ve Büyüme, 1820–1913* (Istanbul: Türkiye Ekonomi ve Toplumsal Vakfı, 1994); Donald Quataert, *Social Disintegration and Popular Resistance in the Ottoman Empire, 1881–1908: Reactions to European Economic Penetration* (New York: New York University Press, 1983).
19 Müge Özoğlu discusses this anxiety from the masculinity standpoint with reference to the declining power of the Ottoman Empire at the turn of the twentieth century in literary works. See Müge Özoğlu, "Modernity as an Ottoman Fetish: Representations of Ottoman Masculinity in Kesik Bıyık," *Masculinities Journal* 6 (2016): 79–101.
20 See Selçuk Akşin Somel, *The Modernization of Public Education in the Ottoman Empire, 1839–1908: Islamization, Autocracy, and Discipline* (Leiden: Brill, 2001).
21 Ibid., 6.
22 Ibid., 7.
23 Ibid., 62–4. I would like to thank Alp Eren Topal for sharing with me his transliteration of *Ahlâk Risalesi*.
24 Benjamin Fortna, "Islamic Morality in Late Ottoman 'Secular' Schools," *International Journal of Middle East Studies* 32, no. 3 (2000): 375.
25 Ibid., 373.
26 Ibid., 375.
27 Betül Açıkgöz, "*The Epistemological Conflict in the Narratives of Elementary School Textbooks (1908–1924)*" (PhD diss. Boğaziçi University, Istanbul, 2012), 80.
28 Ibid., 81.
29 Some descriptive accounts were published on moral decline, social problems, and prostitution during the First World War and the armistice period, predicating a story of an inevitable social and moral disintegration without questioning the

term "moral decline" itself. For instance, see İlbeyi Özer, "Mütareke ve İşgal Yıllarında Osmanlı Devletinde Görülen Sosyal Çöküntü ve Toplumsal Yaşam," *OTAM* 14 (2003): 247–71; Aydın Yetkin, "II. Meşrutiyet Dönemi'nde Toplumsal Ahlak Bunalımı: Fuhuş Meselesi," *Tarihin Peşinde Uluslararası Tarih ve Sosyal Araştırmalar Dergisi* 6 (2011): 21–54.; Cafer Ulu, "I. Dünya Savaşı ve İşgal Sürecinde İstanbul'da Yaşanan Sosyal ve Ahlaki Çözülme 1914–1922," *İstanbul Üniversitesi Tarih Dergisi* 58 (2013): 87–113.

30 Başak Tuğ, *Politics of Honor in Ottoman Anatolia: Sexual Violence and Socio-Legal Surveillance in the Eighteenth Century* (Leiden: Brill, 2017).

31 Gülhan Balsoy, *The Politics of Reproduction in Ottoman Society, 1838–1900* (London: Pickering & Chatto, 2013). On abortion and gender policies in the nineteenth century, see also Tuba Demirci and Selçuk Akşin Somel, "Women's Bodies, Demography, and Public Health: Abortion Policy and Perspectives in the Ottoman Empire of the Nineteenth Century," *Journal of the History of Sexuality* 17, no. 3 (2008): 377–420.

32 Ibid., 121.

33 See Elizabeth Thompson, *Colonial Citizens Republican Rights, Paternal Privilege, and Gender in French Syria and Lebanon* (New York: Columbia University Press, 2000).

34 Ibid., 19.

35 Zafer Toprak, *Türkiye'de Kadın Özgürlüğü ve Feminizm (1908–1935)* (İstanbul: Tarih Vakfı Yurt Yayınları, 2015), 283.

36 Alan Duben and Cem Behar, *Istanbul Households, Marriage, Family, and Fertility, 1880–1940* (New York: Cambridge University Press, 1991), 199.

37 Toprak, *Türkiye'de Kadın Özgürlüğü ve Feminizm (1908–1935)*, 14–16.

38 Vahdeti, "Buhran-ı Vükelâ," *Volkan*, no. 46, 1908, 203, quoted in Tarık Zafer Tunaya, *İslamcılık Akımı* (İstanbul: İstanbul Bilgi Üniversitesi Yayınları, 2003), 109.

39 Amit Bein, *OttomanUlema, Turkish Republic Agents of Change and Guardians of Tradition* (Stanford: Stanford University Press, 2011), 23–4.

40 Erik Jan Zürcher, *Turkey: A Modern History* (London, New York: I.B. Tauris, 2004), 121–2.

41 Abou-El-Haj, "The Ottoman Nasihatname as a Discourse over 'Morality,'" 25. Zarinebaf explains the notion of justice as follows: "The notion of justice in the Ottoman Empire was based on two traditions. The first was the ancient Near Eastern and Iranian (Sassanid) theory of the Circle of Justice that passed from the Seljuks and the Ilkhanids to the Ottomans and formed the legal philosophy of the imperial law codes issued by Ottoman sultans, most notably Mehmed II (1444–6, 1451–81), Bayezid II (1481–1512), and Süleyman Kanuni (1520–66). The second involved the Islamic ethical principles of morality, equity, and social

justice contained in the Qur'an and the Prophet's sayings and deeds that evolved into the shari'a." Fariba Zarinebaf, *Crime and Punishment in Istanbul: 1700–1800* (Berkeley: University of California Press, 2010), 149.

42   Bein, *Ottoman Ulema, Turkish Republic Agents of Change and Guardians of Tradition*, 97.

43   Ibid., 98.

44   See Mustafa Aksakal, *The Ottoman Road to War in 1914: The Ottoman Empire and the First World War* (Cambridge, NY: Cambridge University Press, 2008).

45   Ibid., 14. I shall highlight the latter for the sake of our topic: wartime constituted a laboratory for reformers advocating social reform as a means to regenerate the Ottoman-Muslim community. They were convinced that national revival would only be possible when its social aspects were taken into consideration.

46   Mehmet Beşikçi, "Domestic Aspects of Ottoman Jihad: The Role of Religious Motifs and Religious Agents in the Mobilization of the Ottoman Army," in *Jihad and Islam in World War I*, ed. Erik Jan Zürcher (Leiden: Leiden University Press, 2016), 95–6.

47   Erik Jan Zürcher, *The Young Turk Legacy and Nation Building, from the Ottoman Empire to Atatürk's Turkey* (London, New York: I.B. Tauris, 2010), 176.

48   See Erik Jan Zürcher, "Between Death and Desertion: The Experience of the Ottoman Soldier in World War I," *Turcica* 28 (1996): 235–8; Mehmet Beşikçi, *The Ottoman Mobilization of Manpower in the First World War: Between Voluntarism and Resistance* (Leiden: Brill, 2012).

49   Zürcher, *Turkey*, 120–1.

50   Yiğit Akın, *When the War Came Home: The Ottoman's Great War and the Devastation of an Empire* (Stanford: Stanford University Press, 2018), 5.

51   On the confiscation of Armenian properties, see Uğur Ümit Üngör and Mehmet Polatel, *Confiscation and Destruction: The Young Turk Seizure of Armenian Property* (London, New York: Continuum, 2011); Taner Akçam and Ümit Kurt, *The Spirit of the Laws: The Plunder of Wealth in the Armenian Genocide*, trans. Aram Arkun (New York, Oxford: Berghahn, 2015). Abandoned properties were utilized for many purposes, such as strengthening the Muslim bourgeoisie, providing the needs of the military and state institutions, and for the settlement of the immigrants and refugees, see especially chapters 5 and 6 in Oya Gözel Durmaz, *A City Transformed: Great War, Deportation and Socio-Economic Change in Kayseri (1915–1920)* (Istanbul: Libra Kitap, 2018).

52   Uğur Ümit Üngör, "Orphans, Converts, and Prostitutes: Social Consequences of War and Persecution in the Ottoman Empire, 1914–1923," *War in History* 19, no. 2 (2012): 187.

53   Matthias Bjornlund, "'A Fate Worse than Dying': Sexual Violence during the Armenian Genocide," in *Brutality and Desire: War and Sexuality in Europe's Twentieth Century*, ed. Dagmar Herzog (London, New York: Palgrave Macmillan, 2009).

54 For more information on resettlements during this period, see Fuat Dündar, *Modern Türkiye'nin Şifresi: İttihat ve Terakki'nin Etnisite Mühendisliği (1913–1918)* (Istanbul: İletişim, 2008).
55 See M. Talha Çiçek, *War and State Formation in Syria: Cemal Pasha's Governorate during World War I, 1914–17* (New York: Routledge, 2014).
56 Wartime famine carved out a space for local, national, and international actors to reshape the wartime and postwar political landscape through relief and charity; see Melanie S. Tanielian, *The Charity of War, Famine, Humanitarian Aid, and World War I in the Middle East* (Stanford: Stanford University Press, 2018). On postwar relief as a political contest in Anatolia, see Chris Graten, "The Sick Mandate of Europe: Local and Global Humanitarianism in French Cilicia, 1918–1922," *Journal of the Ottoman and Turkish Studies Association* 3, no. 1 (2016): 165–90.
57 See Toprak, *Ittihad Terakki ve Cihan Harbi* (Istanbul: Homer Kitabevi, 2003).
58 Beşikçi, *The Ottoman Mobilization of Manpower in the First World War*, 7.
59 Ibid.
60 Yiğit Akın, "War, Women, and the State: The Politics of Sacrifice in the Ottoman Empire during the First World War," *Journal of Women's History* 26, no. 3 (2014): 12–35.
61 Ibid., 26.
62 For a detailed analysis of the occupation of Istanbul, see Nur Bilge Criss, *Istanbul under Allied Occupation, 1918–1923* (Leiden: Brill, 1999). On the "nightlife boom" in Istanbul under occupation and its perception by the locals and occupiers, see Daniel MacArthur-Seal, "Intoxication and Imperialism, Nightlife in Occupied Istanbul, 1918–23," *Comparative Studies of South Asia, Africa and the Middle East* 37, no. 2 (2017), 299–313.
63 K. W. Swart, *The Sense of Decadence in Nineteenth-Century France* (The Hague: Springer Science Business Media, 1964), 5.
64 Ibid., 6.
65 Ibid., 3. Edward Gibbon's account of the Roman Empire has been enormously influential for this line of thought. See Gibbon, *The Decline and Fall of the Roman Empire* (London: David Campbell, 1993).
66 Swart, *The Sense of Decadence in Nineteenth-Century France*, 11.
67 Ibid., 18.
68 Ibid., 61.
69 Daniel Pick, *Faces of Degeneration: A European Disorder, c.1848–c.1918. Ideas in Context* (Cambridge: Cambridge University Press, 1989), 2.
70 On the relationship between the social sciences and Darwinism, see M. Asım Karaömerlioğlu, "Darwin ve Sosyal Bilimler," *Birikim,* 251 (March 2010), 111–22.
71 Pick, *Faces of Degeneration*, 20.
72 Ibid., 21.

73 Ibid., 11.
74 Swart, *The Sense of Decadence in Nineteenth-Century France*, x.
75 Robert A. Nye, *Crime, Madness and Politics in Modern France: The Medical Concept of National Decline* (Princeton: Princeton University Press, 2014), 68.
76 Swart, *The Sense of Decadence in Nineteenth-Century France*, 69.
77 Edward Royce, *Classical Social Theory and Modern Society, Marx, Durkheim, Weber* (Lanham: Rowman & Littlefield Publishers, 2015), 55–6.
78 Ibid., 56.
79 Ibid., 65.
80 On the emphasis of science in the Young Turk movement, see Şükrü Hanioğlu, *Preparation for a Revolution, The Young Turks, 1902–1908* (Oxford, New York: Oxford University Press, 2001), 289–311. For the place of sociology in shaping the worldviews of prominent Young Turks and the CUP, see Zafer Toprak, "Osmanlı'da Toplumbilimin Doğuşu," in *Modern Türkiye'de Siyasi Düşünce: Cumhuriyet'e Devreden Düşünce Mirası, Tanzimat ve Meşrutiyet'in Birikimi*, ed. Mehmet Ö Alkan et al. (Istanbul: İletişim Yayınları, 2001), 310–27. For Darwinism and Ottoman intellectuals, see Doğan, *Osmanlı Aydınları ve Sosyal Darwinizm* (Istanbul: Bilgi Üniversitesi Yayınları, 2006). The idea of evolution remained as an important aspect of Turkish nationalism in the Early Republican period; see Asım Karaömerlioğlu and Murat Yolun, "Turkish Nationalism and the Evolutionary Idea (1923–1938)," *Nations and Nationalism* (2020): 1–16.
81 Swart, *The Sense of Decadence in Nineteenth-Century France*, 195–6.
82 Ibid., 198.
83 On eugenics in the early Republican context, see Zafer Toprak, *Darwin'den Dersim'e Cumhuriyet ve Antropoloji* (Istanbul: Doğan Kitap, 2012); Ayça Alemdaroğlu, "Politics of the Body and Eugenic Discourse in Early Republican Turkey," *Body and Society* 11, no. 3 (2005): 61–76; Efe Atabay, "Eugenics, Modernity and the Rationalization of Morality in Early Republican Turkey" (M.A. Thesis, McGill University, 2009); Karaömerlioğlu and Yolun, "Turkish Nationalism," 6–7.
84 See Yücel Yanıkdağ, *Healing the Nation: Prisoners of War, Medicine and Nationalism in Turkey, 1914–1939* (Edinburgh: Edinburgh University Press, 2014).
85 Mark Mazower, *Dark Continent: Europe's Twentieth Century* (London: Penguin Press, 1998), 80.
86 Matthew James Connelly, *Fatal Misconception: The Struggle to Control World Population* (Cambridge: Massachusetts: Harvard University Press, 2008), 46.
87 Adrian Gregory, "Lost Generations: The Impact of Military Casualties on Paris, London, and Berlin," in *Capital Cities at War: Paris, London, Berlin, 1914–1919*, ed. J. M. Winter and Jean-Louis Robert (Cambridge, NY: Cambridge University Press, 1999), 57.

88 Jay M. Winter and Jean-Louis Robert, "Conclusions: Towards a Social History of Capital Cities at War," in *Capital Cities at War: Paris, London, Berlin, 1914–1919*, ed. J. M. Winter and Jean-Louis Robert (Cambridge, NY: Cambridge University Press, 1999).
89 Mazower, *Dark Continent*, 80.
90 Ibid. Maksudyan underlines a different approach to childhood in the years of war, a period told by children of the time as "the end of childhood." In her study on the war experiences of Ottoman children and youth, she discusses how children acquired a new agency during the war. Due to the multiethnic and multireligious composition of the empire, children represented different meanings on Ottoman home front as targets and also agents of nationalist policies, Nazan Maksudyan, *Ottoman Children and Youth During World War I* (New York: Syracuse University Press, 2019).
91 Connelly, *Fatal Misconception*, 47.
92 Pick, *Faces of Degeneration*, 17.
93 Mazower, *Dark Continent*, 82.
94 As discussed by Zürcher, labeling the late Ottoman intelligentsia into three groups "Islamists," "Turkists," or "Westernists" does not reflect the complexity of the Ottoman political spectrum, and such labels do not explain the CUP policies and the inconsistencies within those policies. See the chapter titled "Young Turks, Ottoman Muslims and Turkish Nationalists," in Zürcher, *The Young Turk Legacy and Nation Building*, 213–35.

Chapter 2

1 Throughout this chapter I use the original title of these journals instead of their English translation. I should also note that most authors used a surname that they had chosen even earlier than the Surname Law of 1934. For instance, Ziya Gökalp signed his articles as "Ziya Gök Alp" even in his Yeni Mecmua times (or sometimes only with the name Mehmed Ziya); Ahmed Besim also signed his articles sometimes with the name or sometimes only as "Besim Atalay." Another author, Ahmed Naim, used his family name in the beginning of his name as "Babanzade Ahmed Naim." My use of surnames while referring to these authors should not be considered anachronistic.
2 Masami Arai, *Turkish Nationalism in the Young Turk Era* (Leiden: Brill, 1992), 83. Arai translated the catchphrase of the journal as "life with religion, religion with life," but given that the journal sought to establish a new life in which religious order fit into contemporary society, a more accurate translation that I propose is "a religious life, a lively religion."

3   Tunaya, *İslamcılık Akımı*, 110.
4   Arai, *Turkish Nationalism in the Young Turk Era*, 86.
5   Ibid., 88–90.
6   Some of these articles were transcribed in İsmail Kara, ed., *Türkiye'de İslâmcılık Düşüncesi: Metinler/Kişiler* (İstanbul: Kitabevi, 1997).
7   Ruhi Güler, "İslam Mecmuası (1914–1918) ve İçeriği" M.A. Thesis (İstanbul Üniversitesi, Istanbul, 1995), 14.
8   For a detailed assessment of these discussions, see Mustafa Bakırcı, "II. Meşrutiyet Dönemi Din Sosyolojisinin Önemli Bir Kaynağı: İslam Mecmuası (1914–1918)," Selçuk Üniversitesi İlahiyat Fakültesi Dergisi, 17 (2004): 177–210.
9   See Arai's table of "Classification of Articles in the İslam Mecmuası" in Arai, *Turkish Nationalism in the Young Turk Era*, 87.
10 He signed his articles with his titles School Director from Konya, Maraş, and the İçel Teacher Training Schools (*Dar'ül-muallim*s) respectively. Atalay had acquired eleven years of madrasa education before enrolling in a secular school. After the First World War, as the director of culture (*Hars Müdürü*) he conducted studies on the Turkish language and brought together a book on "pure" Turkish in 1920. Later, Atalay promoted the simplification of the Turkish language as a member of the Turkish Linguistic Society during the 1930s. His translation of the Quran into Turkish in 1941 received the appreciation of İsmet İnönü, then president of the Republic of Turkey. Besim Atalay is known for his studies on language rather than his early career as a writer in late Ottoman journals. Neither a monograph nor a study evaluating his early articles has been published. Even so, discussions on jurisprudence and polygyny overshadowed other articles in İslam Mecmuası, including Atalay's works. It is also interesting to note that Sebilürreşad's writers never addressed Besim Atalay's articles on morality; they considered Ziya Gökalp and Mansurizade Said to be their addressees. The only biographic information on Besim Atalay I can find is a monograph focusing on his studies on language. See Sevgi Özel, *Besim Atalay* (Ankara: Türk Dil Kurumu Yayınları, 1983).
11 A prominent work in English on Ziya Gökalp's thinking is Uriel Heyd, *Foundations of Turkish Nationalism: The Life and Teachings of Ziya Gökalp* (London: Luzac, 1950). Berkes' works deal with Gökalp and secular thought of the time in general, Niyazi Berkes, *The Development of Secularism in Turkey* (Montreal: McGill University Press, 1964); Niyazi Berkes, *Turkish Nationalism and Western Civilization: Selected Essays of Ziya Gökalp* (London: Allen and Unwin, 1959). A recent study assessed Gökalp's views on reform in Islam: Charles Kurzman, ed., *Modernist Islam, 1840–1940: A Sourcebook* (Oxford, New York: Oxford University Press, 2002).
12 Parla also discusses some problematic points of Uriel Heyd's work. For example, Parla criticizes Heyd's interpretation of Gökalp's solidarism and corporatism as a rejection of Western values since this approach of Heyd's equates Western

civilization only with liberalism; see Taha Parla, *The Social and Political Thought of Ziya Gökalp, 1876–1924* (Leiden: Brill, 1985), 66–7. On another note, a far-right nationalist publishing house published simplified version of a compilation of his articles on morality; however, many misinterpretations are evident in this version. Yet, this shows a recent popular interest in Gökalp's views on morality; see Oğuzhan Cengiz and Mehmet Celal Atgın, *Türk Ahlâkı* (Istanbul: Bilge Oğuz, 2013).

13   Kâzım Nami Duru, *Arnavutluk ve Makedonya Hatıralarım* (Istanbul: Sucuoğlu Matbaası, 1959); Kâzım Nami Duru, *Cumhuriyet Devri Hatıralarım* (Istanbul: Sucuoğlu Matbaası, 1958); Kâzım Nami Duru, *"İttihat ve Terakki" Hatıralarım* (Istanbul: Sucuoğlu Matbaası, 1957). He also wrote a monograph on Gökalp: Kâzım Nami Duru, *Ziya Gökalp* (Istanbul: Milli Eğitim, 1949).

14   Kâzım Nami Duru, *Mekteblerde Ahlakı Nasıl Telkin Etmeli?* (Istanbul: Kanaat Matbaası, 1925).

15   The criticism of Tanzimat in both views does not go beyond a cultural criticism that emphasizes a need for authenticity and local values. This is in line with Yalçınkaya's reading of the 1860s Young Ottomans' criticism of the Tanzimat elites with references to Islam and tradition, a discourse that was utilized by the former to challenge high-ranking bureaucracy and its monopoly of power. See, Yalçınkaya, *Learned Patriots*.

16   Ahmet Besim, "Ahlâk: Ahlâk ve Din," *İslam Mecmuası*, no. 10 (1914): 27.

17   Ibid. The works he referred to as "archaic" were the classics on morality in the Muslim and the Ottoman literary world, such as Kınalızâde Ali Efendi's *Ahlâk-ı Alâî* or Nasirüddin Tûsî's *Ahlâk-ı Nâsirî*.

18   Ibid.

19   Ibid. He claims this is the reason for the emergence of different schools in Islam.

20   Ahmed Besim, "Din ve Ahlâk: Mânâ-yı Ahlâk," *İslam Mecmuası*, no. 51 (1917): 16.

21   Ahmed Besim, "Ahlâk ve Din 2," *İslam Mecmuası*, no. 13 (1915): 7.

22   Ibid., 8.

23   Ahmed Besim, "Ahlâk: Din ve Ahlâk 3," *İslam Mecmuası*, no. 15 (1915): 11.

24   Ahmed Besim, "Ahlâk: Ahlâk ve Din," *İslam Mecmuası*, no.10 (1914): 27.

25   Ahmed Besim, "Ahlâk: Din ve Ahlâk, Nazar-ı İslam'da Ahlâk," *İslam Mecmuası*, no. 29 (1915): 7.

26   For instance, he quoted the hadith "*Ne kadar namaz kılan kimseler vardır ki kazançları ancak yorgunluktur,*" which translates as "There are so many of those praying who gain nothing but tiredness." Ahmed Besim, "Din ve Ahlâk, 9: İbadat-ı İslamiyye ve Ahlâk," *İslam Mecmuası*, no. 33 (1915): 14.

27   Ahmed Besim, "Ahlâk: Din ve Ahlâk, Nazar-ı İslam'da Ahlâk," 7.

28   Ahmed Besim, "Ahlâk, Din ve Ahlâk: İbadat-ı İslamiye ve Ahlâk," *İslam Mecmuası*, no. 33 (1915): 14.

29 Ahmed Besim, "Ahlâk ve Din 2," 9–10.
30 Ibid., 10.
31 Ibid., 9.
32 Ibid. He was probably referring to Lucius Quinctius Cincinnatus, the Roman dictator who voluntarily returned to farming after his service.
33 Ibid.
34 Ahmed Besim, "Din ve Ahlâk 11: İbadat-ı İslamiye ve Ahlâk, Oruç, Hac ve Zekat," *İslam Mecmuası*, no. 40 (1915): 8.
35 Muallim Vahyi, "Ahlâk: Müslüman," *İslam Mecmuası*, no. 1 (1914): 20.
36 Ibid., 22.
37 Ibid.
38 Ibid.
39 Ahmed Besim, "Nazar-ı İslam'da Ahlâk 4," *İslam Mecmuası*, no. 20 (1915): 14.
40 Ahmed Besim, "Ahlâk: Din ve Ahlâk 3," 11.
41 Ahmed Besim, "Ahlâk: Din ve Ahlâk 4, Hakikat-i Ahlâk," *İslam Mecmuası*, no. 22 (1915): 11.
42 Ahmed Besim, "Din ve Ahlâk 6," *İslam Mecmuası*, no. 25 (1915): 14.
43 Ibid.
44 Besim Atalay, "Ahlâk Değişir mi?" *İslam Mecmuası*, no. 52 (1916): 10–14.
45 Ibid., 10.
46 Ahmet Besim, "Ahlâk: Din ve Ahlâk 4 Hakikat-i Ahlâk," 12.
47 Ibid., 9.
48 Ziya Gökalp, "İslam Terbiyesi: İslam Terbiyesinin Mahiyeti," *İslam Mecmuası*, no. 1 (1914): 14–17.
49 Ibid.
50 Kazım Nami, "İslam Terbiyesi: Dinî Terbiye," *İslam Mecmuası*, no. 1 (1914): 17.
51 Ibid.
52 Halim Sabit, "Dini Terbiye Heyeti," *İslam Mecmuası*, no. 29 (June 10, 1915): 3–5; "Velayet-i Diniyye: Meşihat-i İslamiyye Teşkilatı," *İslam Mecmuası*, no. 30 (June 24, 1915): 5–8.
53 Halim Sabit, "Velayet-i Diniyye: Meşihat-i İslamiyye Teşkilatı," 5–8.
54 Ibid.
55 Ibid., 8.
56 Halim Sabit, "Dini Terbiye Heyeti," 5.
57 Ibid.
58 On Gökalp's views on Diyanet, see Seyfettin Erşahin, "The Ottoman Foundation of the Turkish Republic's Diyanet: Ziya Gokalp's Diyanet Ishları Nazâratı," *The Muslim World* 98, no. 2–3 (2008): 182–98.
59 Parla, *The Social and Political Thought of Ziya Gökalp*, 40–1.
60 On Sırat-ı Müstakim and Sebilürreşad, see Esther Debus, *Sebilürreşâd: Kemalizm Öncesi ve Sonrası Dönemdeki İslamcı Muhalefete dair Karşılaştırmalı bir Araştırma*,

trans. Atilla Dirim (İstanbul: Libra Yayınevi, 2012); S. Akşin Somel, "Sırat-ı Müstakim: Islamic Modernist Thought in the Ottoman Empire (1908–1912)" (M.A. Thesis, Boğaziçi University, 1987); Tunaya, *İslamcılık Akımı*; Zafer Toprak, "Türkiye'de Fikir Dergiciliğinin Yüz Yılı," in *Türkiye'de Dergiler Ansiklopediler (1849–1984)* (İstanbul: Gelişim Yayınları, 1984), 13–54; Ayşe Polat, "Sırat-ı Müstakim ve Okuyucu Mektupları: Sorulan, Tartışılan, İnşa Edilen İslam," in *İslam'ı Uyandırmak: Meşrutiyetten Cumhuriyet'e İslamcı Düşünce ve Dergiler*, ed. Lütfi Sunar (Istanbul: İlem, 2018), 393–419.

61 Somel, "Sırat-ı Müstakim," 4–5. With respect to the difference between *İslam Mecmuası* and *Sebilürreşad* and their support for the ruling party, it is worth noting that the CUP was not a monolithic party. Within its body many different views were coalesced under a single name. On the other hand, the *Sebilürreşad* writers criticized the nationalists because nationalists were benefiting from modernist interpretations of Islam such as those of Afgani or Abduh to strengthen their own view. See Debus, *Sebilürreşâd*, 51.

62 Somel, "Sırat-ı Müstakim," 5–6.

63 The journal had stopped publication during the war between October 26, 1916, and July 4, 1918. The paper shortages of wartime as well as the censorship of CUP were the reasons of this break. Censorship was lifted from summer 1918 until February 1919.

64 Ahmet Şeyhun, *Islamist Thinkers in the Late Ottoman Empire and Early Turkish Republic* (Leiden: Brill, 2014), 19–20.

65 Ibid., 59.

66 Ahmet Naim, *İslâmda Dava-yı Kavmiyet* (Istanbul: Sebilürreşad Kütüphanesi Neşriyatı, r., 1332).

67 Şeyhun, *Islamist Thinkers in the Late Ottoman Empire and Early Turkish Republic*, 147–52.

68 See, Kara, *Türkiye'de İslamcılık Düşüncesi*, 271–3.

69 Akseki, *Ahlâk İlmi ve İslâm Ahlâkı*, ed. Ali Arslan Aydın (Ankara: Nur Yayınları, 1979); Akseki, *İslâm Dini, İtikat, İbâdet ve Ahlâk* (Ankara: Diyanet İşleri Reisliği Yayınları, 1958).

70 Ahmed Hamdi Aksekili, "Ahlâkiyyat Serisi Mukaddimesi," *Sebilürreşad*, no: 450 (December 4, 1919): 92.

71 These passages were taken from Said Halim Pasha's *Islamization* in manuscript form which were provided to Ahmet Şeyhun by the author's family. Şeyhun, *Islamist Thinkers in the Late Ottoman Empire and Early Turkish Republic*, 104.

72 Ibid., 32–3.

73 Muhammed Ferid Vecdi, "Felsefe: Maddiyun Meslek Felsefesinin Edyana Hücumu," trans. Mehmed Akif, *Sebilürreşad*, no. 298 (June 1914): 209–11; Muhammed Ferid Vecdi, "Felsefe: Felsefe-yi Maddiyun ile Felsefe-yi Ruhiyyunun Çarpışması," trans. Ahmed Hamdi, *Sebilürreşad*, no. 300 (June 1914): 250–2.

74 *Sebilürreşad* published several editorials criticizing the Bolsheviks. For instance, "Bolşevik Fikirleri: Erkân-ı Diniyyeye Karşı Hakarat ve Tecavüz," *Sebilürreşad*, no. 609 (September 1914): 174. The editors often referred to Bolshevism in their critique of Turkish Republican secularism. "Bolşevik Düsturları: Mekteplerde Laik Terbiyeden Maksat Ne İmiş?" *Sebilürreşad*, no. 612 (October 1924): 214–17.

75 İsmail Hakkı Milaslı, "Geri Kalmamızın Sebebi Dinimiz midir? Usülsüzlüğümüz müdür? Daha başka bir şey midir?" *Sebilürreşad*, no. 429–430 (July 1919): 106–7.

76 Ibid.

77 Although it is beyond the scope of this study, the reason why the *Sebilürreşad*'s editors set aside many pages in the journal for quoting another source deserves attention. It might be partly due to the theological background of the writers and their aim to develop certain ideas in defense of religion rather than to comment on recent political developments.

78 "Matbuat: Ahlâk-ı Umumiyenin Islahı Lüzumu ve Hükümetin Vazifesi," *Sebilürreşad*, no. 364 (August 1918): 265–6.

79 Ibid.

80 Ibid.

81 Ibid.

82 Ibid., 266.

83 Sebilürreşad, "Matbuat: Ahlâk Telakkisi," *Sebilürreşad*, no. 626 (December 1919): 232.

84 Ibid., 231.

85 Ibid., 232.

86 Ibid.

87 Ibid.

88 Ibid.

89 Ahmed Cevdet, "Şark ve Garb," Sebilürreşad, no. 452 (December 1919): 118–19.

90 Ibid.

91 Ibid.

92 Ibid.

93 "Decadent Turkey," *Times*, September 11, 1919, 9. I am thankful to Seçil Yılmaz, who shared an electronic copy of this article with me.

94 Seçil Yılmaz, "Love in the Time of Syphilis: Medicine and Sex in the Ottoman Empire, 1860–1922" (PhD Diss., City University of New York, New York, 2016), 273.

95 "Decadent Turkey," *Times*, 9.

96 "Ahvâl-i Sıhhiye Hakkında," *Sebilürreşad*, no: 429–430 (July 1919): 106–7.

97 This debate started with a dispute over the number of venereal disease cases indicated by Abdullah Cevdet. The Ottoman Physicians Society (*Cemiyet-i Ettiba-yi Osmaniye*) claimed that these numbers were exaggerated and incorrect, Yılmaz, "Love in the Time of Syphilis: Medicine and Sex in the Ottoman Empire, 1860–1922," 274–6.

98 "Matbuat: Ahlâk Meselesi," 17.
99 Ibid.
100 M. Şükrü Hanioğlu, "Dar'ül-Hikmeti'l İslamiye," *Encyclopaedia of Islam*, 3, 2016 (Accessed January 6, 2016). http://referenceworks.brillonline.com/entries/encyclopaedia-of-islam-3/*-COM_27738.
101 Ibid. Notably, Mehmet Akif was the chief scribe in this office.
102 "Twenty-six religious scholars served on the board between 1918 and 1922. The board members convened 171 times to discuss 273 different matters." Ibid.
103 Sebilürreşad, "Türk Ocağındaki Münasebetsizlikler Hakkında," no. 452 (December 1919): 119.
104 Ibid.
105 Sebilürreşad, "Konya'da Münteşir Türk Sözü'nün Adâb ve Ahlâka Mugâyir Neşriyatı ve Ahlâka Mugâyir Neşriyat," *Sebilürreşad*, no. 364 (August 1918): 265–6.
106 Ibid.
107 Ibid. "Âlem-i İslam'ın Hastalıkları ve Çareleri."
108 "Memleket Ne Hâlde, Matbuat Ne İle Meşgul," *Sebilürreşad*, no. 372 (October 1918): 149–50.
109 Ibid.
110 Ibid., 149.
111 Ibid., 150.
112 Ibid.
113 Ibid.
114 Ibid. "Mini mini iskarpinler/Ne sevimli güvercinler/Parkelenmiş sokaklarda/Mini mini ayaklarda/Ne gecelerin sesi gelir/Vurunca da neşelidir."
115 See Erol Köroğlu's work on the national literature movement and its development during the war, Erol Köroğlu, *Ottoman Propaganda and Turkish Identity: Literature in Turkey during World War I* (New York: Palgrave Macmillan, 2007). It is possible that *Sebilürreşad*'s editors used this opportunity to criticize nationalist attempts to create a Turkish literary genre and used morality arguments for this purpose.
116 Sebilürreşad, "İslam'ın Mukaddesâtı Aleyhinde Neşriyat," *Sebilürreşad*, no. 298 (July 1914): 227–8.
117 Ahmed Hamdi Akseki, "Tesettür ve Kadın Hakları Konusunda Bilinmesi Elzem Hakikatler," quoted in Kara, *Türkiye'de İslâmcılık Düşüncesi*, 283.
118 Sebilürreşad, "Memleketimizde Ahlâk Meselesi," *Sebilürreşad*, no. 387 (January 1919): 404–6.
119 Ibid.
120 Ibid.
121 Ibid.
122 Ibid.

123 An outer garment that covers the entire body of women. For details, see Reşat Ekrem Koçu, *Türk Giyim, Kuşam ve Süsleme Sözlüğü* (Ankara: Sümerbank Yayınları, 1969), 65–8.
124 Ibid.
125 Ibid.
126 Ibid.
127 Ibid.
128 Ibid.
129 Ibid.
130 Quoted in Şeyhun, *Islamist Thinkers in the Late Ottoman Empire and Early Turkish Republic*, 46–7.
131 Sebilürreşad, "Memleketimizde Ahlâk Meselesi," 404–6.
132 Sebilürreşad, "Kadınların Vaziyeti ve Vezaifleri," *Sebilürreşad*, no. 429–430 (July 1919): 105.
133 Sebilürreşad, "Kadınlarımız Hakkında," *Sebilürreşad*, no. 444 (October 1919): 19.
134 Ibid.
135 Ibid.
136 Ibid.
137 Yahya Kemal, *Siyasi ve Edebi Portreler*, 17–18, quoted in Yamaç, "Basın Tarihinde Yeni Mecmua Muhteva Analizi ve Dizini," x. For the publication history of *Yeni Mecmua*, also see Köroğlu, *Ottoman Propaganda and Turkish Identity*, 93–4.
138 Ibid., 90.
139 Ibid., 100–15.
140 Gökalp, *Türkleşmek, İslamlaşmak, Muasırlaşmak* (Dersaadet: Evkaf-ı İslamiye Matbaası, 1918). In English, see Robert Devereaux, *The Principles of Turkism* (Leiden: E.J. Brill, 1968).
141 "Yeni Hayat" was also the name of Gökalp's book of poetry published by *Yeni Mecmua* in 1918, which reflected his project of national life. Köroğlu, *Ottoman Propaganda and Turkish Identity*, 128.
142 Necmettin Sadak is mostly known with his service as the minister of foreign affairs between 1947 and 1950. In the late Ottoman era, he was one of few graduates in sociology and taught sociology with Gökalp at *Darülfünun* (today Istanbul University). Sadak was a journalist, as well; he founded *Akşam* newspaper in 1918. For more information, see Ali Birinci, "Necmettin Sadık Sadak (1890–1953)," in *Türkiye'de Sosyoloji (İsimler, Eserler)*, ed. M. Çağatay Özdemir, Vol. 1 (Ankara: Phoenix, 2008), 493.
143 Phyllis Stock-Morton, *Moral Education for a Secular Society: The Development of Morale Laïque in Nineteenth Century France* (New York: State University of New York Press, 1988), 125–39.
144 Zürcher, *Turkey*, 131.
145 Parla, *The Social and Political Thought of Ziya Gökalp*, 60.

146 Many studies on the impact of Durkheim on Ottoman-Turkish intellectuals have been published. For more information, see Zafer Toprak, *Türkiye'de Popülizm: 1908–1923* (İstanbul: Doğan Kitap, 2013); Zafer Toprak, "Türkiye'de Durkheim Sosyolojisinin Doğuşu," *Toplumsal Tarih* 238 (October 2013): 22–32; Taha Parla, *The Social and Political Thought of Ziya Gökalp: 1876–1924*.

147 Zafer Toprak discusses this in the context of "social revolution" in Gökalp's thought. Social revolution was the second step in the advancement of reform in Ottoman society following the political revolution of 1908. Zafer Toprak, "Osmanlı'da Toplumbilimin Doğuşu," in *Modern Türkiye'de Siyasi Düşünce: Cumhuriyet'e Devreden Düşünce Mirası, Tanzimat ve Meşrutiyet'in Birikimi*, ed. Mehmet Ö Alkan et al. (Istanbul: İletişim Yayınları, 2001), 310–27.

148 See, Anton A. Wesselingh, "Emile Durkheim, Citizenship and Modern Education," in *Durkheim and Modern Education*, ed. Geoffrey Walford and W. S. F. Pickering (London: Routledge, 1998), 33–46; W. Halls, "The Cultural and Educational Influence of Durkheim, 1900–1945," *Durkheimian Studies* 2 (1996): 122.

149 Stock-Morton, *Moral Education for a Secular Society*, 128.

150 Ibid., 5.

151 Ibid., 26.

152 Ibid., 134–5.

153 Edward Royce, *Classical Social Theory and Modern Society*, 57–8.

154 Stock-Morton, *Moral Education for a Secular Society*, 127.

155 Ibid., 129.

156 Ziya Gökalp, "Ahlâk Buhranı," *Yeni Mecmua*, no. 7 (August 23, 1917): 122.

157 Ibid.

158 Ibid.

159 Ibid.

160 Ibid.

161 İsmail Hakkı, "Ahlâk Mücahedeleri," *Yeni Mecmua*, no. 62 (September 26, 1918): 187–8.

162 Ziya Gökalp, "İctimaiyyat: Şahsî Ahlâk," *Yeni Mecmua*, no. 8 (August 30, 1917): 141.

163 Ibid.

164 Ziya Gökalp, "İctimâiyyat: Cinsî Ahlâk," *Yeni Mecmua*, no. 9 (September 6, 1914): 168.

165 Ibid.

166 Ziya Gökalp, "Aile Ahlakı: Şövalye Aşkı ve Feminizm," *Yeni Mecmua*, no. 19 (November 15, 1917): 364.

167 Ahmed Mithad, "Mesleki Zümreler ve Ahlaki Hayat," *Yeni Mecmua*, no. 65 (November 12, 1918): 258–9.

168 Ziya Gökalp, "İctimaiyyat: Cinsi Ahlâk," no: 9.

169 Necmettin Sadak, "Umûmî Ahlâk, Meslekî Ahlâk," *Yeni Mecmua*, no. 25 (December 27, 1917): 496.

170 Ziya Gökalp, "Ahlâk Buhranı," 122.
171 Refik Halid "Harb Zengini," *Yeni Mecmua*, no. 42 (May 2, 1918): 301.
172 Ibid.
173 For example, see Ahmed Mithad, "Mesleki Zümreler ve Ahlakî Hayat," 258–9; Necmettin Sadak, "Umumi Ahlâk, Mesleki Ahlâk," 496; Tekin Alp, "Tesanüdcülük: Harp Zenginleri Meselesi," *Yeni Mecmua*, no. 42 (May 2, 1918): 313.
174 Necmettin Sadak, ibid.
175 Ibid.
176 Ibid.
177 Nazan Maksudyan, *Orphans and Destitute Children in the Late Ottoman Empire* (Syracuse: Syracuse University Press, 2014), 9.
178 Ibid.
179 See Füsun Üstel, *Makbul Vatandaşın Peşinde: II. Meşrutiyet'ten Bugüne Vatandaşlık Eğitimi* (Istanbul: İletişim, 2009).
180 Niyazi Berkes, *The Development of Secularism in Turkey*, 412.
181 Sadak, "Terbiye Meselesi: Genç Kızlarımızın Terbiyesi," *Yeni Mecmua*, no. 1 (July 12, 1917): 15–16.
182 Necmettin Sadak, "İspor Tehlikesi," *Yeni Mecmua*, no. 24 (December 20, 1917): 473.
183 Ernest Lewis, "Fikir Hayatı: Milli Terbiyeye Dair," *Yeni Mecmua*, no. 33 (February 21, 1918): 132.
184 Necmettin Sadak, "Vatan Terbiyesi," *Yeni Mecmua*, no. 18 (October 8, 1917): 354.
185 Woman authors of the time also discussed the centrality of this topic in morality debates in their writings. While some of them questioned the unequal moral expectations that were set from men and women, some others stressed the need for social reform that would relax strict moral codes constituting an obstacle in the way of woman's freedom. See my research on women's writings on morality and moral decline which explores how women writers approached woman-related morality discussions and how they pursued the problem of moral decline, Çiğdem Oğuz, "'The Homeland Will Not Be Saved Merely by Chastity': Women's Agency, Nationalism, and Morality in the Late Ottoman Empire," in "Women's Agency in the Late Ottoman Empire," special issue of the *Journal of the Ottoman and Turkish Studies Association*, Vol. 6, no. 2 (Fall 2019): 91–111.

Chapter 3

1 Susan Grayzel, *Women and the First World War* (Harlow: Longman, 2002), 62.
2 Angela Woollacott, "'Khaki Fever' and Its Control: Gender, Class, Age and Sexual Morality on the British Homefront in the First World War," *Journal of Contemporary History* 29, no. 2 (1994): 325.

3   Ibid.
4   Ibid., 327–35.
5   Susan Grayzel, "Mothers, Marraines, and Prostitutes, Morale and Morality in First World War France," *The International History Review* 19, no. 1 (1997): 72.
6   Ute Daniel, *The War from within, German Working-Class Women in the First World War* (Oxford, New York: Berg, 1997), 160.
7   Ibid., 166.
8   Ibid.
9   Ibid., 162–3.
10 Early accounts emphasized that working during the war played an "emancipatory" role in women's lives; see Yalman, *Turkey in the World War*, 231–9.
11 Nicole A. N. M. Van Os, "*Feminism, Philanthropy and Patriotism: Female Associational Life in the Ottoman Empire*" (PhD diss., Leiden University, Leiden, 2013), 401–8.
12 Yaprak Zihnioğlu, *Kadınsız İnkılap, Nezihe Muhiddin, Kadınlar Halk Fırkası, Kadın Birliği* (Istanbul: Metis Yayınları, 2003), 42–97; Elizabeth Frierson, "Women in Late Ottoman Intellectual History," in *Late Ottoman Society: The Intellectual Legacy*, ed. Elisabeth Özdalga (London and New York: RoutledgeCurzon, 2005), 135–60.
13 Van Os, *Feminism, Philanthropy and Patriotism*, 285.
14 I. F. W. Beckett, *Home Front, 1914–1918: How Britain Survived the Great War* (Richmond: National Archives, 2006), 98.
15 Laura Lee Downs, *Manufacturing Inequality, Gender Division in the French and British Metalworking Industries, 1914–1939* (Ithaca: Cornell University Press, 1995), 140–1.
16 Deborah Thom, *Nice Girls and Rude Girls, Women Workers in World War I* (London, New York: I.B. Tauris, 2000), 20.
17 Grayzel, *Women and the First World War*, 70–2.
18 Ahmed Rasim, *Eski Fuhuş Hayatı: Fuhş-i Âtik* (Istanbul: Avrupa Yakası Yayınları, 2007) (1st edition 1922), 209–10.
19 Grayzel, *Women and the First World War*, 71.
20 Ibid., 72.
21 Steward Journey, "Prostitution, International Encyclopedia of the First World War (WW1)," in *International Encyclopedia of the First World War*, ed. Oliver Janz et al., 2017 (Accessed April 25, 2017). https://encyclopedia.1914-1918-online.net/article/prostitution.
22 Grayzel, *Women and the First World War*, 67.
23 Meg Albrinck, "Humanitarians and He-Men," in *Picture This: World War I Posters and Visual Culture*, ed. Pearl James (Lincoln, London: University of Nebraska Press, 2009), 317.

24 See Robert L. Nelson, "German Comrades-Slavic Whores: Images in the German Soldier Newspapers of the First World War," in *Home/Front The Military, War, and Gender in the Twentieth-Century Germany*, ed. Karen Hagemann and Stefanie Schüler Springorum (Oxford, NY: Berg, 2002), 67–87.
25 Christian Koller, "Enemy Images: Race and Gender Stereotypes in the Discussion on Colonial Troops. A Franco-German Comparison, 1914–1923," in *Home/Front The Military, War, and Gender in the Twentieth-Century Germany*, ed. Karen Hagemann and Stefanie Schüler Springorum (Oxford, NY: Berg, 2002), 142–3.
26 Jovana Knezevic, "Prostitutes as a Threat to National Honor in Habsburg-Occupied Serbia during the Great War," *Journal of the History of Sexuality* 20, no. 2 (2011): 315.
27 For a detailed assessment of security practices and concepts from the eighteenth to the twentieth centuries in the Ottoman Empire, see the edited work of Lévy, Özbek, and Toumarkine, eds., *Osmanlı'da Asayiş, Suç ve Ceza: 18. - 20. Yüzyıllar* (Istanbul: Tarih Vakfı Yurt Yayınları, 2007).
28 In the earlier periods, prostitutes were consistently banished from one neighborhood to another as a punishment. They were free to live within the same city; see Elyse Semerdjian, *"Off the Straight Path": Illicit Sex, Law and Community in Ottoman Aleppo* (New York: Syracuse University Press, 2008).
29 On the application of martial law in the Balkans, see Barış Zeren, "The Formation of Constitutional Rule: The Politics of Ottomanism between de Jure and de Facto (1908–1913)" (PhD diss. Boğaziçi University, Istanbul, 2017).
30 Osman Köksal, "Osmanlı Devleti'nde Sıkıyönetim ile İlgili Mevzuat Üzerine bir Deneme," *Osmanlı Tarihi Araştırma ve Uygulama Merkezi Dergisi OTAM* 12 (2001): 157.
31 Osman Köksal, "Tarihsel Süreci İçerisinde Bir Özel Yargı Organı Olarak Dîvân-ı Harb-i Örfîler,(1877–1922)" (PhD diss., Ankara Üniversitesi, Ankara, 1996), 16.
32 Ibid.
33 Ibid., 10.
34 Ibid., 36–7.
35 Noemi Lévy-Aksu, "An Ottoman Variation on the State of Siege, The Invention of the idare-i örfiyye during the First Constitutional Period," *New Perspectives on Turkey* 55 (2016): 20.
36 Köksal, "Osmanlı Devleti'nde Sıkıyönetim ile İlgili Mevzuat Üzerine Bir Deneme," 169.
37 "İdare-i Örfiye Kararnamesi," *Düstur*, I, no. 4 (1879): 71–2.
38 Ibid.
39 Stanford J. Shaw, *The Ottoman Empire in World War I* (Ankara: Turkish Historical Society, 2006), 172–3.

40 Köksal, "Tarihsel Süreci İçerisinde Bir Özel Yargı Organı Olarak Divan-ı Harb-i Örfîler (1877–1922)," 21.
41 Shaw, *The Ottoman Empire in World War I*, 172–3.
42 BOA. DH. EUM. ADL. 33/23, 1335 Ş 25.
43 Deniz Dölek Sever, "War and Imperial Capital: Public Order, Crime and Punishment in Istanbul, 1914–1918" (PhD diss., Middle East Technical University, Ankara, 2015), 29.
44 On the history of regulation of prostitution in the Ottoman Empire, see Zafer Toprak, "İstanbul'da Fuhuş ve Salgın Hastalıklar," *Toplumsal Tarih* 7, no. 39 (1987): 159–68; Müge Özbek, "The Regulation of Prostitution in Beyoğlu (1875–1915)," *Middle Eastern Studies* 46, no. 4 (2010): 555–68; Mark D. Wyers, *"Wicked" Istanbul: The Regulation of Prostitution in the Early Turkish Republic* (Istanbul: Libra Yayınevi, 2012). Toprak later published a more detailed version of the aforementioned article in his book; Toprak, *Türkiye'de Kadın Özgürlüğü ve Feminizm (1908–1935)*, 113–53.
45 On the regulation of prostitution during the First World War on the Ottoman homefront, see Çiğdem Oğuz, "Prostitution (Ottoman Empire)," *International Encyclopedia of the First World War*, 2017 (Accessed February 1, 2017). https://encyclopedia.1914-1918-online.net/article/prostitution_ottoman_empire?version=1.0.
46 Ahmed Rasim, *Eski Fuhuş Hayatı*, 209–10.
47 Yalman, *Turkey in the World War*, 244.
48 BOA. DH.HMŞ. 11/27 12 Teşrinisani 1333 (November 12, 1917) "Emrâz-ı Zühreviyenin Men'i Sirayetine Dair Neşr Olunan Nizamnâmeye Mütealik Talimâtnâme." A shortened Turkish translation of the regulation is available in Halim Alyot, *Türkiye'de Zabıta, Tarihî Gelişim ve Bugünkü Durum* (Ankara: Kanaat Basımevi, 1947), 570–86.
49 Wyers, *"Wicked" Istanbul: The Regulation of Prostitution in the Early Turkish Republic*, 67.
50 Toprak, *Türkiye'de Kadın Özgürlüğü ve Feminizm (1908–1935)*, 117.
51 Judith Smart, "Sex, the State and the 'Scarlet Scourge': Gender, Citizenship and Venereal Diseases Regulation in Australia during the Great War," *Women's History Review* 7, no. 1 (March 1, 1998): 25.
52 Toprak, *Türkiye'de Kadın Özgürlüğü ve Feminizm (1908–1935)*, 114–15.
53 Yılmaz, "Love in the Time of Syphilis: Medicine and Sex in the Ottoman Empire, 1860–1922," 280–1.
54 Ibid., 260.
55 Seçil Yılmaz, "Threats to Public Order and Health: Mobile Men as Syphilis Vectors in Late Ottoman Medical Discourse and Practice," *Journal of Middle East Women's Studies* 13, no. 2 (2017): 222–43.

56 *Kadınları Çalıştırma Cemiyeti İslamiyesi Nizamnamesi*. A copy of the regulation can be found in BOA. DH.İ.UM.EK. 37/6 (9).
57 If a potential groom was unable to provide a living for the new family, the organization took on the responsibility of finding him a job. The salaries of women who did not agree to the arranged marriages were decreased by 15 percent and women were fired from the organization if there was any further disagreement. Those who married received a 20 percent increase in their daily wages plus an additional 20 percent increase for every child she bore. In order to match couples, the names and backgrounds of candidates were published in newspapers. Spectacular public weddings were promoted to encourage single people to marry. Yalman, *Turkey in the World War*, 236. See also Toprak, "The Family, Feminism, and the State during the Young Turk Period, 1908–1918," in *Premiere Rencontre Internationale Sur L'Empire Ottoman et La Turquie Moderne*, ed. Edhem Eldem (Istanbul: ISIS, 1991: 441–52); Toprak, *Türkiye'de Kadın Özgürlüğü ve Feminizm (1908-1935)*; Yavuz Selim Karakışla, *Women, War and Work in the Ottoman Empire* (Istanbul: Ottoman Bank Archives and Research Centre, 2005); Tiğinçe Oktar, *Osmanlı Toplumunda Kadının Çalışma Yaşamı, Osmanlı Kadınları Çalıştırma Cemiyet-i İslamiyesi* (Istanbul: Bilim Teknik Yayınevi, 1998).
58 Oktar, *Osmanlı Toplumunda Kadının Çalışma Yaşamı*, 88.
59 Ibid., 80.
60 Elif Mahir Metinsoy, *Ottoman Women during World War I: Everyday Experiences, Politics, and Conflict* (Cambridge: Cambridge University Press), 125–34.
61 In his article published after the earlier version of my study, Stefan Hock argues that the deportation of prostitutes was aimed to "engineer radical changes in the composition of Ottoman society." However, prostitution was not abolished and not all prostitutes were "punished" to this end at the time; prostitution was rather regulated. Those who remained outside the regulation (those without a license), who engaged in trafficking in women, and who procured Muslim women were banished to other parts. Concerning the "ethnic composition" issue, the banishment of sex work agents (especially the owners of the brothels) from Istanbul was not an operation to change "ethnic composition" of the city. Rather than radical changes in terms of social engineering, banishment was an assertion of authority after years of Capitulations' immunity as a demonstration of power. From this point of view, unlike Hock argues, Ottoman experience has a significant difference from that of the empire's European cobelligerents. Stefan Hock, "To Bring about a 'Moral of Renewal': The Deportation of Sex Workers in the Ottoman Empire during the First World War," *Journal of the History of Sexuality*, 28, no. 3 (2019): 457–82.
62 As discussed by Deniz Dölek Sever, during the war, the Ottoman government issued measures to control civilian travel on the home front. Travel permits were reintroduced and new security units were established to control people's

movement. "Undesirables" such as vagabonds, beggars, and idlers—most of which were poor people—were sent away from Istanbul as they were regarded as the "usual suspects." See Dölek Sever, "War and Imperial Capital: Public Order, Crime and Punishment in Istanbul, 1914–1918," 152–206.

63 BOA. DH.ŞFR. 477/72 1331 H 14 (June 27, 1915).
64 DH.EUM.ADL. 21/35 1334 N 08 (July 9, 1916).
65 Ibid.
66 DH. EUM. 6. ŞB. 54/59 1335 C 16 (March 10, 1917).
67 DH.EUM.ADL. 18/8 1334 C 12 (December 26, 1915).
68 DH.EUM.ADL. 33/23 1335 Ş 25 (June 16, 1917).
69 Ibid.
70 Ibid.
71 DH. EUM. 5. Şb. 9/26 1333 Ra 29 (December 21, 1914).
72 Ibid.
73 DH.EUM.SSM 1335 N 25 11/74 (July 15, 1917).
74 DH.EUM.ADL. 28/38 1335 Ra 20 (March 4, 1916).
75 DH.EUM. 3. Şb. 25/53 1336 Ş 09 (May 20, 1918).
76 DH. EUM. 6. Şb. 18/52 1335 L 17 (August 6, 1917).
77 Ibid.
78 "Curb White Slavery in Constantinople: Ambassador Morgenthau's Efforts Effectively Seconded by the Sultan's Police," *New York Times*, February 27, 1915. Also discussed in Wyers, *"Wicked" Istanbul: The Regulation of Prostitution in the Early Turkish Republic*, 90–1.
79 Ibid., 86.
80 In the framework of political contest and morality, Egypt offers a fruitful analysis on the relation between sex work, nationalism, and colonialism. In colonial Egypt, Francesca Biancani shows how the nationalist independence projects pursued prostitution and its protection by the Capitulations at the center of the colonial domination representing the lack of national hegemony over social, sexual, and moral politics of the country; see Francesca Biancani, *Sex Work in Colonial Egypt: Women, Modernity and the Global Economy* (London: I.B. Tauris, 2018). Although my documents use the term "trafficking in women" and I have not added further discussion here, as recent studies on sex work show, the term is a discursive strategy of most abolitionists, nongovernmental organizations, and the governments to disregard the agency of sex workers. Recent studies consider the term "migration for work" rather than "trafficking." For a discussion, see M. R. García, E. van N. Meerkerk, and L. H. van Voss, "Selling Sex in World Cities, 1600s–2000s: An Introduction," in *Selling Sex in the City: A Global History of Prostitution, 1600s–2000s*, ed. M. R. García, E. van N. Meerkerk, L. H. van Voss (Leiden: Brill, 2017): 1–21.

81 It is possible to observe this discourse in various sources including journal articles and literary works. For instance, an article titled "The Issue of Morality" in Sebilürreşad argued that immorality was "instilled into the Muslim nation by foreign hands." See "Memleketimizde Ahlâk Mes'elesi," 404–6. I discuss this issue further in the Conclusion chapter.

82 Toprak, *Türkiye'de Kadın Özgürlüğü ve Feminizm* (1908–35), 115. Frith summarizes what people from different countries called syphilis: "Syphilis had a variety of names, usually people naming it after an enemy or a country they thought responsible for it. The French called it the 'Neapolitan disease', the 'disease of Naples' or the 'Spanish disease', and later grande verole or grosse verole, the 'great pox', the English and Italians called it the 'French disease', the 'Gallic disease', the 'morbus Gallicus', or the 'French pox', the Germans called it the 'French evil', the Scottish called it the 'grandgore', the Russians called it the 'Polish disease', the Polish and the Persians called it the 'Turkish disease', the Turkish called it the 'Christian disease', the Tahitians called it the 'British disease', in India it was called the 'Portuguese disease', in Japan it was called the 'Chinese pox', and there are some references to it being called the 'Persian fire,'" John Frith, "Syphilis—Its Early History and Treatment until Penicillin and the Debate on Its Origins," *Journal of Military and Veterans' Health* 20, no. 4 (2012): 49.

83 Yakup Kadri Karaosmanoğlu, *Sodom ve Gomore* (1st edition 1924) (Istanbul: İletişim Yayınları, 2003). For other examples from literary works on the occupation, see Mehmet Törenek, *Türk Romanında İşgal Istanbul'u* (Istanbul: Kitabevi, 2002).

84 Irvin Cemil Schick, "Nationalism Meets the Sex Trade: Istanbul's District of Beyoğlu/Pera during the Early Twentieth Century," paper presented at *Amherst and Hampshire Colleges Workshop*, Amherst College, 2009.

85 Ibid., 5.

86 Arus Yumul, "'A Prostitute Lodging in the Bosom of Turkishness,' Istanbul's Pera and Its Representation," *Journal of Intercultural Studies* 30, no. 1 (2009): 66.

87 Hülya Yıldız, "Limits of the Imaginable in the Early Turkish Novel, Non-Muslim Prostitutes and Their Ottoman Muslim Clients," *Texas Studies in Literature and Language* 54, no. 4 (2012): 540.

88 Rıfat Bali, *The Jews and Prostitution in Constantinople, 1854–1922* (Istanbul: Isis Press, 2008).

89 Ibid., 12–14.

90 Pappenheim, *Sisyphus-Arbeit Reisebriefe aus den Jahren 1911 und 1912* (Leipzig: Linder, 1924), 50, quoted in: Bali, *The Jews and Prostitution in Constantinople, 1854–1922*, 36.

91 "In all of his novels Flaubert associates the Orient with the escapism of sexual fantasy. Emma Bavaey and Frederic Moreau pine for what in their drab (or

harried) bourgeois lives they do not have, and what they realize they want comes easily to their daydreams packed inside Oriental cliches: harems, princesses, princes, slaves, veils, dancing girls and boys, sherbets, ointments, and so on. The repertoire is familiar, not so much because it reminds us of Flaubert's own voyages in and obsession with the Orient, but because, once again, the association is clearly made between the Orient and the freedom of licentious sex," Edward Said, *Orientalism* (New York: Vintage Books, 1979), 190.

92 On the reproduction of sexual and cultural differences within the discourse of Orientalism, see Meyda Yeğenoğlu, *Colonial Fantasies: Towards a Feminist Reading of Orientalism* (Cambridge, NY: Cambridge University Press, 1998).

93 Wyers, *"Wicked" Istanbul: The Regulation of Prostitution in the Early Turkish Republic*, 94.

94 Malte Fuhrmann, "'Western Perversions' at the Threshold of Felicity: The European Prostitutes of Galata-Pera (1870–1915)," *History and Anthropology* 21, no. 2 (2010): 164.

95 Ibid., 164–5.

96 Ibid., 168.

97 Quoted in Bali, *The Jews and Prostitution in Constantinople, 1854–1922*, 78. Some archival documents support the argument regarding the particular attention that Ottoman authorities paid to preventing Muslim women from engaging in prostitution. There is a case demonstrating that even Talat Pasha was involved in to rescue a daughter of Pasha who was to be sent to her ill-reputed mother in Ankara. Talat Pasha intervened to save this girl from her mother and offered her a job in a workshop, BOA. DH. EUM.ADL. 6/8 14 Haz 1331 (June 27, 1915). Furthermore, it seems that policemen paid special attention when a Muslim woman began working in the Beyoğlu brothels. When the police heard that a certain Fatma, the daughter of a deceased colonel, was living in a brothel in Beyoğlu, officers stormed the brothel and took everybody into custody to investigate who had encouraged her to prostitute herself. See BOA. DH.EUM. EMN 74/6 1332 C 27 (April 23, 1914).

98 Wyers, *"Wicked" Istanbul: The Regulation of Prostitution in the Early Turkish Republic*, 87.

99 Bertha Pappenheim's words are worth quoting here: "*The German Embassy has set itself against my desire to either undermine or [somehow] break through the Capitulatory rights [of Europeans in the Ottoman Empire]! They deem it unnecessary [to do so simply] on behalf of the few German girls who are in circulation. As for the Greek, Catholic and Jewish [girls], they aren't worth the effort to move heaven and earth!!?*" Pappenheim, *Sisyphus-Arbeit Reisebriefe aus den Jahren 1911 und 1912*, Leipzig: Verlag Paul E. Linder, 1924, 58–60, quoted in: Bali, *The Jews and Prostitution in Constantinople, 1854–1922*, 40.

100 BOA. HR. İD. 1585/41 (June 9, 1914).
101 Ibid.
102 Wyers, *"Wicked" Istanbul: The Regulation of Prostitution in the Early Turkish Republic*, 88.
103 BOA. DH.İD. 89-1 1329 Ra 7 (April 1, 1911).
104 Henry Morgenthau, *Ambassador Morgenthau's Story* (New York: Doubleday, Page Company, 1918), 324.
105 Ibid., 325.
106 BOA. DH.EUM.ADL 12/16 1334 M 13 (November 21, 1915).
107 BOA. DH.EUM. 5. Şb. 27/46 1334 L 06 (August 6, 1916).
108 Liat Kozma mentions Madam Dina as "Sarina Glaser (aka Dina Sarina)," one of the notorious brothel owners at the time when she was interviewed by the League of Nations' trafficking in women investigator Paul Kinsie in 1924–5. Kinsie posed as a procurer and talked to various actors of sex work across the Mediterranean. He was surprised by Madam Dina's courage to take up her disputes with the procurers to the court in Istanbul; see Liat Kozma, *Global Women, Colonial Ports: Prostitution in the Interwar Middle East* (Albany, NY: State University of New York Press, 2017), 94–5.
109 BOA. DH.EUM.ADL 12/31 1334 M 24 (December 2, 1915).
110 BOA. DH.EUM.5.Şb. 22/47 1334 Ca 28 (May 2, 1916).
111 BOA. DH.EUM.ADL. 49/26 1335 Ra 6 (January 19, 1917).
112 BOA. DH.EUM.ADL. 48/13 1335 Ca 30 (March 24, 1917).
113 BOA. DH.EUM.ADL. 49/20 1334 Z 25 (September 23, 1916).
114 Ibid.
115 The war shaped a stricter concept of citizenship in belligerent countries. The status of enemy alien and political and social stigma that it brought about further exacerbated ethnic divisions and made transnational lives impossible. On the topic, see Daniela L. Caglioti, *Enemy Aliens and National Belonging from the French Revolution to the First World War* (Cambridge: Cambridge University Press, 2020).
116 "Ecnebilerin Memalik-i Osmaniye'de Seyahat ve İkametleri Hakkında Kanun-u Muvakkat," *Düstur* 2, no. 7 (1918): 484–5.
117 Ibid.
118 A certain Michael Moses Salamovitz, alias Michel Pasha, was indicated as the person who ran the synagogue to which traffickers attend in Morgenthau's reports that were cited in Rifat Bali's work. It is possible he was the same person. Bali, *The Jews and Prostitution in Constantinople, 1854–1922*, 55.
119 BOA. DH. EUM. ADL. 14/34 1334 Ra 20 (January 26, 1916).
120 BOA. DH. EUM. 5., ŞB., 80/57 (June 4, 1914).
121 ATASE, 277/1136 001 12.
122 Ibid.

123 Ibid.
124 On administrative decisions regarding banishment, see Feridun Ata, "I. Dünya Savaşı İçinde Bozkır'a Yapılan Sürgünler," *Türk Kültürü İncelemeleri Dergisi* 17 (2007): 51–64. Whether foreigners were subject to courts martial orders deserves further investigation. During the First World War, military law was imposed on foreigners, showing a trend of "extraterritoriality" in the application of military law. This point, indeed, caused heated debate prior to the war between the Ottoman government and foreign powers. See Noemi Levy-Aksu's work for further discussion. Lévy-Aksu, "An Ottoman Variation on the State of Siege." See also Zeren's study in which he discussed extraterritoriality in law in the framework of the establishment of constitutional rule in the Ottoman Balkans. Zeren, "The Formation of Constitutional Rule: The Politics of Ottomanism between de Jure and de Facto (1908–1913)."
125 BOA. DH. İ. UM. 29-1/15 1333 Ra 16 (February 1, 1915).
126 BOA. DH.EUM.ECB. 4/45 1334 C 21 (April 25, 1916).
127 BOA. DH.İ.UM. 29-1/4 1333 S 13 (December 31, 1914).
128 BOA. DH. İD. 61-1/46 1333 S 25 (January 12, 1915).
129 BOA. DH.İD: 61-1/44 25 Kanunievvel 1330 (January 7, 1915).
130 BOA. DH.SN.THR. 69/68 1334 N 14 (June 16, 1916).
131 BOA. DH. EUM. 2. Şb. 26/2 1334 L 12 (August 12, 1916).
132 BOA. DH. EUM. 5. ŞB. 19/1 24 Ağustos 1331 (September 6, 1915).
133 Wyers, *"Wicked" Istanbul: The Regulation of Prostitution in the Early Turkish Republic*, 177–9. The League of Nations 1927 report on the trafficking in women severely criticized Turkish authorities for being tolerant of traffickers. Ibid., 107–8.

Chapter 4

1 One exception to this critique was Germany, the Ottoman ally during the war. Mehmet Akif admired the way the German Emperor and commanders expressed their gratitude to God on every occasion, and he wrote that this was something that should be expected from pious Muslims. He complained that the Germans had become an example for the Muslims other than vice versa. Mehmed Akif, "Harb-i Hâziredan Alınan Dersler," *Sebilürreşad*, no. 432 (September 1914): 311.
2 "Kanun-i Cezanın Doksan Dokuzuncu Maddesinin Altıncı Cumadelahire 1329 Tarihli Dördüncü Zeyli Mucibince Riayet Edilmesi Lazım Gelen Ba'zı Kavaid Hakkında Kararname," *Düstur* 2, no. 4 (1913): 311.
3 Dölek Sever's study on public order and crime in Istanbul during the First World War offers a valuable analysis of both the legal framework of maintenance of public order in Ottoman capital and the impact of these legal measures on

civilians on a daily basis. See Deniz Dölek Sever, "War and Imperial Capital: Public Order, Crime and Punishment in Istanbul."

4   Rudi Matthee, "Alcohol in the Islamic Middle East, Ambivalence and Ambiguity," *Past & Present* 222, no. supp. 9 (2014): 112.
5   The period in question was marked by "social fluidity and the gradual disintegration of existing hierarchies" owing to domestic migration that was a consequence of population growth and the dissolution of the *tımar* land system. Kırlı, "The Struggle over Space," 42.
6   Ibid., 42-3.
7   Ibid., 49.
8   For more information, see Cengiz Kırlı, *Sultan ve Kamuoyu Osmanlı Modernleşme Sürecinde "Havadis Jurnalleri"(1840-1844)* (Istanbul: Türkiye İş Bankası, 2009).
9   Yıldız, "Limits of the Imaginable in the Early Turkish Novel," 555. Regarding initial introduction of cinema and cinema-going in the Ottoman Empire, see Özge Çeliktemel-Thomen, "The Curtain of Dreams: Early Cinema in Istanbul (1896-1923)" (M.A. Thesis, Central European University, Budapest, 2009).
10 Zarinebaf gives a detailed account of how the kefalet system worked; see Zarinebaf, *Crime and Punishment in Istanbul*, 132-3.
11 Avner Wishnitzer, "Into the Dark, Power, Light, and Nocturnal Life in 18th-Century Istanbul," 46, no. 3 (2014): 518.
12 Nurçin İleri, "A Nocturnal History of Fin de Siécle Istanbul" (PhD diss., Binghamton University, Binghamton, 2015), 24.
13 Ibid., 204-5.
14 For example, see Karaosmanoğlu, *Sodom ve Gomore*.
15 BOA. DH.EUM. 7. Şb. 1333 Ra 3 (3/1) (January 19, 1915).
16 Ibid.
17 Ali Osman Koçkuzu, *Çanakkale Cephesinde Bir Müderris, Abdullah Fevzi Efendi, Hâtıralar* (Istanbul: İz Yayıncılık, 2010), 112.
18 A certain Abdi Hulusi wrote a letter to the ministry listing the houses being used for prostitution. He stated his aim in writing this letter as "to serve humanity," BOA. DH. EUM. 3. Şb. 8/74 1333 Za 11 (September 20, 1915).
19 BOA. DH. EUM. 6. Şb. 42/52 (3) 17 Ağustos 1334 (August 17, 1918).
20 This letter, indeed, seems to have been inspired by İsmail Canbulat's, the new minister of interior affairs, promises as he declared to take strict measures against prostitution while in office. See Chapter 2.
21 In 1911, a new article was issued as a supplement to Article 202 of the Ottoman Penal Code stipulating imprisonment for a period from one month to one year for the act of women dancing. See İleri, "A Nocturnal History of Fin de Siécle Istanbul," 266.
22 A case demonstrates the power of "public enthusiasm" vis-à-vis the violation of public morality. In Isparta, the local gendarme commander (*jandarma bölük*

kumandanı) Kazım Efendi, the retired lieutenant (*mülâzım*) Hacı Bey, and the telegraph bureau officer Mehmed Şevket Efendi were arrested after public protest of women dancing in Kazım Efendi's house, BOA. DH. H. 48/5 1331 Ca 04 (April 24, 1913).

23 Archival correspondence gives a sample case on the topic. In the town of Mecidözü, a member of the local administrative council (*meclis-i idare âzâsı*), Pirzade İbrahim; the director of the Subsistance Office (*mal müdürü*), Hakkı; and the commander for tracking down the deserters (*firarî takip müfrezesi kumandanı*), Captain İbrahim, were caught watching women dancing, and their case was transferred to the courts martial. See BOA. DH. EUM. KLU. 12/30. 1335 R 05 (January 29, 1917). Unfortunately I could not detail this case here since this file is under restoration in the archives and only this summary is available.

24 Salim Tamari, *Year of the Locust: A Soldier's Diary and the Erasure of Palestine's Ottoman Past* (Berkeley: University of California Press, 2011).

25 The title "Residence Inspector" refers to an Ottoman military rank *Menzil Müfettişi* which can also be translated as "Station Inspector."

26 Tamari, *Year of the Locust*, 111–12.

27 Abigail Jacobson, "Negotiating Ottomanism in Times of War: Jerusalem during World War I through the Eyes of a Local Muslim Resident," *International Journal of Middle East Studies* 40, no. 1 (2008): 69–88.

28 Cited in: Thompson, *Colonial Citizens*, 27.

29 Teitelbaum, "The Man Who Would Be Caliph: Sharifian Propaganda in World War I," 290–1.

30 Toprak, *Türkiye'de Milli İktisat, 1908–1918*, 174 (1st edition in 1982). Zürcher discusses whether "millî" refers to Turkish nationalism, Ottomanism, or Islamism in Young Turk social and economic policies and concludes that the Unionists' policies were primarily motivated by the idea of promoting an "Ottoman Muslim" state, Zürcher, *The Young Turk Legacy and Nation Building*, 230–1.

31 Feroz Ahmad, *İttihatçılıktan Kemalizme*, trans. Fatmagül Berktay (Istanbul: Kaynak Yayınları, 1999), 44–5.

32 Toprak, *Türkiye'de Milli İktisat, 1908–1918*, 538.

33 Vehbi Koç (1901–96), patriarch of one of the wealthiest families in contemporary Turkey, displays in his memoirs how transporting goods from Ankara to Istanbul brought him a good profit during the war years. Vehbi Koç, *Hayat Hikâyem* (Istanbul: Apa Ofset Basımevi, 1973), 20–1.

34 For a companion of these literary works, see Seçil Deren Van Het Hof, "Erken Dönem Cumhuriyet Romanında Zenginler ve Zenginlik," *Kültür ve İletişim* 13, no. 2 (2010): 81–106.

35 For a representative story, see A. Sermet Muhtar Alus, *Harp Zengininin Gelini* (Istanbul: Kanaat Kütüphanesi, 1934).

36 Leyla and her family in Yakup Kadri's *Sodom ve Gomore* is a perfect example of this typology. See Karaosmanoğlu, *Sodom ve Gomore*.
37 Van Het Hof, "Erken Dönem Cumhuriyet Romanında Zenginler ve Zenginlik," 96.
38 Yiğit Akın, "War Profiteers and the Ottoman Home Front during World War I," *World War I in the Middle East and North Africa*, 2012 (Accessed February 6, 2017). https://blogs.commons.georgetown.edu/world-war-i-in-the-middle-east/seminar-participants/web-projects/yigit-akin-war-profiteers-and-the-ottoman-home-front-during-world-war-i/
39 Robert, "The Image of the Profiteer," in *Capital Cities at War: Paris, London, Berlin, 1914–1919*, ed. J. M. Winter and Jean-Louis Robert (New York: Cambridge University Press, 1999), 132.
40 Jens Hanssen discusses this argument focusing on Beirut; see Jens Hanssen, "Public Morality and Marginality in Fin de siècle Beirut," in *Outside In: On the Margins of the Modern Middle East*, ed. Eugene Rogan (London: I.B. Tauris, 2001), 201. Nurçin İleri also discusses this point in her study: "Entertainment venues and other public places such as Turkish baths or printing houses were considered as 'habitats of crime' because the rebels and criminals could blend in public in these venues." İleri, "A Nocturnal History of Fin de Siécle Istanbul," 207.
41 For a brief assessment of the topic in Turkish, see Çiğdem Oğuz, "Millî Mesele ve Maddî Gereksinim Arasında: Birinci Dünya Savaşı'nda Eğlence Yerlerini Düzenleme Çabaları," *Toplumsal Tarih* 267 (March 2016): 86–90.
42 BOA. DH.MTV. 35/7 1333 S 04 (December 22, 1914).
43 I borrowed this description from Jens Hanssen. Hanssen, "Public Morality and Marginality in Fin de Siècle Beirut," 198.
44 Nadir Özbek, "Defining the Public Sphere during the Late Ottoman Empire: War, Mass Mobilization and the Young Turk Regime (1908–18)," *Middle Eastern Studies* 43, no. 5 (2007): 801–7.
45 Sevengil, *Türk Tiyatrosu Tarihi: Meşrutiyet Tiyatrosu*, Vol. 5. (Istanbul: Milli Eğitim Basımevi, 1959), 227.
46 BOA. DH. UMVM. 116/40 1335 Ca 20 (April 13, 1917). During Ramadan, when night time became particularly active, inspectors of the Poorhouse visited the theaters themselves and collected this revenue on a daily basis; see Nuran, Yıldırım, *İstanbul Darülaceze Müessesesi Tarihi* (Istanbul: Darülaceze Vakfı, 1996), 124.
47 BOA. BEO 4482/336127 1335 Za 11 (September 28, 1917).
48 Apart from these taxes there were also license tax, stamp tax, and a tax issued by the Ottoman Public Debt Administration (Düyun-u Umumiye). An actor, Burhaneddin Bey, submitted a petition to the Ministry of Interior Affairs regarding the excessive taxation of theaters, and he wrote that these taxes were the main obstacle to the development of local theater initiatives because they were only imposed on local companies. Yıldırım, *İstanbul Darülaceze Müessesesi Tarihi*, 124.

49 BOA. A.) DVN. MKL. 64/27 April 6, 1918.
50 It is possible to find letters from theater directors from distant provinces such as Basra complaining that they are unable to run their companies anymore because of the heavy taxes, BOA. DH. H. 1332.4.27 17/40 (March 25, 1914).
51 Quoted in: Sevengil, *Türk Tiyatrosu Tarihi: Meşrutiyet Tiyatrosu*, 182.
52 Ibid.
53 Halit Fahri Ozansoy, *Darülbedayi Devrinin Eski Günlerinde* (Istanbul: Ak Kitabevi, 1964), 55.
54 Ertuğrul Muhsin, "Garpta Tiyatroculuk, Bizde Tiyatroculuk," *Temaşa* no. 9 (September 26, 1918): 5.
55 Turhan Turgut, "I. Dünya Savaşı'nda Osmanlı Posta Sansürü," *Toplumsal Tarih* 243 (March 2014): 88–92.
56 Ibid. I thank Gizem Tongo Overfield Shaw, who directed my attention to this transcribed, simplified version of "Instruction of Censorship," which can be found online: Türk Filatelli Akademisi, *1330 (1914) Senesinde Selimiye Askerî Matbaada Basılan "Sansür Talimatnamesi,"* October 22, 2016 (Accessed February 20, 2017). http://turkfilateliakademisi.org/wp-content/uploads/2016/10/sansur.pdf.
57 BOA. DH. EUM. 5. Şb. 9/51 1333 R 07 (February 22, 1915).
58 Ibid.
59 BOA. DH.EUM. 6. Şb. 38/12 1336 Ş 18 (May 29, 1918).
60 Ibid.
61 The ministry asked the opinions of local police regarding the feasibility of regulations; see BOA. DH.EUM.MEM 72/29 1334 S 24 (January 1, 1916). The Ministry of Interior Affairs asked the Ministry of Foreign Affairs to send examples of regulations being implemented in other countries such as Bulgaria, Sweden, and Austria; see BOA. DH.EUM.VRK 29/8 1336 Za 14 (August 21, 1918); DH.EUM.VRK 29/7 1336 Za 13 (August 20, 1918); and DH.EUM.VRK 29/3 1336 L 25 (August 3, 1918).
62 BOA. DH.EUM.6.Şb. 31/29 1336 Ca 05 (March 18, 1918).
63 Ibid. It is often argued that the Ottoman wartime government had no respect for the law or law-making processes, and Enver Pasha's orders were implemented suddenly. This case here shows a tension between the military and bureaucratic authorities on the legislation procedures and reveals the inner bureaucratic circles' functioning despite the "need" for extraordinary and "justified" measures.
64 BOA. DH. EUM. VRK 28/51 1336 C 4 (March 17, 1918).
65 Francois Georgeon, "Ottomans and Drinkers: The Consumption of Alcohol in Istanbul in the Nineteenth Century," in *Outside In: On the Margins of the Modern Middle East*, ed. Eugene Rogan (London: I.B. Tauris, 2001), 14.
66 Kırlı, "The Struggle over Space," 58.
67 İleri, "A Nocturnal History of Fin de Siécle Istanbul," 232.
68 Ibid.

69 Hanssen, "Public Morality and Marginality in Fin-de-siècle Beirut," 200.
70 Ibid., 203. Closing hours were particularly important with regard to regulations on alcohol consumption and the reorganization of entertainment venues. Nurçin İleri asserts that attempts of authorities to close the venues on time stemmed from their assumption that a strict closing hour regulation would preserve the balance between morality and modernity. İleri, "A Nocturnal History of Fin de Siécle Istanbul," 208.
71 Hanssen, "Public Morality and Marginality in Fin-de-siècle Beirut," 201.
72 Georgeon, "Ottomans and Drinkers," 10.
73 Matthee, "Alcohol in the Islamic Middle East," 112.
74 Georgeon, "Ottomans and Drinkers," 16–17.
75 Ibid.
76 MacArthur-Seal, "Intoxication and Imperialism, Nightlife in Occupied Istanbul, 1918–23," 300.
77 Emine Ö. Evered and Kyle T. Evered, "From Rakı to Ayran: Regulating the Place and Practice of Drinking in Turkey," *Space and Polity* 20, no. 1 (2016): 43. In addition, this measure also curbed the interests of non-Muslim alcohol sellers. As the law eliminated most private enterprises, it also served the purpose of establishing a state monopoly (*tekel*) on alcohol. See Onur Karahanoğulları, *Birinci Meclisin İçki Yasağı (Men-i Müskirat Kanunu)* (Ankara: Phoenix, 2007).
78 Ibid., 44.
79 Yalman, *Turkey in the World War*, 242–3.
80 "Evlâd-ı Şühedânın Ta'lim ve Terbiyesiçün Vücuda Getirilecek Mü'essesat Mesarifine Muktezî Vâridat Hakkında Kanun-u Muvakkat," *Düstur* 1, no. 7, 642–3.
81 *MMZC*, Term 3, Vol. 4 Year: 1, 19.
82 Ibid.
83 Ibid.
84 Ibid.
85 Gambling was subject to punishment of up to six months imprisonment and a fine according to the 242nd Article of the 1858 Ottoman Penal Code; see İleri, "A Nocturnal History of Fin de Siécle Istanbul," 244.
86 Yalman, *Turkey in the World War*, 243.
87 *Tanin*, "Kumar Oynayanlar Hakkında," August 31, 1918.

Chapter 5

1 Sigmund Freud quoted these lines of the famous eighteenth-century poet-philosopher Schiller as a starting point for his ego-instinct and object-instinct drive theory: "In what was at first my utter perplexity, I took as my starting-point a

saying of the poet-philosopher, Schiller, that 'hunger and love are what moves the world'. Hunger could be taken to represent the instincts which aim at preserving the individual; while love strives after objects, and its chief function, favoured in every way by nature, is the preservation of the species." Sigmund Freud, *Civilization and Its Discontents*, trans. Joan Riviere (New York: J. Cape & H. Smith, 1930), 34.

2   Edward J. Erickson, *Ordered to Die: A Military History of the Ottomans* (Westport: Greenwood Press, 2001), 211.
3   I owe this formulation to the work of Elizabeth Thompson in which she casts light on the political and social reflections of the gender crisis in terms of authority and identity. In her work, she used the term "civic order" to evaluate a broader context of state-society interaction: "The civic order embodies norms and institutions that govern relations among citizens and between citizens and the state. It is within the civic order that the terms of citizenship and state power are both expressed and continually renegotiated among agents of the formal state apparatus, its unofficial agents, and their clients." Thompson, *Colonial Citizens*, 1.
4   Grayzel, *Women and the First World War*, 64.
5   On Family Aid in several countries, see Daniel, *The War from within*; Susan Grayzel, *Women's Identities at War: Gender, Motherhood, and Politics in Britain and France during the First World War* (Chapel Hill: University of North Carolina Press, 1999); Susan Pedersen, *Family, Dependence, and the Origins of the Welfare State: Britain and France, 1914–1945* (Cambridge, NY: Cambridge University Press, 1995).
6   See Daniel, *The War from within*, 143–7; Grayzel, *Women and the First World War*, 67.
7   Nicole A. N. M. Van Os, "Taking Care of Soldiers' Families: The Ottoman State and the Muinsiz Aile Maaşı," in *Arming the State: Military Conscription in the Middle East and Central Asia, 1775–1925*, ed. Erik Jan Zürcher (London, New York: I.B. Tauris, 1999), 96–7; Akın, "When the War Came Home," 32.
8   See Beşikçi, *The Ottoman Mobilization of Manpower in the First World War*, 8.
9   In villages, the situation worsened as well due to the lack of manpower and the high taxes on products, Van Os, "Taking Care of Soldiers' Families: The Ottoman State and the Muinsiz Aile Maaşı," 102. In his memoirs, İrfan Orga tells how they treated families in the revenue office in Istanbul. His mother, after being insulted by the officers, did not go there to collect the aid and instead sent Orga to receive it. When he went to the office, a man who helped him talk to the officer physically abused him. After the incident, none among the family members visited the office again. He says the allowance they received was anyway not enough to live on due to increasing prices. İrfan Orga, *Bir Türk Ailesinin Öyküsü*, trans. Arın Bayraktaroğlu (Istanbul: Ana Yayıncılık, 2002), 149–50.

10 Yiğit Akın, "The Ottoman Home Front during World War I, Everyday Politics, Society, and Culture" (PhD diss., Ohio State University, Columbus, 2011), 160.
11 Enver Pasha's decision: DH.I.UM.EK. 23/51.
12 Yalman, *Turkey in the World War*, 246.
13 Grayzel, *Women and the First World War*, 117.
14 Akın, "When the War Came Home," 158.
15 Toprak, "The Family, Feminism, and the State during the Young Turk Period, 1908–1918," 441–52.
16 Yet, traditional gender roles persisted, holding women back from achieving equality. For a discussion on the emancipation of women both in early Turkish Republican and contemporary contexts, see Deniz Kandiyoti, "Emancipated but Unliberated?" Reflections on the Turkish Case," *Feminist Studies* 13, no. 2 (1987): 317–38; Yeşim Arat, "From Emancipation to Liberation: The Changing Role of Women in Turkey's Public Realm," *Journal of International Affairs* 54, no. 1 (2000): 107–23.
17 Daniel, *The War from within*, 127.
18 Ibid., 138.
19 Toprak, *Türkiye'de Popülizm*, 264.
20 Duben and Behar, *Istanbul Households*.
21 Ibid., 200–1.
22 Başak Tuğ, "The Claims on Modernity and Tradition: Marriage in Turkey in the 1910s and the 1920s" (M.A. Thesis, Boğaziçi University, Istanbul, 2000), 99.
23 Toprak, *Türkiye'de Kadın Özgürlüğü ve Feminizm (1908–1935)*, 14–16; Toprak, *Türkiye'de Popülizm*, 263–4.
24 I should also add that while in contemporary Turkish the word *tecavüz* means rape, in the Ottoman context it meant "crossing the lines" and violating the rights of someone else. For the dictionary meaning of the word, see Sami, *Kâmûs-i Türkî*, 481.
25 Zeynep Kutluata, "Ottoman Women and the State during World War I" (PhD diss., Sabancı University, Istanbul, 2014), 186.
26 Mahir Metinsoy, *Ottoman Women and World War I*, 7.
27 See Oxford Islamic Studies Online for the definition *hadd* in Islam: "Limit or prohibition; pl. *hudud*. A punishment fixed in the Quran and hadith for crimes considered to be against the rights of God. The six crimes for which punishments are fixed are theft (amputation of the hand), illicit sexual relations (death by stoning or one hundred lashes), making unproven accusations of illicit sex (eighty lashes), drinking intoxicants (eighty lashes), apostasy (death or banishment), and highway robbery (death). Strict requirements for evidence (including eyewitnesses) have severely limited the application of *hudud* penalties. Punishment for all other crimes is left to the discretion of the court; these punishments are called *ta'zir*." "Hadd," in *The Oxford Dictionary of Islam*, ed. John

L. Esposito. *Oxford Islamic Studies Online* (Accessed 2 May 2017). http://www.oxfordislamicstudies.com/article/opr/t125/e757. On the discussion of *hadd* and *zina*, see Amira Sonbol, "Rape and Law in Ottoman and Modern Egypt," 214–32.

28 Sulhi Dönmezer, *Ceza Hukuku, Hususî Kısım, Umumî Adap ve Aile Nizamı Aleyhinde Cürümler* (Istanbul: Istanbul Üniversitesi Yayınları, 1961), 19–21. For prophetic and sectarian traditions of punishment in *zina* cases, see Sonbol, "Rape and Law in Ottoman and Modern Egypt," in *Women in the Ottoman Empire: Middle Eastern Women in the Early Modern Era*, ed. Madeline C. Zilfi (Leiden, New York: Brill, 1997), 215–19.

29 Belkıs Konan, "Osmanlı Hukukunda Tecavüz Suçu," *Osmanlı Tarihi Araştırma ve Uygulama Merkezi Dergisi OTAM* 29 (2011): 152–5.

30 Ibid., 157–62. Elyse Semerdjian, "Gender Violence in Kanunnames and Fetvas of the Sixteenth Century," in *Beyond the Exotic: Women's Histories in Islamic Societies*, ed. Amira El-Azhary Sonbol (Cairo: The American University in Cairo Press, 2005), 180–97.

31 Zübeyde Güneş Yağcı, "Osmanlı Taşrasında Kadına Yönelik Cinsel Suçlarda Adalet Arama Geleneği," *Kadın 2000* 6, no. 2 (2005): 51–81.

32 See, Semerdjian, "*Off the Straigh Path*."

33 See especially the case of child bride Ine's story, Peirce, *Morality Tales*, 129–42.

34 Konan, "Osmanlı Hukukunda Tecavüz Suçu," 162–3; Sulhi Dönmezer, *Umumî Adab ve Aile Nizamı Aleyhinde Cürümler* (Istanbul: Istanbul Üniversitesi Yayınları, 1950), 27–8.

35 Konan, "Osmanlı Hukukunda Tecavüz Suçu," 168. This aspect of law was also discussed in the case of Egypt, see Sonbol, "Rape and Law in Ottoman and Modern Egypt," 225.

36 For a transliterated version of the articles, see Ahmet Akgündüz, *Akgündüz, Mukayeseli İslam ve Osmanlı Hukuku Külliyatı* (Diyarbakır: Dicle Üniversitesi Hukuk Fakültesi, 1986), 864–6.

37 Konan, "Osmanlı Hukukunda Tecavüz Suçu," 162–6; Dönmezer, *Umumî Adab ve Aile Nizamı Aleyhinde Cürümler*, 27–8.

38 Dönmezer, *Ceza Hukuku*, 31–32.

39 Dönmezer, *Umumi Adab ve Aile Nizamı Aleyhinde Cürümler*, 20–8.

40 Ibid., 24.

41 Emphasis on population growth was particularly evident in the penal codes of fascist countries; see Maria Sophia Quine, *Population Politics in Twentieth-Century Europe: Fascist Dictatorships and Liberal Democracies* (London: Routledge, 1996).

42 BOA. DH.H. 43/66 4 Nisan 1329 (April 17, 1913).

43 BOA. DH.H. 46/01 (04) 21 Eylül 1329 (September 21, 1913).

44 BOA. DH.H. 48/06 (026) 17 Te 1328 (October 30, 1912).

45 Ibid.

46 Akın, *When the War Came Home*, 22.

47 BOA.DH.EUM.MTK 79/34 1333 S 16 (January 3, 1915).
48 *Düstur*, Vol. 2, No. 7, 716.
49 BOA. DH. EUM. ADL 23/31, 26 Temmuz 1332 (August 8, 1916).
50 Kutluata, "Ottoman Women and the State during World War I," 11.
51 Akın, *When the War Came Home*, 144–62.
52 Mahir Metinsoy, *Ottoman Women during World War I*.
53 See Tuğ, *Politics of Honor in Ottoman Anatolia*.
54 BOA. DH. EUM. 2. Şb. 35/1 (003) 11 Teşrinisani 1331 (November 24, 1915). The letter begins with "we, the three of us, are soldiers' wives"; however, it was signed by only two women.
55 BOA.DH.EUM. 2. Şb. 35/1 (102) 12 Kanunuevvel 1330 (December 25, 1914).
56 BOA.DH.EUM.2. Şb. 35/1 (104) 9 Şubat 1330 (February 22, 1915).
57 BOA.DH.EUM. 2. Şb. 35/1 (92). 27 Kanunuevvel 1330 (January 4, 1915).
58 For the original statement see *MMZC*, Term 3, Vol. 1, Year. 1, 21 December 1914, 26.
59 BOA. DH. EUM. 2. Şb. 35/1 (106) 12 Şubat 1330 (February 25, 1915).
60 BOA. DH. EUM. ADL. 32/28 (011) 1335 B 16 (May 8, 1917).
61 BOA. DH. EUM. 2. Şb. 35/1 (028) 17 Kanunuevvel 1331 (December 30, 1915).
62 For instance, in a telegram eleven men from Malatya complained to the Ministry of Interior Affairs that their "*honor was trampled by a few gendarmeries in the region*"; see BOA.DH.EUM. 2. Şb. 35/1 (071) 18 Ağustos 1331 (August 31, 1915). The ministry received not only cases of sexual assault but also cases of property violation and homicide cases for which the members of the military were accused. For a homicide case in which two soldiers attacked and murdered two women, see BOA. BEO. 4495/337074 11 Kanunuevvel 1333 (December 11, 1917); for a case of the violation of private property by gendarme and its investigation, which was instigated upon the receipt of a telegram from five women (soldiers' wives) from Bursa, see BOA. DH. EUM. 2. Şb. 35/1 (034). Eventually, the Directorate of Police issued a circular to all provinces on May 27, 1915, ordering that attacks on soldiers' properties be prevented. See BOA. DH. EUM. 2. Şb. 35/1 (142) 14 Mayıs 1331 (May 27, 1915).
63 BOA.DH.I.UM EK. 36/3 13 Haziran 1333 (June 13, 1917). Also discussed in, Akın, "When the War Came Home," 150.
64 BOA. İ. DUİT 171/12 7 Mayıs 1332 (Mayıs 20, 1916).
65 BOA. İ. DUİT. 174/20 2 Haziran 1333 (Haziran 2, 1917).
66 BOA. İ. DUİT. 173/59 21 Teşrinievvel 1332 (November 3, 1916).
67 BOA. İ. DUİT. 171/99 9 Temmuz 1332 (July 22, 1916).
68 BOA. İ. DUİT. 171/68 26 Haziran 1332 (July 9, 1916).
69 BOA. İ. DUİT. 171/10 7 Mayıs 1332 (May 20, 1916).
70 BOA. İ. DUİT. 171/28 11 Mayıs 1332 (May 24, 1916).
71 BOA. İ. DUİT. 171/7 27 Mayıs 1332 (June 9, 1916).

72 For such cases see, BOA. İ. DUİT. 171/41 11 Mayıs 1332 (May 24, 1916), İ.DUİT. 171/35 18 Mayıs 1332 (May 31, 1916), İ. DUİT. 171/33 15 Mayıs 1332 (May 28, 1916).
73 BOA. İ. DUİT. 171/66 22 Haziran 1332 (July 5, 1916).
74 Kutluata, "Ottoman Women and the State during World War I," 189.
75 On Armenian orphans and Armenian women after the deportation, see Üngör, "Orphans, Converts, and Prostitutes"; Maksudyan considers Armenian children's survival and resilience strategies and emphasizes their agency; see Maksudyan, *Ottoman Children and Youth during World War I*, 105–36.
76 Bjornlund, "A Fate Worse than Dying," 25.
77 Kutluata, "Ottoman Women and the State during World War," 75–6.
78 Ibid., 92.
79 Kutluata, "Ottoman Women and the State during World War I," 159.
80 Todd, "'The Soldier's Wife Who Ran Away with the Russian,' Sexual Infidelities in World War I Germany," *Central European History* 44, no. 2 (2011): 277.
81 Grayzel, *Women and the First World War*, 67. Todd called this situation "press pillory." See Todd, "'The Soldier's Wife Who Ran Away with the Russian,'" 269.
82 Ibid., 264.
83 Ibid., 271.
84 Grayzel, *Women and the First World War*, 74.
85 Ibid., 76.
86 Ibid., 72.
87 BOA. BEO. 4430/332225 13 Nisan 1332 (April 26, 1916).
88 Quoted in: Akın, "When the War Came Home," 98.
89 BOA. MV. 203/34 1334 Za 15 (Eylül 13, 1916).
90 For instance, Judith Tucker concentrated on whether the Family Law was a step toward gender equality and the limitation of male social power. She compared the old and new regimes with regard to marital rights, marriage obligations, and female-initiated divorce in Ottoman Syria and Palestine. She concluded that the Ottoman Family Law of 1917 did not expand women's right to divorce because the previous application of the Hanafi doctrine was already quite flexible. See Tucker, "Revisiting Reform: Women and the Ottoman Law of Family Rights, 1917," *The Arab Studies Journal* 4, no. 2 (1996): 4–17. A comprehensive review of the literature on the Family Decree of 1917 is beyond the scope of this study. For a survey of this literature, see Nihal Altınbaş, "Marriage and Divorce in Early Twentieth Century Ottoman Society: The Law of Family Rights of 1917" (PhD diss., Bilkent University, Ankara, 2014), 2–9. On an analysis of the Family Decree from a Foucauldian point of changing understanding of *governmentality*, see Darina Martykánová, "Matching Sharia and 'Governmentality' Muslim Marriage Legislation in the Late Ottoman Empire," in *Institutional Change and Stability: Conflicts, Transitions and Social Values*, ed. Andrea Gémes, Florencia Peyrou, and Ioannis Xydopoulos (Pisa: Pisa University Press, 2009), 153–75.

91 This question, as far as I could tell, was posed in one of the first accounts of the Family Decree: Ziyaeddin Fındıkoğlu, "Aile Hukukumuzun Tedvini Meselesi," in *Tedris Hayatının Otuzuncu Yıldönümü Hatırası Olmak Üzere Medeni Hukuk Ordinaryüs Profesörü Ebül'ulâ Mardin'e Armağan*, ed. Istanbul Üniversitesi Hukuk Fakültesi (Istanbul: Istanbul Üniversitesi Yayınları, 1944), 687–738. In fact, during the Tanzimat era several steps were taken by the government to remove the burden of traditions such as "brideprice" from marriage ceremonies, Mehmet Ö. Alkan, "Tanzimat'tan Sonra 'Kadın'ın Hukuksal Statüsü," *Toplum ve Bilim* 50 (1990): 90–1; İlber Ortaylı, "Ottoman Family Law and the State in the Nineteenth Century," *OTAM* I (1990): 327. The fact that the Tanzimat bypassed a family reform does not mean that marriage and family had remained outside Ottoman policy making. For instance, Karen M. Kern's study shows how the Ottoman marriage ban of 1874 between Iranian men and Ottoman women played an important role in controlling the demographic composition in the frontier provinces of Iraq for the sake of Ottoman sovereignty; see Karen M. Kern, *Imperial Citizen: Marriage and Citizenship in the Ottoman Frontier Provinces of Iraq* (Syracuse: Syracuse University Press, 2011).

92 Nihan Altınbaş, "Marriage and Divorce in the Late Ottoman Empire: Social Upheaval, Women's Rights, and the Need for New Family Law," *Journal of Family History* 39, no. 2 (2014): 114–25.

93 Ibid., 116.

94 Ortaylı, "Ottoman Family Law and the State in the Nineteenth Century."

95 Ibid., 321–2.

96 Ibid., 322.

97 Ibid., 324.

98 Fındıkoğlu, "Aile Hukukumuzun Tedvini Meselesi," 709.

99 M. Akif Aydın, *İslâm-Osmanlı Aile Hukuku* (Istanbul: Marmara Üniversitesi İlahiyat Fakültesi Vakfı Yayınları, 1985), 178.

100 For a good summary of these literary works and a sociological perspective, see Şerif Mardin, "Super Westernization in Urban Life in the Ottoman Empire in the Last Quarter of the Nineteenth Century," in *Turkey: Geographic and Social Perspectives*, ed. Peter Benedict et al. (Leiden: Brill, 1974), 403–46. For an epistemological evaluation of Tanzimat novels, see Jale Parla, *Babalar ve Oğullar, Tanzimat Romanının Epistemolojik Temelleri* (Istanbul: İletişim Yayınları, 1990). In Cem Behar and Alan Duben's work one can follow how family tragedies were reflected in the narratives of the turn-of-the-century novelists. See *Duben and Behar, Istanbul Households*. Also see Zafer Toprak's analysis of novels focused on family and women in the context of the late nineteenth century and the early twentieth century: Toprak, *Türkiye'de Kadın Özgürlüğü ve Feminizm* (1908–1935).

101 Also see Martykánová, "Matching Sharia and 'Governmentality,'" 163–4.

102 He coined the term *ictimâî usûl-u fıkh* as a method of harmonizing religious interpretation with social needs and customs in society. Accordingly, he claimed

the customs and needs should be more central in lawmaking. See the discussion between Islamists and Turkish nationalists on the sources of lawmaking: Şener, "İctimai Usul-i Fıkh Tartışmaları," *AÜ İslam İlimleri Enstitüsü Dergisi* V (1982): 231–47.

103 Mansurizade wrote: "Just as neither telegraphs nor telephones need a fatwa, nor are they subject to any Sharia provision, the Sharia could not prescribe permissibility in matters of marriage, divorce, and polygamy. The legislator can very well enact laws on them in accordance with the desires of the nation and of the age." See Mansurizade Said, "Taaddüd-ü Zevcat İslamiyette Men Olunabilir," *İslam Mecmuası*, no. 8 (1914): 233–8. Also discussed in Berkes, *The Development of Secularism in Turkey*, 391.

104 Eyal Ginio, *The Ottoman Culture of Defeat: The Balkan Wars and Their Aftermath* (Oxford, New York: Oxford University Press, 2016), 131.

105 Ibid., 121.

106 "*Vatanın selameti için yapılacak bu teşebbüslerde evham vatana hıyanetliktir.*" Mükerrem Belkıs, "Muzur Adetleri Yıkmak Farzdır," *Kadınlar Dünyası*, no. 83, 1329 (1913): 2.

107 Çakır, "Meşrutiyet Devri Kadınlarının Aile Anlayışı," in *Sosyo-kültürel Değişme Sürecinde Türk Ailesi*, ed. Ezel Erverdi and Hakkı Dursun Yıldız (Ankara: T.C. Başbakanlık Aile Araştırma Kurumu, 1992), 230–44 (internet edition assigned page numbers). Çakır's pioneering work shed light on women's opinions and feminism of the time, Serpil Çakır, *Osmanlı Kadın Hareketi* (Istanbul: Metis Yayınları, 1994).

108 Ziya Gökalp, "Aile Ahlakı-3: Konak," *Yeni Mecmua*, no. 12–17, 1917.

109 Tüccarzade İbrahim Hilmi, *Avrupalılaşmak*, ed. Osman Kafadar and Faruk Öztürk (Ankara: Gündoğan yayınları), 86.

110 T.C. Başbakanlık Aile Araştırma Kurumu, "Münakahat ve Müfarakat Kararnamesi Esbab-ı Mucibe Layihası," 295–307. All citations from the justificatory text are taken from this source. Page numbers in the internet edition of the book are not inserted; therefore, I have used automatically assigned order of the pdf file in citing the pages.

111 Aydın, *İslâm-Osmanlı Aile Hukuku*, 192.

112 Celal Nuri addressed this problem in his work *Kadınlarımız (Our women)* in 1911. According to him, the vast autonomy of the husband in Islamic Law contributed to the degeneration of Muslim families. As there were no legal impositions such as civil law limiting the authority of the husband in cases of divorce, remarriage, and illegitimate children, the family remained in disarray; see Celal Nuri, *Kadınlarımız (1st edition 1911)* (Ankara: Kültür Bakanlığı, 1993).

113 For instance, on April 17, 1913, a certain Aişe wrote a petition from Kastamonu claiming that village elders were forcing her to marry someone else since she had not received news from her husband, who had been in the military service for a while. Although this case was during the Balkan Wars, such instances presumably

increased during the First World War see DH.H. 43/61 4 Nisan 1329 (April 17, 1913). In another case, a soldier claimed that his fiancée had been forced to marry, and he asked an official investigation. The Ministry of Interior Affairs decided to investigate the roles of the imam, *muhtar*, and village elders and to punish them; see DH.H. 47/63 (May 27, 1913).
114 Altınbaş, "Marriage and Divorce," 36–7.
115 Mahir Metinsoy argues the decree served to the purposes of reassuring soldiers in captivity by making divorce difficult in the absence of men, Mahir Metinsoy, *Ottoman Women During World War I*, 190–1.
116 Koçkuzu, *Çanakkale Cephesinde Bir Müderris*, 156.
117 Ibid., 179.
118 Ibid., 182–3.
119 On February 14, 1915, the Council of Ministers issued an official decree enacting mandatory retirement of amoral (*suî ahlâk*) or incompetent (*adem-i liyakat*) members of the military. Although not expounded upon further in the document, such instances concerned immorality; see MV. 196/75 1333 Ra 29 (February 14, 1915).
120 Aydın, *İslâm-Osmanlı Aile Hukuku*, 192. Also see Scott Rank's article on the famous debate between Fatma Aliye and Mahmud Es'ad on polygamy in which Mahmud Es'ad defended polygamy as a means of maintaining a balanced ratio of women and men in the population. He also argued that men instinctively tend to marry multiple women, which according to him prevents immorality in society, Rank, "Polygamy and Religious Polemics in the Late Ottoman Empire."
121 Stock-Morton, *Moral Education for a Secular Society*, 133.
122 Tamari, *Year of the Locust*, 7. Tanielian also argues that war had a paradoxical formative and destructive impact in the areas of gender, local communal relationships, family. The war relief and welfare organizations to confront the famine in the Middle East on the Ottoman home front consolidated local ties and strengthened women's role in the politics in Lebanon as a consequence of the Ottoman government's reliance on women in war relief; see Tanielian, *The Charity of War*.

Chapter 6

1 "Ahlâk Mes'eleleri," *Tanin*, September 14, 1918; "Adâb-ı Umûmîye Mes'eleleri," *Tanin*, September 16, 1918.
2 Halide Edib, *Memoirs of Halide Edib* (London; New York: The Century Co., 1926), 387.
3 Ibid.

4 Hülya Adak, "The Protracted Purging of the Tyranny of Nationalism: Turkish Egodocuments and the Possibilities of Armenian-Turkish Reconciliation," in *The Armenian Genocide, Turkey and Europe* (*Der Völkermord an Den Armeniern, Die Türkei und Europa*), ed. Hans-Lukas Kieser and Elmar Plozza (Zürich: Chronos, 2006), 108–9.

5 For the records of trials, see Osman Selim Kocahanoğlu, *İttihat Terakki'nin Sorgulanması ve Yargılanması* (Istanbul: Temel Yayınları, 1998).

6 Çetinoğlu documents a list of names in an unpublished paper; see Sait Çetinoğlu, "Teşkilat-ı Mahsusa'dan Kemalist Rejime Gelen Kadrolar Üzerine Bir Deneme," unpublished paper, 2006 (Accessed April 28, 2020). https://www.academia.edu/41763607/Te%C5%9Fkilat-%C4%B1_Mahsusadan_Kemalist_Rejime_Gelen_Kadrolar_%C3%9Czerine_Bir_Deneme. Göçek also gives a list in her book and discusses Çetinoğlu's another work, see Fatma Müge Göçek, *Denial of Violence: Ottoman Past, Turkish Present, and Collective Violence against the Armenians, 1789–2009* (New York: Oxford University Press, 2015), 471–3.

7 For instance see the article, S. M. Tevfik, "İslam Siyasetine Muhtacız," *Sebilürreşad*, 15, no. 376 (October 18, 1918): 229–31.

8 Kohar Mazlımyan, "Türk Kadını Savaş Yıllarında Ne Yaptı?," *Hay Gin*, 14, 16 May 1920, trans. Lerna Ekmekçioğlu, *Kültür ve Siyasette Feminist Yaklaşımlar*, no. 2, February 2007 (Accessed April 26, 2020). http://www.feministyaklasimlar.org/sayi-02-subat-2007/turk-kadini-savas-yillari-boyunca-ne-yapti/

9 Adak, "The Protracted Purging of the Tyranny of Nationalism," 111.

10 Belge documents this approach in Turkish literary works; see Murat Belge, *Edebiyatta Ermeniler* (Istanbul: İletişim Yayınları, 2013) 23–4. I thank Özgür Türesay for bringing this work to my attention.

11 Lerna Ekmekçioğlu, *Recovering Armenia: The Limits of Belonging in Post-Genocide Turkey* (Stanford: Stanford University Press, 2016) 147.

12 See the study conducted on the identification of Turks and Kurds who saved and helped Armenians at the time, Burçin Gerçek, "Turkish Rescuers: Report on Turks who Reached Out to Armenians in 1915," The International Raoul Wallenberg Foundation, 2010 (Accessed April 28, 2020). https://www.raoulwallenberg.net/wp-content/files_mf/1435335304ReportTurkishrescuerscomplete.pdf I thank Mehmet Polatel for bringing this report and other relevant sources to my attention.

13 *Meclis-i Ayan Zabıt Ceridesi*, Term 3, Vol. 1, Year: 2, November 30, 1915, 133–7.

14 Göçek, *Denial of Violence*, 477–8.

15 Ibid., 463.

16 On "Turkish-Islamist Synthesis," see Binnaz Toprak, "Religion as State Ideology in a Secular Setting: The Turkish-Islamic Synthesis," in *Aspects of Religion in Secular Turkey*, ed. Malcolm Wagstaff (Durham: The University of Durham Occasional

Paper Series No. 40, 1990), 10–15. This ideology contributed to the increasing role of religion in society and politics leading to the rise of Erdoğan and his party to power; see Mustafa Şen, "Transformation of Turkish Islamism and the Rise of the Justice and Development Party," *Turkish Studies* 11, no. 1 (2010): 59–84.

17 For compilations recently published by the aforementioned publication houses, see Umut Kaya, *Tanzimat'tan Cumhuriyet'e Osmanlı'da Ahlâk Eğitimi*; Bayraktar, *Son Dönem Osmanlı Ahlâk Terbiyecileri ve Ahlâk Terbiyesi* (Istanbul: Dem Yayınları, 2013).

18 The Islamist writer M. Ertuğrul Düzdağ edits the series. Online access to the journal is available via the Bağcılar Municipality's website, "*Sırâtımüstakim*," Bağcılar Belediyesi, 2017 (Accessed April 20, 2020). http://www.bagcilar.bel.tr/kategori/1137/6/siratimustakim.aspx).

19 *Türkiye Cumhuriyeti Cumhurbaşkanlığı*, "Asım'ın Neslini Ayağa Kaldırmanın Mücadelesini Veriyoruz," December 26, 2015 (Accessed April 10, 2020). https://www.tccb.gov.tr/haberler/410/37428/asimin-neslini-ayaga-kaldirmanin-mucadelesini-veriyoruz.html.

20 Asım M. Karaömerlioğlu, "Ateşle Oynamanın Cilveleri: Nüfus Mühendisliğinden Gezi Parkı Direnişine," *T24*, July 19, 2013 (Accessed July 19, 2013). http://t24.com.tr/haber/atesle-oynamanin-cilveleri-nufusmuhendisliginden-gezi-direnisine,234718.

21 For a short summary of these events in English, see Berivan Orucoglu, "Why Turkey's Mother of All Corruption Scandals Refuses to Go Away," *Foreign Policy*, January 6, 2015 (Accessed April 15, 2020). https://foreignpolicy.com/2015/01/06/why-turkeys-mother-of-all-corruption-scandals-refuses-to-go-away/

22 Kamil Yılmaz, Mehmet Alper Sözer, "17/25 December Graft Probe in Turkey and Understanding Erdogan's Invincibility: A Critical Discourse Analysis (CDA)," *Sicurezza, Terrorismo e Società*, Issue 1 (2015): 55–79.

23 "Erdoğan Berkin Elvan'ı Terörist İlan Etti Annesini de Yuhalattı," *Cumhuriyet*, March 14, 2014 (Accessed April 11, 2020). http://www.cumhuriyet.com.tr/video/erdogan-berkin-elvani-terorist-ilan-etti-annesini-de-yuhalatti-50743.

24 Serbay Mansuroğlu, "Karaman'da 45 Öğrenciye Tecavüz," *BirGün*, March 12, 2016 (Accessed April 5, 2020). https://www.birgun.net/haber/karaman-da-45-erkek-ogrenciye-tecavuz-106150; Selin Girit, "Turkey Child Abuse: Scandal Shocks Karaman" *BBC*, April 19, 2016 (Accessed April 7, 2020). https://www.bbc.com/news/world-europe-36071773.

25 The map of these relations is available here: (Accessed April 8, 2020). https://graphcommons.com/graphs/eb5af8a7-e9ea-466d-a0ff-5e746e1060a4?auto=true, last updated 2016.

26 Many articles can be found on the issue. To cite a few that inspired my study, see Levent Gültekin, "Türkiye'nin Ahlak Sorunu," *Diken*, November 4, 2015 (Accessed November 4, 2015). http://www.diken.com.tr/turkiyenin-ahlak-sorunu/; Polat S.

Alpman, "Ahlak Meselesi," *Birikim*, 4 July 2019 (Accessed April 15, 2020). https://www.birikimdergisi.com/haftalik/9589/ahlak-meselesi; Yavuz Çobanoğlu, "İslamcı Ahlak ya da Ütopyadan Distopyaya Evrilen Bir Peri Masalının Hal-i Pür Melali," *BirGün*, April 3, 2016 (Accessed April 5, 2016). https://www.birgun.net/haber/islamci-ahlak-ya-da-utopyadan-distopyaya-evrilen-bir-peri-masalinin-hal-i-p%C3%BBr-melali-108021. Upon receiving comments stating that "true Islam" commands pure morality thus morality in Islam is different from that of the pragmatic approach of Islamists, Çobanoğlu wrote another article pointing the Islamic doctrine's subjective morality, see Çobanoğlu, "İslam Ahlakı ile İslamcı Ahlak Farklı mı?," *BirGün*, May 19, 2016 (Accessed May 19, 2016). http://www.birgun.net/haber-detay/islam-ahlaki-ile-islamci-ahlak-farkli-mi-116735.html

27 A think-tank organization supported by the government circles, SETA (*Siyaset, Ekonomi ve Toplum Araştırmaları Vakfı*, Foundation for Political, Economic and Social Research) published a recent analysis on *Manevi Rehberlik*, see Merve Reyhan Baygeldi, "Türkiye'de Modern Sorunlara Dini bir Çözüm Olarak Manevi Danışmanlık Uygulaması Mevcut Durum ve Öneriler," *Analiz*, 234, April 2018.

28 Ibid., p. 27.

29 "Diyanetin Bütçesi Sekiz Bakanlığı Geride Bıraktı," *T24*, October 24, 2019 (Accessed March 25, 2020). https://t24.com.tr/haber/diyanet-in-2020-butcesi-sekiz-bakanligi-geride-birakti-butcenin-125-milyon-lirasi-derneklere-aktarilacak,845137

30 "Son 18 Yılda Rakıya Yüzde 1800 Zam Geldi, Vergi Geliri Yüzde 650 Arttı," *BirGün*, February 20, 2020 (Accessed March 30, 2020). https://www.birgun.net/haber/son-18-yilda-rakiya-yuzde-1800-zam-geldi-vergi-geliri-yuzde-650-artti-288709.

31 "Ya İçki İçenler Olmasaydı Ne Yapacaktınız?" *Odatv*, January 22, 2020 (Accessed March 30, 2020). https://odatv.com/ya-icki-icenler-olmasaydi-ne-yapacaktiniz-22012039.html.

32 "Türkiye'nin En Büyük Sorununun Ahlak Sorunu Olması," *Ekşisözlük*, 2018 (Accessed April 25, 2020). https://eksisozluk.com/turkiyenin-en-buyuk-sorunun-ahlak-sorunu-olmasi–5645634. The entry that is cited here belongs to the user "talavtiyerik."

Bibliography

Archival Sources

ATASE (Genelkurmay Askerî Tarih ve Stratejik Etüd Başkanlığı Arşivi)
277/1136 001 12
BOA (Başbakanlık Osmanlı Arşivleri)
A.)DVN. MKL. 64/27
BEO. 4430/332225
BEO. 4495/337074
DH. EUM. 2. Şb. 26/2, 35/1 (028)/(034)/(106)/(142)/(003)/(071)/(92)/(102)/(104)
DH. EUM. 3. Şb. 8/74, 25/53
DH. EUM. 5. Şb. 19/1, 9/51, 80/57, 27/46, 22/47, 9/26
DH. EUM. 6. Şb. 42/52 (3), 38/12, 54/59, 18/52
DH. EUM. 7. Şb. 3/1
DH. EUM. ADL. 32/28 (011), 14/34, 6/8, 12/16, 12/31, 33/23, 18/8, 21/35, 28/38, 33/23, 23/31
DH. EUM. ECB. 4/45
DH. EUM. EMN 74/6
DH. EUM. KLU. 12/30
DH. EUM. MEM 72/29
DH. EUM. MTK 79/34
DH. EUM. SSM 11/74
DH. EUM. VRK 29/8, 29/7, 29/3, 28/51
DH. H. 43/66, 46/01 (04), 48/06 (026), 48/5, 43/61
DH. HMŞ. 11/27
DH. İ. UM 29-1/15
DH. İ. UM. EK. 37/6 (9), 36/33, 36/3
DH. İ.UM. 29-1/4
DH. İD: 61-1/44, 61-1/46, 89-1
DH. MTV. 35/7
DH. ŞFR. 477/72
DH. UMVM. 116/40
HR. İD. 1585/41
İ. DUİT. 171 (66/10/12/28/68/7/99/59/41/35/33), 174/20
MV. 196/75, 203/34

Periodicals and Newspapers

"Adâb-ı Umûmîye Mes'eleleri." *Tanin* (September 16 Eylül 1918).
"Ahlâk Mes'eleleri." *Tanin* (September 14, 1918).
"Ahlâk Mes'elesl." *Sebilürreşad*, no: 444 (October 1919).
"Ahvâl-i Sıhhiye Hakkında." *Sebilürreşad*, no: 429–430 (July 1919).
"Bolşevik Düsturları: Mekteplerde Laik Terbiyeden Maksat Ne İmiş?" *Sebilürreşad*, no: 612 (October 1924): 214–17.
"Bolşevik Fikirleri: Erkân-ı Diniyyeye Karşı Hakarat ve Tecavüz." *Sebilürreşad*, no: 609 (September 1914): 174.
"Curb White Slavery in Constantinople: Ambassador Morgenthau's Efforts Effectively Seconded by the Sultan's Police." *The New York Times* (February 27, 1915).
"Decadent Turkey." *Times* (September 11, 1919): 9.
"İslamın Mukaddesatı Aleyhinde Neşriyat." *Sebilürreşad*, no: 298 (July 1914): 227–8.
"Kadınlarımız Hakkında." *Sebilürreşad*, no: 444 (October 1919): 19.
"Kadınların Vaziyeti ve Vezaifleri." *Sebilürreşad*, no: 429–430 (July 1919): 105.
"Konya'da Münteşir 'Türk Sözü'nün Adâb ve Ahlâka Mugayir Neşriyatı ve Ahlâka Mugâyir Neşriyat." *Sebilürreşad*, no: 364 (August 1918): 265–6.
"Kumar Oynayanlar Hakkında." *Tanin* (August 31, 1918).
"Matbuat: Ahlâk Telakkisi." *Sebilürreşad*, no: 626 (December 1919): 232.
"Matbuat: Ahlâk-ı Umumiyenin Islahı Lüzumu ve Hükümetin Vazifesi." *Sebilürreşad*, no: 364 (August 1918): 265–6.
"Matbuat: Ahlâk-ı Umumiyenin Islahı Lüzumu ve Hükümetin Vazifesi." *Sebilürreşad*, no: 364 (August 1918): 265–6.
"Memleket Ne Halde, Matbuat Ne İle Meşgul." *Sebilürreşad*, no: 372 (October 1918): 149–50.
"Memleketimizde Ahlâk Meselesi." *Sebilürreşad*, no: 387 (January 1919): 404–6.
"Türk Ocağındaki Münasebetsizlikler Hakkında." *Sebilürreşad*, no: 452 (December 1919).
Ahmed Besim. "Ahlâk Değişir mi?" *İslam Mecmuası*, no: 52 (March 14, 1916): 10–14.
Ahmed Besim. "Ahlâk, Din ve Ahlâk: İbadat-ı İslamiye ve Ahlâk." *İslam Mecmuası*, no: 32 (July 29, 1915): 8–10.
Ahmed Besim. "Ahlâk: Ahlâk ve Din." *İslam Mecmuası*, no: 10 (June 18, 1914): 16–19.
Ahmed Besim. "Ahlâk: Din ve Ahlâk 3." *İslam Mecmuası*, no: 15 (November 19, 1915): 11–13.
Ahmed Besim. "Ahlâk: Din ve Ahlâk 4, Hakikat-i Ahlâk." *İslam Mecmuası*, no: 22 (February 25, 1915): 8–11.
Ahmed Besim. "Ahlâk: Din ve Ahlâk, Nazar-ı İslam'da Ahlâk." *İslam Mecmuası*, no: 29 (June 10, 1915): 5–7.
Ahmed Besim. "Din ve Ahlâk 6." *İslam Mecmuası*, no: 25 (April 15, 1915): 11–12.
Ahmed Besim. "Din ve Ahlâk, 9, İbadat-ı İslamiyye ve Ahlak." *İslam Mecmuası*, no: 33 (August 11, 1915): 11–12.

Ahmed Besim. "Din ve Ahlâk 11: İbadat-ı İslamiye ve Ahlâk, Oruç, Hac ve Zekat." *İslam Mecmuası*, no: 40 (December 2, 1915): 8.

Ahmed Besim. "Din ve Ahlâk: Mânâ-yı Ahlâk." *İslam Mecmuası*, no. 51 (February 8, 1917): 14–16.

Ahmed Besim. "Nazar-ı İslam'da Ahlâk 4." *İslam Mecmuası*, no: 20 (January 28, 1915): 11–12.

Ahmed Hamdi Aksekili. "Ahlâkiyyat Serisi Mukaddimesi." *Sebilürreşad*, no: 450 (December 4, 1919): 92.

Ahmed Mithad. "Mesleki Zümreler ve Ahlakî Hayat." *Yeni Mecmua*, no: 65 (November 12, 1918): 258–9.

Ertuğrul Muhsin. "Garpta Tiyatroculuk, Bizde Tiyatroculuk." *Temaşa*, no: 9 (September 26, 1918): 5.

Halim Sabit. "Dini Terbiye Heyeti." *İslam Mecmuası*, no: 2 (June 10, 1915): 3–5.

Halim Sabit. "Velayet-i Diniyye: Meşihat-i İslamiyye Teşkilatı." *İslam Mecmuası*, no: 30 (June 24, 1915): 5–8.

İsmail Hakkı. "Ahlâk Mücahadeleri." *Yeni Mecmua*, no: 62 (September 26, 1918): 187–8.

İsmail Hakkı Milaslı. "Geri Kalmamızın Sebebi Dinimiz midir? Usülsüzlüğümüz müdür? Daha başka bir şey midir?" *Sebilürreşad*, no: 429–430 (July 1919): 106–7.

Kazım Nami. "İslam Terbiyesi: Dinî Terbiye." *İslam Mecmuası*, no: 1 (February 12, 1914): 17–20.

Lewis, Ernest. "Fikir Hayatı: Millî Terbiyeye Dair." *Yeni Mecmua*, no: 33 (February 21, 1918): 132–5.

Mansurizade Said. "Taaddüd-ü Zevcat İslamiyette Men Olunabilir." *İslam Mecmuası*, no: 8 (May 21, 1914): 233–8.

Mehmed Akif. "Harb-i Hâzıradan Alınan Dersler." *Sebilürreşad*, no: 432 (September 1914): 311.

Muallim Vahyi. "Ahlâk: Müslüman." *İslam Mecmuası*, no: 1 (February 12, 1914): 20–5.

Muhammed Ferid Vecdi. "Felsefe: Felsefe-yi Maddiyun ile Felsefe-yi Ruhiyyunun Çarpışması." Translated by Ahmed Hamdi, *Sebilürreşad*, no: 300 (June 1914): 250–2.

Muhammed Ferid Vecdi. "Felsefe: Maddiyun Meslek Felsefesinin Edyana Hücumu." Translated by Mehmed Akif, *Sebilürreşad*, no: 298 (June 1914): 209–11.

Mükerrem Belkıs. "Muzır Adetler." *Kadınlar Dünyası*, no: 83 (July 8, 1913): 49–50.

Necmettin Sadak. "İspor Tehlikesi." *Yeni Mecmua*, no: 24 (December 20, 1917): 473.

Necmettin Sadak. "Terbiye Meselesi: Genç Kızlarımızın Terbiyesi." *Yeni Mecmua*, no: 1 (July 12, 1917): 15–16.

Necmettin Sadak. "Umûmî Ahlâk, Meslekî Ahlâk." *Yeni Mecmua*, no: 25 (December 27, 1917): 496–8.

Necmettin Sadak. "Vatan Terbiyesi." *Yeni Mecmua*, no: 18 (October 8, 1917): 354.

Refik Halit. "Harb Zengini." *Yeni Mecmua*, no: 42 (May 2, 1918): 301–2.

S. M. Tevfik. "İslam Siyasetine Muhtacız." *Sebilürreşad*, no: 376 (October 18, 1918): 229–31.

Tekin Alp. "Tesanüdcülük: Harp Zenginleri Meselesi." *Yeni Mecmua*, no: 42 (May 2, 1918): 313.

Ziya Gökalp. "Ahlâk Buhranı." *Yeni Mecmua*, no: 7 (August 23, 1917): 122–4.
Ziya Gökalp. "Aile Ahlâkı: Şövalye Aşkı ve Feminizm." *Yeni Mecmua*, no: 19 (November 15, 1917): 391–4.
Ziya Gökalp. "Aile Ahlâkı-3: Konak." *Yeni Mecmua*, no: 12 (September 27, 1917): 221–3.
Ziya Gökalp. "İctimaiyyat: Cinsî Ahlâk." *Yeni Mecmua*, no: 9 (September 6, 1914): 168.
Ziya Gökalp. "İctimaiyyat: Şahsî Ahlâk." *Yeni Mecmua*, no: 8 (August 30, 1917): 141.
Ziya Gökalp. "İslam Terbiyesi: İslam Terbiyesinin Mahiyeti." *İslam Mecmuası*, no: 1 (February 12, 1914): 14–17.

Books and Articles

Abou-El-Haj, Rifaʻat Ali. *Formation of the Modern State: The Ottoman Empire, Sixteenth to Eighteenth Centuries*. Syracuse: Syracuse University Press, 2005.
Abou-El-Haj, Rifaʻat Ali. "The Ottoman Nasihatname as a Discourse over 'Morality'." In *Mélanges Professeur Robert Mantran*, edited by Abdeljelil Temimi, 17–30. Zaghouan: Cermondi, 1988.
Açıkgöz, Betül. "The Epistemological Conflict in the Narratives of Elementary School Textbooks (1908–1924): Islamic and Secular Insights into Education." PhD diss., Boğaziçi University, 2012.
Adak, Hülya. "The Protracted Purging of the Tyranny of Nationalism: Turkish Egodocuments and the Possibilities of Armenian-Turkish Reconciliation." In *The Armenian Genocide, Turkey and Europe (Der Völkermord an Den Armeniern, Die Türkei und Europa)*, edited by Hans-Lukas Kieser and Elmar Plozza, 107–16. Zürich: Chronos, 2006.
Ahmad, Feroz. *İttihatçılıktan Kemalizme*. Translated by Fatmagül Berktay. Istanbul: Kaynak Yayınları, 1999.
Ahmed Rasim. *Eski Fuhuş Hayatı: Fuhş-i Âtik*. Istanbul: Avrupa Yakası Yayınları, 2007.
Ahmet Mithad. *Felâtun Bey İle Râkım Efendi*. Istanbul: Kırk Anbar Matbaası, 1875.
Ahmet Mithad Efendi. *Felâtun Bey and Râkim Efendi: An Ottoman Novel*. Translated by Melih Levi and Monica M. Ringer. Syracuse: Syracuse University Press, 2016.
Ahmet Naim. *İslâmda Dava-yı Kavmiyet*. Istanbul: Sebilürreşad Kütüphanesi Neşriyatı, r. 1332.
Akçam, Taner and Ümit Kurt. *The Spirit of the Laws: The Plunder of Wealth in the Armenian Genocide* Translated by Aram Arkun. New York, Oxford: Berghahn, 2015.
Akgündüz, Ahmet. *Mukayeseli İslam ve Osmanlı Hukuku Külliyatı*. Diyarbakır: Dicle Üniversitesi Hukuk Fakültesi, 1986.
Akın, Yiğit. "The Ottoman Home Front during World War I: Everyday Politics, Society, and Culture." PhD diss., Ohio State University, 2011.
Akın, Yiğit. "War Profiteers and the Ottoman Home Front during World War I." *World War I in the Middle East and North Africa*, 2012. https://blogs.commons.georgetown.edu/world-war-i-in-the-middle-east/seminar-participants/web-projects/yigit-akin-war-profiteers-and-the-ottoman-home-front-during-world-war-i/.

Akın, Yiğit. "War, Women, and the State: The Politics of Sacrifice in the Ottoman Empire During the First World War." *Journal of Women's History* 26, no. 3 (2014): 12–35.

Akın, Yiğit. *When the War Came Home: The Ottomans' Great War and the Devastation of an Empire*. Stanford: Stanford University Press, 2018.

Aksakal, Mustafa. *The Ottoman Road to War in 1914: The Ottoman Empire and the First World War*. Cambridge, NY: Cambridge University Press, 2008.

Akseki, Ahmet Hamdi. *Ahlâk ilmi ve İslâm Ahlâkı: Ahlâk dersleri*. Edited by Ali Arslan Aydın. Ankara: Nur Yayınları, 1979.

Akseki, Ahmet Hamdi. *İslâm Dini, İtikat, İbâdet ve Ahlâk*. Ankara: Diyanet İşleri Reisliği Yayınları, 1958.

Albrinck, Meg. "Humanitarians and He-Men." In *Picture This: World War I Posters and Visual Culture*, edited by Pearl James, 312–39. Lincoln, London: University of Nebraska Press, 2009.

Alemdaroğlu, Ayça. "Politics of the Body and Eugenic Discourse in Early Republican Turkey." *Body and Society* 11, no. 3 (2005): 61–76.

Alkan, Mehmet Ö. "Tanzimat'tan Sonra 'Kadın'ın Hukuksal Statüsü." *Toplum ve Bilim* 50 (1990): 85–95.

Alpman, Polat S. "Ahlak Meselesi." *Birikim*, July 4, 2019. https://www.birikimdergisi.com/haftalik/9589/ahlak-meselesi

Altınbaş, Nihan. "Marriage and Divorce in Early Twentieth Century Ottoman Society: The Law of Family Rights of 1917." PhD diss., Bilkent University, 2014.

Altınbaş, Nihan. "Marriage and Divorce in the Late Ottoman Empire: Social Upheaval, Women's Rights, and the Need for New Family Law." *Journal of Family History* 39, no. 2 (2014): 114–25.

Alus, A. Sermet Muhtar. *Harp Zengininin Gelini*. Istanbul: Kanaat Kütüphanesi, 1934.

Alyot, Halim. *Türkiye'de Zabıta: Tarihî Gelişim ve Bugünkü Durum*. Ankara: Kanaat Basımevi, 1947.

Arai, Masami. *Turkish Nationalism in the Young Turk Era*. Leiden: Brill, 1992.

Arat, Yeşim. "From Emancipation to Liberation: The Changing Role of Women in Turkey's Public Realm." *Journal of International Affairs* 54, no. 1 (2000): 107–23.

Ata, Feridun. "I. Dünya Savaşı İçinde Bozkır'a Yapılan Sürgünler." *Türk Kültürü İncelemeleri Dergisi* 17 (2007): 51–64.

Atabay, Efe. "Eugenics, Modernity and the Rationalization of Morality in Early Republican Turkey." M.A. Thesis, McGill University, 2009.

Aydın, M. Âkif. *İslâm-Osmanlı Aile Hukuku*. Istanbul: Marmara Üniversitesi İlahiyat Fakültesi Vakfı Yayınları, 1985.

Bakırcı, Mustafa. "II. Meşrutiyet Dönemi Din Sosyolojisinin Önemli Bir Kaynağı: İslam Mecmuası (1914–1918)." *Selçuk Üniversitesi İlahiyat Fakültesi Dergisi* 17 (2004): 177–210.

Bali, Rıfat. *The Jews and Prostitution in Constantinople, 1854–1922*. Istanbul: Isis Press, 2008.

Balsoy, Gülhan. *The Politics of Reproduction in Ottoman Society 1838–1900.* London: Pickering & Chatto, 2013.

Baygeldi, Merve Reyhan. "Türkiye'de Modern Sorunlara Dini bir Çözüm Olarak Manevi Danışmanlık Uygulaması Mevcut Durum ve Öneriler." *Analiz* 234 (April 2018).

Bayraktar, Faruk M. *Son Dönem Osmanlı Ahlâk Terbiyecileri ve Ahlâk Terbiyesi.* Istanbul: Ensar Neşriyat, 2015.

Beckett, I. F. W. *Home Front, 1914–1918: How Britain Survived the Great War.* Richmond: National Archives, 2006.

Bein, Amit. *Ottoman Ulema, Turkish Republic Agents of Change and Guardians of Tradition.* Stanford: Stanford University Press, 2011.

Belge, Murat. *Edebiyatta Ermeniler.* Istanbul: İletişim Yayınları, 2013.

Berkes, Niyazi. *The Development of Secularism in Turkey.* Montreal: McGill University Press, 1964.

Berkes, Niyazi. *Turkish Nationalism and Western Civilization: Selected Essays of Ziya Gökalp.* London: Allen and Unwin, 1959.

Beşikçi, Mehmet. "Domestic Aspects of Ottoman Jihad: The Role of Religious Motifs and Religious Agents in the Mobilization of the Ottoman Army." In *Jihad and Islam in World War I*, edited by Erik Jan Zürcher, 95–115. Leiden: Leiden University Press, 2016.

Beşikçi, Mehmet. *The Ottoman Mobilization of Manpower in the First World War: Between Voluntarism and Resistance.* Leiden: Brill, 2012.

Biancani, Francesca. *Sex Work in Colonial Egypt: Women, Modernity and the Global Economy.* London, I.B. Tauris, 2018.

Birinci, Ali. "Necmettin Sadık Sadak (1890–1953)." In *Türkiye'de Sosyoloji (İsimler, Eserler)*, edited by M. Çağatay Özdemir, Vol. 1. Ankara: Phoenix, 2008.

Bjornlund, Matthias. "'A Fate Worse than Dying': Sexual Violence during the Armenian Genocide." In *Brutality and Desire: War and Sexuality in Europe's Twentieth Century*, edited by Dagmar Herzog, 16–59. London, New York: Palgrave Macmillan, 2009.

Caglioti, Daniela L. *Enemy Aliens and National Belonging from the French Revolution to the First World War.* Cambridge: Cambridge University Press, 2020.

Çağrıcı, Mustafa. *Anahatlarıyla İslâm Ahlâkı.* Istanbul: Ensar Neşriyat, 2000.

Çakır, Serpil. "Meşrutiyet Devri Kadınlarının Aile Anlayışı." In *Sosyo-kültürel Değişme Sürecinde Türk Ailesi*, edited by Ezel Erverdi and Hakkı Dursun Yıldız, 230–44. Ankara: T.C. Başbakanlık Aile Araştırma Kurumu, 1992.

Çakır, Serpil. *Osmanlı Kadın Hareketi.* Istanbul: Metis Yayınları, 1994.

Çeliktemel-Thomen, Özde. "The Curtain of Dreams: Early Cinema in Istanbul (1896–1923)." M.A. Thesis, Central European University, 2009.

Cengiz, Oğuzhan, and Mehmet Celal Atgın. *Türk Ahlâkı.* Istanbul: Bilge Oğuz, 2013.

Çetinoğlu, Sait. "Teşkilat-ı Mahsusa'dan Kemalist Rejime Gelen Kadrolar Üzerine Bir Deneme." Unpublished Paper, 2006. https://www.academia.edu/41763607/Te%C5%9Fkilat-%C4%B1_Mahsusadan_Kemalist_Rejime_Gelen_Kadrolar_%C3%9Czerine_Bir_Deneme.

Ceyhan, Abdullah. *Sırat-ı Müstakim ve Sebilürreşad Mecmuaları Fihristi*. Ankara: Diyanet İşleri Başkanlığı Yayınları, 1991.
Connelly, Matthew James. *Fatal Misconception: The Struggle to Control World Population*. Cambridge, MA: Harvard University Press, 2008.
Çobanoğlu, Yavuz. "İslam Ahlakı ile İslamcı Ahlak Farklı mı?" *BirGün*, May 19, 2016. http://www.birgun.net/haber-detay/islam-ahlaki-ile-islamci-ahlak-farkli-mi-116735.html
Çobanoğlu, Yavuz. "İslamcı Ahlak ya da Ütopyadan Distopyaya Evrilen Bir Peri Masalının Hal-i Pür Melali." *BirGün*, April 3, 2016. https://www.birgun.net/haber/islamci-ahlak-ya-da-utopyadan-distopyaya-evrilen-bir-peri-masalinin-hal-i-p%C3%BBr-melali-108021.
Criss, Nur Bilge. *Istanbul under Allied Occupation, 1918–1923*. Leiden: Brill, 1999.
Daniel, Ute. *The War from within: German Working-Class Women in the First World War*. Oxford, NY: Berg, 1997.
Debus, Esther. *Sebilürreşâd: Kemalizm Öncesi ve Sonrası Dönemdeki İslamcı Muhalefete Dair Karşılaştırmalı bir Araştırma*. Translated by Atilla Dirim. Istanbul: Libra Yayınevi, 2012.
"Definition of Morality." *Oxford Dictionaries*. 2017. https://en.oxforddictionaries.com/definition/morality.
Demirci, Tuba and Selçuk Akşin Somel. "Women's Bodies, Demography, and Public Health: Abortion Policy and Perspectives in the Ottoman Empire of the Nineteenth Century." *Journal of the History of Sexuality* 17, no. 3 (2008): 377–420.
Demirdirek, Aynur. *Osmanlı Kadınlarının Hayat Hakkı Arayışının Bir Hikayesi*. Ankara: İmge Kitabevi, 1993.
Deren Van Het Hof, Seçil. "Erken Dönem Cumhuriyet Romanında Zenginler ve Zenginlik." *Kültür ve İletişim* 13, no. 2 (2010): 81–106.
Devereaux, Robert. *The Principles of Turkism*. Leiden: E. J. Brill, 1968.
Doğan, Atila. *Osmanlı Aydınları ve Sosyal Darwinizm*. Istanbul: Bilgi Üniversitesi Yayınları, 2006.
Dölek Sever, Deniz. "War and Imperial Capital: Public Order, Crime and Punishment in Istanbul, 1914–1918." PhD diss., Middle East Technical University, 2015.
Dönmezer, Sulhi. *Ceza Hukuku: Hususî Kısım, Umumî Adab ve Aile Nizamı Aleyhinde Cürümler*. Istanbul: Istanbul Üniversitesi Yayınları, 1961.
Dönmezer, Sulhi. *Umumî Adab ve Aile Nizamı Aleyhinde Cürümler*. Istanbul: Istanbul Üniversitesi Yayınları, 1950.
Downs, Laura Lee. *Manufacturing Inequality: Gender Division in the French and British Metalworking Industries, 1914–1939*. Ithaca: Cornell University Press, 1995.
Duben, Alan, and Cem Behar. *Istanbul Households: Marriage, Family, and Fertility, 1880–1940*. New York: Cambridge University Press, 1991.
Duru, Kâzım Nami. *Arnavutluk ve Makedonya Hatıralarım*. Istanbul: Sucuoğlu Matbaası, 1959.
Duru, Kâzım Nami. *Cumhuriyet Devri Hatıralarım*. Istanbul: Sucuoğlu Matbaası, 1958.

Duru, Kâzım Nami. "*İttihat ve Terakki" Hatıralarım*. Istanbul: Sucuoğlu Matbaası, 1957.
Duru, Kâzım Nami. *Mekteplerde Ahlakı Nasıl Telkin Etmeli?* Istanbul: Kanaat Matbaası, 1925.
Duru, Kâzım Nami. *Ziya Gökalp*. Istanbul: Milli Eğitim, 1949.
Dündar, Fuat. *Modern Türkiye'nin Şifresi: İttihat ve Terakki'nin Etnisite Mühendisliği (1913-1918)*. Istanbul: İletişim, 2008.
Düstur. Vol. 1. No. 4. Dersaadet: Matbaa-yı Amire, 1296.
Düstur. Vol. 2. No. 4. Dersaadet: Matbaa-yı Amire, 1331.
Düstur. Vol. 2. No. 7. Dersaadet: Matbaa-yı Amire, 1336.
Düzdağ, M. Ertuğrul, Mustafa İsmet Uzun, Bağcılar Belediyesi. "Sırâtımüstakim." *Bağcılar Belediyesi*, 2017. http://www.bagcilar.bel.tr/kategori/1137/6/siratimustakim.aspx
Ekmekçioğlu, Lerna. *Recovering Armenia: The Limits of Belonging in Post-Genocide Turkey*. Stanford: Stanford University Press, 2016.
Emraz-ı Zühreviyenin Men'i Sirayetine Dair Neşr Olunan Nizamnameye Mütealik Talimatname. Istanbul: Matbaa-yı Amire, 1915.
Erdem, Hüsameddin. *Son Devir Osmanlı Düşüncesinde Ahlâk: Tanzimattan Cumhuriyete Kadar*. Istanbul: Dem Yayınları, 2006.
Erem, Onur and Haziran Eğitim Komisyonu. Ensar Vakfı İlişkileri, 2016. https://graphcommons.com/graphs/eb5af8a7-e9ea-466d-a0ff-5e746e1060a4?auto=true
Erickson, Edward J. *Ordered to Die: A History of the Ottoman Army in the First World War*. Westport: Greenwood Press, 2001.
Erşahin, Seyfettin. "The Ottoman Foundation of the Turkish Republic's Diyanet: Ziya Gokalp's Diyanet Ishları Nazâratı." *The Muslim World* 98, no. 2-3 (2008): 182-98.
Evered, Emine Ö., and Kyle T. Evered. "From Rakı to Ayran: Regulating the Place and Practice of Drinking in Turkey." *Space and Polity* 20, no. 1 (2016): 39-58.
Fındıkoğlu, Ziyaeddin. "Aile Hukukumuzun Tedvini Meselesi." In *Tedris Hayatının Otuzuncu Yıldönümü Hatırası Olmak Üzere Medeni Hukuk Ordinaryüs Profesörü Ebül'ulâ Mardin'e Armağan*, 687-738. Istanbul: Istanbul Üniversitesi yayınları, 1944.
Fortna, Benjamin. "Islamic Morality in Late Ottoman 'Secular' Schools." *International Journal of Middle East Studies* 32, no. 3 (2000): 369-93.
Freud, Sigmund. *Civilization and Its Discontents*. Translated by Joan Riviere. New York: J. Cape & H. Smith, 1930.
Frierson, Elizabeth. "Women in Late Ottoman Intellectual History." In *Late Ottoman Society: The Intellectual Legacy*, edited by Elisabeth Özdalga, 135-60. London and New York: RoutledgeCurzon, 2005.
Frith, John. "Syphilis: Its Early History and Treatment until Penicillin and the Debate on Its Origins." *Journal of Military and Veterans' Health* 20, no. 4 (2012): 49-56.
Fuhrmann, Malte. "'Western Perversions' at the Threshold of Felicity: The European Prostitutes of Galata-Pera (1870-1915)." *History and Anthropology* 21, no. 2 (2010): 159-72.
García, M. R., E. van N. Meerkerk, L. H. van Voss. *Selling Sex in World Cities, 1600s-2000s: An Introduction, in, Selling Sex in the City: A Global History of*

Prostitution, 1600s–2000s, edited by M. R. García, E. van N. Meerkerk, L. H. van Voss, 1–21. Leiden: Brill, 2017.

Georgeon, Francois. "Ottomans and Drinkers: The Consumption of Alcohol in Istanbul in the Nineteenth Century." In *Outside in: On the Margins of the Modern Middle East*, edited by Eugene Rogan, 7–30. London: I.B. Tauris, 2001.

Gerçek, Burçin. "Turkish Rescuers: Report on Turks Who Reached Out to Armenians in 1915." The International Raoul Wallenberg Foundation, 2010. https://www.raoulwallenberg.net/wp-content/files_mf/1435335304ReportTurkishrescuerscomplete.pdf

Gibbon, Edward. *The Decline and Fall of the Roman Empire*. London: David Campbell, 1993.

Ginio, Eyal. *The Ottoman Culture of Defeat: The Balkan Wars and Their Aftermath*. Oxford, New York: Oxford University Press, 2016.

Girit, Selin. "Turkey Child Abuse: Scandal Shocks Karaman." *BBC*, April 19, 2016 (Accessed April 7, 2020). https://www.bbc.com/news/world-europe-36071773

Göçek, Fatma Müge. *Denial of Violence: Ottoman Past, Turkish Present, and Collective Violence against the Armenians, 1789–2009*. New York: Oxford University Press, 2015.

Gökalp, Ziya. *Türkleşmek, İslamlaşmak, Muasırlaşmak*. Dersaadet: Evkaf-ı İslamiye Matbaası, 1918.

Gözel Durmaz, Oya. *A City Transformed: Great War, Deportation and Socio-Economic Change in Kayseri (1915–1920)*. Istanbul: Libra Kitap, 2018.

Gültekin, Levent. "Türkiye'nin Ahlak Sorunu." *Diken*, November 4, 2015. http://www.diken.com.tr/turkiyenin-ahlak-sorunu/

Graten, Chris. "The Sick Mandate of Europe: Local and Global Humanitarianism in French Cilicia, 1918–1922." *Journal of the Ottoman and Turkish Studies Association* 3, no. 1 (2016): 165–90.

Grayzel, Susan R. "Mothers, Marraines, and Prostitutes: Morale and Morality in First World War France." *The International History Review* 19, no. 1 (1997): 66–82.

Grayzel, Susan R. *Women and the First World War*. Harlow: Longman, 2002.

Grayzel, Susan R. *Women's Identities at War: Gender, Motherhood, and Politics in Britain and France during the First World War*. Chapel Hill: University of North Carolina Press, 1999.

Gregory, Adrian. "Lost Generations: The Impact of Military Casualties on Paris, London, and Berlin." In *Capital Cities at War: Paris, London, Berlin, 1914–1919*, edited by J. M. Winter and Jean-Louis Robert, 57–104. Cambridge, NY: Cambridge University Press, 1999.

Güler, Ruhi. "İslam Mecmuası (1914–1918) ve İçeriği." M.A. Thesis, Istanbul Üniversitesi, 1995.

"Hadd." *Oxford Islamic Studies Online*. 2017. http://www.oxfordislamicstudies.com/article/opr/t125/e757.

Halide Edib, *Memoirs of Halide Edib*. New York; London: The Century Co., 1926.

Halls, W. "The Cultural and Educational Influence of Durkheim, 1900–1945." *Durkheimian Studies* 2 (1996): 122–32.

Hanioğlu, M. Şükrü. "Darü'l-Hikmeti'l İslamiye." *Encyclopaedia of Islam*. 3, 2016. http://referenceworks.brillonline.com/entries/encyclopaedia-of-islam-3/*-COM_27738.

Hanioğlu, M. Şükrü. *Preparation for a Revolution: The Young Turks, 1902–1908*. Oxford, New York: Oxford University Press, 2001.

Hanssen, Jens. "Public Morality and Marginality in Fin de siècle Beirut." In *Outside In: On the Margins of the Modern Middle East*, edited by Eugene Rogan, 183–211. London: I.B. Tauris, 2001.

Heyd, Uriel. *Foundations of Turkish Nationalism: The Life and Teachings of Ziya Gökalp*. London: Luzac, 1950.

Hock, Stefan. "'To Bring about a Moral of Renewal': The Deportation of Sex Workers in the Ottoman Empire during the First World War." *Journal of the History of Sexuality* 28, no. 3 (2019): 457–82.

"Hukuk-ı Aile Kararnamesi: Münâkehât, Müfârekât, Esbâb-ı Mûcibe Lâyihası." In *Sosyo-kültürel Değişme Sürecinde Türk Ailesi 3*, edited by Ezel Erverdi and Hakkı Dursun Yıldız, 281–307. Ankara: T.C. Başbakanlık Aile Araştırma Kurumu, 1992.

İleri, Nurçin. "A Nocturnal History of Fin de Siécle Istanbul." PhD. diss., Binghamton University, 2015.

Jacobson, Abigail. "Negotiating Ottomanism in Times of War: Jerusalem during World War I through the Eyes of a Local Muslim Resident." *International Journal of Middle East Studies* 40, no. 1 (2008): 69–88.

Journey, Steward. "Prostitution." In *International Encyclopedia of the First World War*, edited by Oliver Janz, Ute Daniel, Heather Jones, Jennifer Keene, Alan Kramer, and Bill Nasson, 2017. https://encyclopedia.1914-1918-online.net/article/prostitution.

Kadınları Çalıştırma Cemiyeti İslamiyesi Nizamnamesi. Dersaadet: Matbaa-yı Askeriye, 1332.

Kandiyoti, Deniz A. "Emancipated but Unliberated? Reflections on the Turkish Case." *Feminist Studies* 13, no. 2 (1987): 317–38.

Kara, İsmail. *Türkiye'de İslâmcılık Düşüncesi: Metinler, Kişiler*. Istanbul: Kitabevi, 1997.

Karahanoğulları, Onur. *Birinci Meclisin İçki Yasağı (Men-i Müskirat Kanunu)*. Ankara: Phoenix, 2007.

Karakışla, Yavuz Selim. *Women, War and Work in the Ottoman Empire: Society for the Employment of Ottoman Muslim Women (1916–1923)*. Istanbul: Ottoman Bank Archives and Research Centre, 2005.

Karaömerlioğlu, Asım M. "Ateşle Oynamanın Cilveleri: Nüfus Mühendisliğinden Gezi Parkı Direnişine." *T24*, July 19, 2013. http://t24.com.tr/haber/atesle-oynamanin-cilveleri-nufus-muhendisliginden-gezi-direnisine,234718.

Karaömerlioğlu, Asım M. "Darwin ve Sosyal Bilimler." *Birikim* 251 (March 2010): 111–22.

Karaömerlioğlu, Asım and Murat Yolun. "Turkish Nationalism and the Evolutionary Idea (1923–1938)." *Nations and Nationalism* 26 (2020): 1–16.

Karaosmanoğlu, Yakup Kadri. *Sodom ve Gomore*. Istanbul: İletişim Yayınları, 2003.
Kaya, Umut. *Tanzimat'tan Cumhuriyet'e Osmanlı'da Ahlâk Eğitimi*. Istanbul: Değerler Eğitim Merkezi Yayınları, 2013.
Kern, Karen M. *Imperial Citizen: Marriage and Citizenship in the Ottoman Frontier Provinces of Iraq*. Syracuse: Syracuse University Press, 2011.
Kırlı, Cengiz. "The Struggle over Space: Coffeehouses of Ottoman Istanbul, 1780–1845," PhD diss., Binghamton University, 2000.
Kırlı, Cengiz. *Sultan ve Kamuoyu: Osmanlı Modernleşme Sürecinde "Havadis Jurnalleri"(1840–1844)*. Istanbul: Türkiye İş Bankası, 2009.
Knezevic, Jovana. "Prostitutes as a Threat to National Honor in Habsburg-Occupied Serbia during the Great War." *Journal of the History of Sexuality* 20, no. 2 (2011): 312–35.
Kocahanoğlu, Osman Selim. *İttihat Terakki'nin Sorgulanması ve Yargılanması*. Istanbul: Temel Yayınları, 1998.
Koçkuzu, Ali Osman, ed. *Çanakkale Cephesinde Bir Müderris: Abdullah Fevzi Efendi, Hâtıralar*. Istanbul: İz Yayıncılık, 2010.
Koç, Vehbi. *Hayat Hikâyem*. Istanbul: Apa Ofset Basımevi, 1973.
Koçu, Reşat Ekrem. *Türk Giyim, Kuşam ve Süslenme Sözlüğü*. Ankara: Sümerbank Yayınları, 1969.
Köksal, Osman. "Osmanlı Devleti'nde Sıkıyönetim ile İlgili Mevzuat Üzerine Bir Deneme." *Osmanlı Tarihi Araştırma ve Uygulama Merkezi Dergisi OTAM* 12 (2001): 157–71.
Köksal, Osman. "Tarihsel Süreci İçerisinde Bir Özel Yargı Organı Olarak Divan-ı Harb-i Örfiler, (1877–1922)." PhD. diss., Ankara Üniversitesi, 1996.
Koller, Christian. "Enemy Images: Race and Gender Stereotypes in the Discussion on Colonial Troops. A Franco-German Comparison, 1914–1923." In *Home/Front The Military, War, and Gender in the Twentieth-Century Germany*, edited by Karen Hagemann and Stefanie Schüler Springorum, 139–115. Oxford, New York: Berg, 2002.
Konan, Belkıs. "Osmanlı Hukukunda Tecavüz Suçu." *Osmanlı Tarihi Araştırma ve Uygulama Merkezi Dergisi OTAM* 29 (2011): 149–72.
Köroğlu, Erol. *Ottoman Propaganda and Turkish Identity: Literature in Turkey during World War I*. New York: Palgrave Macmillan, 2007.
Kozma, Liat. *Global Women, Colonial Ports: Prostitution in the Interwar Middle East*. Albany, NY: State University of New York Press, 2017.
Kurzman, Charles, *Modernist Islam, 1840–1940: A Sourcebook*. Oxford, New York: Oxford University Press, 2002.
Kutluata, Zeynep. "Birinci Dünya Savaşı'nda Ermeni Kadınların Yazdıkları Arzuhaller." *Kültür ve Siyasette Feminist Yaklaşımlar* 27 (2015): 5–17.
Kutluata, Zeynep. "Ottoman Women and the State during World War I." PhD diss., Sabancı University, 2014.
Lévy-Aksu, Noémi. "An Ottoman Variation on the State of Siege: The Invention of the idare-i örfiyye during the First Constitutional Period." *New Perspectives on Turkey* 55 (2016): 5–28.

Lévy, Noémi, Nadir Özbek, and Alexandre Toumarkine, eds. *Osmanlı'da Asayiş, Suç ve Ceza: 18. - 20. Yüzyıllar*. Istanbul: Tarih Vakfı Yurt Yayınları, 2007.

MacArthur-Seal, Daniel-Joseph. "Intoxication and Imperialism: Nightlife in Occupied Istanbul, 1918–23." *Comparative Studies of South Asia, Africa and the Middle East* 37, no. 2 (2017): 299–313.

Mahir Metinsoy, Elif. "Osmanlı Kadınlarının Gıda ve Erzak Savaşı." *Toplumsal Tarih* 243 (2014): 25–8.

Mahir Metinsoy, Elif. *Ottoman Women during World War I: Everyday Experiences, Politics, and Conflict*. Cambridge: Cambridge University Press, 2018.

Maksudyan, Nazan. *Ottoman Children and Youth during World War I*. New York: Syracuse University Press, 2019.

Maksudyan, Nazan. *Orphans and Destitute Children in the Late Ottoman Empire*. Syracuse: Syracuse University Press, 2014.

Mansuroğlu, Serbay. "Karaman'da 45 Öğrenciye Tecavüz." *BirGün*, March 12, 2016. https://www.birgun.net/haber/karaman-da-45-erkek-ogrenciye-tecavuz-106150

Mardin, Şerif. "Super Westernization in Urban Life in the Ottoman Empire in the Last Quarter of the Nineteenth Century." In *Turkey: Geographic and Social Perspectives*, edited by Peter Benedict, Erol Tümertekin, and Fatma Mansur, 403–46. Leiden: Brill, 1974.

Martykánová, Darina. "Matching Sharia and 'Governmentality': Muslim Marriage Legislation in the Late Ottoman Empire." In *Institutional Change and Stability: Conflicts, Transitions and Social Values*, edited by Andrea Gémes, Florencia Peyrou, and Ioannis Xydopoulos, 153–75. Pisa: Pisa University Press, 2009.

Matthee, Rudi. "Alcohol in the Islamic Middle East: Ambivalence and Ambiguity." *Past & Present* 222, no. supp. 9 (2014): 100–25.

Mazlımyan, Kohar. "Türk Kadını Savaş Yıllarında Ne Yaptı?" *Hay Gin*, 14, 16 May 1920, translated by Lerna Ekmekçioğlu, *Kültür ve Siyasette Feminist Yaklaşımlar*, no. 2, February 2007. http://www.feministyaklasimlar.org/sayi-02-subat-2007/turk-kadini-savas-yillari-boyunca-ne-yapti/

Mazower, Mark. *Dark Continent: Europe's Twentieth Century*. London: Penguin Press, 1998.

Meclis-i Ayan Zabıt Ceridesi. Term 3, Vol. 1, Year 2, 1915.

Meclis-i Mebusan Zabıt Ceridesi. Term 3, Vol. 4, Year 1, 1917.

Morgenthau, Henry. *Ambassador Morgenthau's Story*. New York: Doubleday, Page Company, 1918.

"Münakahat ve Müfarakat Kararnamesi Esbâb-ı Mucîbe Lâyihası." In *Sosyokültürel Değişme Sürecinde Türk Ailesi*, III: 295–307. Ankara: T.C. Başbakanlık Aile Araştırma Kurumu, 1992.

Nelson, Robert L. "German Comrades-Slavic Whores: Images in the German Soldier Newspapers of the First World War." In *Home/Front The Military, War, and Gender in the Twentieth-Century Germany*, edited by Karen Hagemann and Stefanie Schüler Springorum, 69–87. Oxford, New York: Berg, 2002.

Nuri, Celal. *Kadınlarımız*. Ankara: Kültür Bakanlığı, 1993.
Nye, Robert A. *Crime, Madness and Politics in Modern France The Medical Concept of National Decline*. Princeton: Princeton University Press, 2014.
Oğuz, Çiğdem. "Millî Mesele ve Maddî Gereksinim Arasında: Birinci Dünya Savaşı'nda Eğlence Yerlerini Düzenleme Çabaları." *Toplumsal Tarih* 267 (March 2016): 86–90.
Oğuz, Çiğdem. "'The Homeland Will Not Be Saved Merely by Chastity': Women's Agency, Nationalism, and Morality in the Late Ottoman Empire." In "Women's Agency in the Late Ottoman Empire," *special issue of the Journal of the Ottoman and Turkish Studies Association* 6, no. 2 (Fall 2019): 91–111.
Oğuz, Çiğdem. "Prostitution (Ottoman Empire)." In *International Encyclopedia of the First World War*, edited by Oliver Janz, Ute Daniel, Heather Jones, Jennifer Keene, Alan Kramer, and Bill Nasson, 2017. https://encyclopedia.1914-1918-online.net/article/prostitution_ottoman_empire?version=1.0.
Oktar, Tiğinçe. *Osmanlı Toplumunda Kadının Çalışma Yaşamı: Osmanlı Kadınları Çalıştırma Cemiyet-i İslamiyesi*. Istanbul: Bilim Teknik Yayınevi, 1998.
Orga, Irfan. *Bir Türk Ailesinin Öyküsü*. Translated by Arın Bayraktaroğlu. Istanbul: Ana Yayıncılık, 2002.
Ortaylı, İlber. "Ottoman Family Law and the State in the Nineteenth Century." *OTAM*, no. 1 (1990): 321–32.
Orucoglu, Berivan. "Why Turkey's Mother of All Corruption Scandals Refuses to Go Away." *Foreign Policy*, January 6, 2015. https://foreignpolicy.com/2015/01/06/why-turkeys-mother-of-all-corruption-scandals-refuses-to-go-away/
Ozansoy, Halit Fahri. *Darülbedayi Devrinin Eski Günlerinde*. Istanbul: Ak Kitabevi, 1964.
Özbek, Müge. "The Regulation of Prostitution in Beyoğlu (1875–1915)." *Middle Eastern Studies* 46, no. 4 (2010): 555–68.
Özbek, Nadir. "Defining the Public Sphere during the Late Ottoman Empire: War, Mass Mobilization and the Young Turk Regime (1908–18)." *Middle Eastern Studies* 43, no. 5 (2007): 795–809.
Özel, Sevgi. *Besim Atalay*. Ankara: Türk Dil Kurumu Yayınları, 1983.
Özer, İlbeyi. "Mütareke ve İşgal Yıllarında Osmanlı Devletinde Görülen Sosyal Çöküntü ve Toplumsal Yaşam." *OTAM* 14 (2003): 247–71.
Özoğlu, Müge. "Modernity as an Ottoman Fetish: Representations of Ottoman Masculinity in Kesik Bıyık." *Masculinities Journal* 6 (2016): 79–101.
Pamuk, Şevket. *Osmanlı Ekonomisinde Bağımlılık ve Büyüme, 1820–1913*. Istanbul: Türkiye Ekonomi ve Toplumsal Vakfı, 1994.
Parla, Jale. *Babalar ve Oğullar: Tanzimat Romanının Epistemolojik Temelleri*. Istanbul: İletişim Yayınları, 1990.
Parla, Taha. *The Social and Political Thought of Ziya Gökalp: 1876–1924*. Leiden: Brill, 1985.

Pedersen, Susan. *Family, Dependence, and the Origins of the Welfare State: Britain and France, 1914–1945*. Cambridge, NY: Cambridge University Press, 1995.

Pick, Daniel. *Faces of Degeneration: A European Disorder, c.1848–c.1918. Ideas in Context*. Cambridge: Cambridge University Press, 1989.

Polat, Ayşe. "Sırat-ı Müstakim ve Okuyucu Mektupları: Sorulan, Tartışılan, İnşa Edilen İslam." In *İslam'ı Uyandırmak: Meşrutiyetten Cumhuriyet'e İslamcı Düşünce ve Dergiler*, edited by Lütfi Sunar, 393–419. Istanbul: İlem, 2018.

Quataert, Donald. "Clothing Laws, State, and Society in the Ottoman Empire, 1720–1829." *International Journal of Middle East Studies* 29, no. 3 (August 1997): 403–25.

Quataert, Donald. *Social Disintegration and Popular Resistance in the Ottoman Empire, 1881–1908: Reactions to European Economic Penetration*. New York: New York University Press, 1983.

Quine, Maria Sophia. *Population Politics in Twentieth-Century Europe: Fascist Dictatorships and Liberal Democracies*. London: Routledge, 1996.

Rank, Scott. "Polygamy and Religious Polemics in the Late Ottoman Empire: Fatma Aliye and Mahmud Es'ad's Ta'addüd-i Zevcât'a Zeyl." *Cihannüma: Tarih ve Coğrafya Araştırmaları Dergisi* 1, no. 2 (2015): 61–79.

Robert, Jean-Louis. "The Image of the Profiteer." In *Capital Cities at War: Paris, London, Berlin, 1914–1919*, edited by J. M. Winter and Jean-Louis Robert, 104–33. New York: Cambridge University Press, 1999.

Royce, Edward. *Classical Social Theory and Modern Society: Marx, Durkheim, Weber*. Lanham: Rowman & Littlefield Publishers, 2015.

Said, Edward W. *Orientalism*. New York: Vintage Books, 1979.

Sami, Şemseddin. *Kâmûs-i Türkî*. Dersaadet: İkdam Matbaası, 1886.

Schick, Irvin Cemil. "Nationalism Meets the Sex Trade: Istanbul's District of Beyoğlu/Pera during the Early Twentieth Century." Paper presented at *Amherst and Hampshire Colleges Workshop*. Amherst College, 2009.

Semerdjian, Elyse. "Gender Violence in Kanunnames and Fetvas of the Sixteenth Century." In *Beyond the Exotic: Women's Histories in Islamic Societies*, edited by Amira El-Azhary Sonbol, 180–97. Cairo: The American University in Cairo Press, 2005.

Semerdjian, Elyse. *"Off the Straight Path": Illicit Sex, Law and Community in Ottoman Aleppo*. New York: Syracuse University Press, 2008.

Şen, Mustafa. "Transformation of Turkish Islamism and the Rise of the Justice and Development Party." *Turkish Studies* 11, no. 1 (2010): 59–84.

Şener, Abdülkadir. "İctimai Usul-i Fıkh Tartışmaları." *AÜ İslam İlimleri Enstitüsü Dergisi* Vol. 5 (1982): 231–47.

Sevengil, Refik Ahmet. *Türk Tiyatrosu Tarihi: Meşrutiyet Tiyatrosu*. Vol. 5. Istanbul: Milli Eğitim Basımevi, 1959.

Şeyhun, Ahmet. *Islamist Thinkers in the Late Ottoman Empire and Early Turkish Republic*. Boston, Leiden: Brill, 2014.

Shaw, Stanford J. *The Ottoman Empire in World War I*. Ankara: Turkish Historical Society, 2006.

Smart, Judith. "Sex, the State and the 'Scarlet Scourge': Gender, Citizenship and Venereal Diseases Regulation in Australia during the Great War." *Women's History Review* 7, no. 1 (March 1, 1998): 5.

Somel, Selçuk Akşin. *The Modernization of Public Education in the Ottoman Empire, 1839-1908: Islamization, Autocracy, and Discipline*. Leiden: Brill, 2001.

Somel, Selçuk Akşin. "Sırat-ı Müstakim: Islamic Modernist Thought in the Ottoman Empire (1908-1912)." M.A. Thesis, Boğaziçi University, 1987.

Sonbol, Amira. "Rape and Law in Ottoman and Modern Egypt." In *Women in the Ottoman Empire: Middle Eastern Women in the Early Modern Era*, edited by Madeline C. Zilfi, 214-31. Leiden, New York: Brill, 1997.

Stock-Morton, Phyllis. *Moral Education for a Secular Society: The Development of Morale Laïque in Nineteenth Century France*. New York: State University of New York Press, 1988.

Swart, K. W. *The Sense of Decadence in Nineteenth-Century France*. The Hague: Springer Science Business Media, 1964.

Tamari, Salim. *Year of the Locust: A Soldier's Diary and the Erasure of Palestine's Ottoman Past*. Berkeley: University of California Press, 2011.

Tanielian, Melanie S. *The Charity of War, Famine, Humanitarian Aid, and World War I in the Middle East*. Stanford: Stanford University Press, 2018.

Teitelbaum, Joshua. "The Man Who Would Be Caliph: Sharifian Propaganda in World War I." In *Jihad and Islam in World War I: Studies on the Ottoman Jihad on the Centenary of Snouck Hurgronje's "Holy War Made in Germany,"* edited by Erik J. Zürcher, 275-304. Leiden: Leiden University Press, 2016.

Tezcan, Baki. "Ethics as a Domain to Discuss the Political: Kınalızâde Ali Efendi's Ahlâk-ı Alâî." In *International Congress on Learning and Education in the Ottoman World: Istanbul, 12-15 April 1999*, edited by Ali Çaksu, 109-21. Istanbul: IRCICA, 2001.

Thom, Deborah. *Nice Girls and Rude Girls: Women Workers in World War I*. London, New York: I.B. Tauris, 2000.

Thompson, Elizabeth. *Colonial Citizens: Republican Rights, Paternal Privilege, and Gender in French Syria and Lebanon*. New York: Columbia University Press, 2000.

"1330 (1914) Senesinde Selimiye Askerî Matbaada Basılan 'Sansür Talimatnamesi.'" *Türk Filatelli Akademisi*. 2016. http://turkfilateliakademisi.org/wp-content/uploads/2016/10/sansur.pdf.

Todd, Lisa M. "'The Soldier's Wife Who Ran Away with the Russian': Sexual Infidelities in World War I Germany." *Central European History* 44, no. 2 (2011): 257-78.

Topal, Alp Eren. "From Decline to Progress: Ottoman Concepts of Reform 1600-1876." PhD diss., Bilkent University, 2017.

Toprak, Binnaz. "Religion as State Ideology in a Secular Setting: The Turkish-Islamic Synthesis." In *Aspects of Religion in Secular Turkey*, edited by Malcolm Wagstaff, 10-15. The University of Durham Occasional Paper Series No. 40, 1990.

Toprak, Zafer. *Darwin'den Dersim'e: Cumhuriyet ve Antropoloji*. Istanbul: Doğan Kitap, 2012.
Toprak, Zafer. "The Family, Feminism, and the State during the Young Turk Period, 1908-1918." In *Premiere Rencontre Internationale Sur L'Empire Ottoman et La Turquie Moderne*, edited by Edhem Eldem, 441-52. Istanbul: ISIS, 1991.
Toprak, Zafer. "İstanbul'da Fuhuş ve Salgın Hastalıklar." *Toplumsal Tarih* 7, no. 39 (1987): 159-68.
Toprak, Zafer. *İttihad Terakki ve Cihan Harbi*. Istanbul: Homer Kitabevi, 2003.
Toprak, Zafer. "Osmanlı'da Toplumbilimin Doğuşu." In *Modern Türkiye'de Siyasi Düşünce: Cumhuriyet'e Devreden Düşünce Mirası, Tanzimat ve Meşrutiyet'in Birikimi*, edited by Mehmet Ö. Alkan, Murat Belge, Ahmet İnsel, Tanıl Bora, Murat Gültekingil, Ahmet Çiğdem, Murat Yılmaz, and Ömer Laçiner, 310-27. Istanbul: İletişim Yayınları, 2001.
Toprak, Zafer. "Türkiye'de Durkheim Sosyolojisinin Doğuşu." *Toplumsal Tarih* 238 (October 2013): 22-32.
Toprak, Zafer. "Türkiye'de Fikir Dergiciliğinin Yüz Yılı." In *Türkiye'de Dergiler Ansiklopediler (1849-1984)*, Istanbul: Gelişim Yayınları, 1984.
Toprak, Zafer. *Türkiye'de Kadın Özgürlüğü ve Feminizm (1908-1935)*. Istanbul: Tarih Vakfı Yurt Yayınları, 2015.
Toprak, Zafer. *Türkiye'de Milli İktisat, 1908-1918*. Istanbul: Doğan Kitap, 2012.
Toprak, Zafer. *Türkiye'de Popülizm: 1908-1923*. Istanbul: Doğan Kitap, 2013.
Törenek, Mehmet, *Türk Romanında İşgal İstanbul'u*. Istanbul: Kitabevi, 2002.
Tüccarzade, İbrahim Hilmi. *Avrupalılaşmak*. Edited by Osman Kafadar and Faruk Öztürk. Ankara: Gündoğan yayınları, 1997.
Tucker, Judith E. "Revisiting Reform: Women and the Ottoman Law of Family Rights, 1917." *The Arab Studies Journal* 4, no. 2 (1996): 4-17.
Tuğ, Başak. "The Claims on Modernity and Tradition: Marriage in Turkey in the 1910s and the 1920s." M.A. Thesis, Boğaziçi University, 2000.
Tuğ, Başak. *Politics of Honor in Ottoman Anatolia: Sexual Violence and Socio-Legal Surveillance in the Eighteenth Century* (Leiden: Brill, 2017).
Tunaya, Tarık Zafer. *İslamcılık Akımı*. Istanbul: Istanbul Bilgi Üniversitesi Yayınları, 2003.
Turgut, Turhan. "I. Dünya Savaşı'nda Osmanlı Posta Sansürü." *Toplumsal Tarih* 243 (March 2014): 88-92.
Türkiye Cumhuriyeti Cumhurbaşkanlığı. "Asım'ın Neslini Ayağa Kaldırmanın Mücadelesini Veriyoruz." December 26, 2015. https://www.tccb.gov.tr/haberler/410/37428/asimin-neslini-ayaga-kaldirmanin-mucadelesini-veriyoruz.html
Ulu, Cafer. "I. Dünya Savaşı ve İşgal Sürecinde İstanbul'da Yaşanan Sosyal ve Ahlaki Çözülme 1914-1922." *Istanbul Üniversitesi Tarih Dergisi* 58 (2013): 87-113.
Üngör, Uğur Ümit and Mehmet Polatel. *Confiscation and Destruction: The Young Turk Seizure of Armenian Property*. London, New York: Continuum, 2011.

Üngör, Uğur Ümit and Mehmet Polatel. "Orphans, Converts, and Prostitutes: Social Consequences of War and Persecution in the Ottoman Empire, 1914–1923." *War in History* 19, no. 2 (2012): 173–92.

Üstel, Füsun. *Makbul Vatandaşın Peşinde: II. Meşrutiyet'ten Bugüne Vatandaşlık Eğitimi*. Istanbul: İletişim, 2009.

Van Os, Nicole A. N. M. "*Feminism, Philanthropy and Patriotism: Female Associational Life in the Ottoman Empire*." PhD diss., Leiden University, 2013.

Van Os, Nicole A. N. M. "Taking Care of Soldiers' Families: The Ottoman State and the Muinsiz Aile Maaşı." In *Arming the State: Military Conscription in the Middle East and Central Asia, 1775–1925*, edited by Erik Jan Zürcher, 95–109. London, New York: I.B. Tauris, 1999.

Wesselingh, Anton A. "Emile Durkheim, Citizenship and Modern Education." In *Durkheim and Modern Education*, edited by Geoffrey Walford and W. S. F. Pickering, 33–46. London: Routledge, 1998.

Winter, Jay, M., and Jean-Louis Robert. "Conclusions: Towards a Social History of Capital Cities at War." In *Capital Cities at War: Paris, London, Berlin, 1914–1919*, edited by J. M. Winter and Jean-Louis Robert, 525–55. Cambridge, NY: Cambridge University Press, 1999.

Wishnitzer, Avner. "Into the Dark: Power, Light, and Nocturnal Life in 18th-Century Istanbul." 46, no. 3 (2014): 513–31.

Woollacott, Angela. "'Khaki Fever' and Its Control: Gender, Class, Age and Sexual Morality on the British Homefront in the First World War." *Journal of Contemporary History* 29, no. 2 (1994): 325–47.

Wyers, Mark David. "*Wicked" Istanbul: The Regulation of Prostitution in the Early Turkish Republic*. Istanbul: Libra Yayınevi, 2012.

Yağcı, Zübeyde Güneş. "Osmanlı Taşrasında Kadına Yönelik Cinsel Suçlarda Adalet Arama Geleneği." *Kadın 2000* 6, no. 2 (2005): 51–81.

Yahya Kemal. *Siyasi ve Edebi Portreler*. Istanbul: Istanbul Fetih Cemiyeti, 1986.

Yalçınkaya, M. Alper. *Learned Patriots: Debating Science, State, and Society in the Nineteenth-Century Ottoman Empire*. Chicago: University of Chicago Press, 2015.

Yalman, Ahmet Emin. *Turkey in the World War*. New Haven: Yale University Press, 1930.

Yamaç, Zehra. "Basın Tarihinde Yeni Mecmua Muhteva Analizi ve Dizini." M.A. Thesis, Istanbul Üniversitesi, 1991.

Yanıkdağ, Yücel. *Healing the Nation: Prisoners of War, Medicine and Nationalism in Turkey, 1914–1939*. Edinburgh: Edinburgh University Press, 2014.

Yavuz, Yusuf Şevki. "Ferid Vecdi." *TDV İslam Ansiklopedisi* 12 (1995): 393–5.

Yeğenoğlu, Meyda. *Colonial Fantasies: Towards a Feminist Reading of Orientalism*. Cambridge, NY: Cambridge University Press, 1998.

Yetkin, Aydın. "II. Meşrutiyet Dönemi'nde Toplumsal Ahlâk Bunalımı: Fuhuş Meselesi." *Tarihin Peşinde Uluslararası Tarih ve Sosyal Araştırmalar Dergisi* 6 (2011): 21–54.

Yıldırım, Nuran. *İstanbul Darülaceze Müessesesi Tarihi*. Istanbul: Darülaceze Vakfı, 1996.

Yıldız, Hülya. "Limits of the Imaginable in the Early Turkish Novel: Non-Muslim Prostitutes and Their Ottoman Muslim Clients." *Texas Studies in Literature and Language* 54, no. 4 (2012): 533–62.

Yılmaz, Kamil Mehmet Alper Sözer. "17/25 December Graft Probe in Turkey and Understanding Erdogan's Invincibility: A Critical Discourse Analysis (CDA)." *Sicurezza, Terrorismo e Società*, Issue 1 (2015): 55–79.

Yılmaz, Seçil. "Love in the Time of Syphilis: Medicine and Sex in the Ottoman Empire, 1860–1922." PhD diss., City University of New York, 2016.

Yılmaz, Seçil. "Threats to Public Order and Health: Mobile Men as Syphilis Vectors in Late Ottoman Medical Discourse and Practice." *Journal of Middle East Women's Studies*, 13, no. 2 (2017): 222–43.

Yumul, Arus. "'A Prostitute Lodging in the Bosom of Turkishness': Istanbul's Pera and Its Representation." *Journal of Intercultural Studies* 30, no. 1 (2009): 57–72.

Zarinebaf, Fariba. *Crime and Punishment in Istanbul: 1700–1800*. Berkeley: University of California Press, 2010.

Zeren, Barış. "The Formation of Constitutional Rule: The Politics of Ottomanism between de Jure and de Facto (1908–1913)." PhD diss., Boğaziçi University, 2017.

Zihnioğlu, Yaprak. *Kadınsız İnkılap: Nezihe Muhiddin, Kadınlar Halk Fırkası, Kadın Birliği*. Istanbul: Metis Yayınları, 2003.

Zürcher, Erik Jan. "Between Death and Desertion: The Experience of the Ottoman Soldier in World War I," *Turcica* 28 (1996): 235–58.

Zürcher, Erik Jan. *The Young Turk Legacy and Nation Building: From the Ottoman Empire to Atatürk's Turkey*. London, New York: I.B. Tauris, 2010.

Zürcher, Erik Jan. *Turkey: A Modern History*. 3rd edition. London, New York: I.B. Tauris, 2004.

Index

abductions 19, 126, 129, 132–4, 143, 147
Abdülhamid II 10, 111
Abdullah Cevdet 42–3, 108
Abdullah Fevzi Efendi 101–2, 146
Adalet ve Kalkınma Partisi (AKP) 158–9, 160–1
adultery 18, 37, 117, 120–1, 134–8, 143, 146
Adultery Bill 116, 123, 131, 135, 138, 147
Ahlâk-ı Alâî 4
Ahmed Besim (Atalay) 24–5, 29–32, 53, 162
Ahmed Emin (Yalman) 1, 75, 112, 130, 134
Ahmed Hamdi (Akseki) 35–7, 47, 158
Ahmed Midhat 5
Ahmed Midhat (Metya) 60
Ahmed Naim (Babanzade) 35
alcoholism 14, 42
Anatolia 12–13, 21, 42, 44, 74, 78, 84, 92, 114, 124, 126, 143, 154
Anatolian 84
    cities 124
    countryside 132
    massacres 156
    town 160
Ankara government 3, 122
Arab
    leaders 12
    revolt 11, 36, 103
    soldiers 103
    vilayets 12
Arabs 10, 12
Armenian 109
    Armenians 134, 153–5
    Assassins 154–5
    community 12, 172
    deportation 153, 155
    feminist 156
    and genocide 11, 12, 154
    girls and women 12, 94, 134–5, 155–6
    issue 12

and orphans 155
persecution of 155
petitions 134
population 16
prostitution 12
woman journals 155
Auguste Comte 15, 55
Austria-Hungary 10
Austrian 88

Balkan Wars 7, 10–11, 34, 103, 118, 123–4, 142, 145, 153
banishment 17, 72, 78, 80, 82–3, 87–9, 92, 95, 121, 131
Beirut 12, 111
Britain 10, 41, 66–8, 118, 122
Bulgaria 11

capitulations 83
    abolition of 17, 71, 83, 86–7, 90, 92, 95, 107, 111, 151, 154
Cemal Pasha 10, 12, 101–3, 154
censorship 12, 37, 39, 41, 44–7, 109, 152, 156
    Commission 109
    Instruction of Censorship (Sansür Tâlimâtnâmesi) 109
Central Powers 10–11
citizenship 18, 62, 76, 88, 90–1, 93–4, 126, 135, 150, 151, 154–5
    Ottoman 18, 71, 83, 90, 93, 95
coffeehouses 5, 99–101, 111
Committee of Union and Progress (CUP) 2–3, 8–11, 35–6, 39, 44, 51, 62, 103–4, 107, 154–5
conspicuous consumption 18, 97–9, 103
crime 14, 19, 58, 66, 73–4, 88, 90–1, 116, 121–2, 125, 132–3, 135, 138, 154, 160
    of adultery 121
    rape 121
    sexual 7, 121, 126
crisis of family 8, 141

Dar'ül-Hikmet'il-İslamiye 9, 37, 44
Dârülbedâyi 108
Darwinism 58
decadence 6, 10, 13–16, 42
degeneration 6, 14–17, 19, 26, 32, 46, 74, 141, 143–4
  of moral order 99
Deir ez-Zor 12
desertion 11, 118, 137
division of labor 15, 33, 53, 56–7, 59–61
Diyanet işleri 33–4, 36, 158, 161
Donanma Cemiyeti 107
Durkheim 15, 33, 53–6, 147
  Durkheimian sociology 39, 147
  and division of labor 33

Early Turkish Republic 8, 34, 84, 154
Egypt 12, 35–6, 38
enemy alien 18, 71, 90, 94
Entente Powers 10, 20, 90, 92
Enver Pasha 10, 110, 118, 131–3, 154
Esbab-ı mucibe layihası 140, 143–5
Eşref Edib 34
European
  capitalism 6
  cultural influence 97, 100
  literary products 4
  morality 1, 26, 36, 114
  powers 10

family reform 19, 117, 139–43, 147
female sexuality 7, 20, 77, 150
Ferid Vecdi 34, 38
France 10, 15, 55, 66, 68, 84, 135
French Revolution 15, 60

gambling 18, 39, 42–43, 97, 99–101, 105, 111, 113–14, 151
gender 5, 85, 152–3
  anxiety 8
  relations 4, 67
  roles 7, 37, 67, 117, 120
  segregation 9, 41, 49, 59, 67, 77, 100
  violence 12, 121–2
  and war 116–17
Germany 10, 20, 66, 68, 70, 118, 135
Gezi Park 158–9
  protests 160
  protestors 159–60
Greeks 12, 155

Halim Sabit 24–5, 32–4
Hamidian
  era 6–7
  public schools 7
  regime 36, 46
Hilâl-ı Ahmer 67, 107
honor 3, 7, 19, 40, 49, 68, 70, 77, 87, 93, 103, 116, 124, 126–31, 136–7, 142

idare-i örfiyye 72, 78
  kararnâmesi 73
İkdam 41, 43
immorality 2–3, 10, 18, 20–1, 23, 37–9, 41, 43, 45–6, 48–50, 57, 61, 65, 68, 70–2, 74, 78–9, 83, 85–7, 90, 94–5, 97–103, 105, 122, 128, 151, 153–4
İslam Mecmuası 17, 23, 24–7, 29–34, 53, 157
Islamic
  jurisprudence 25, 56
  law 8, 25, 27, 37, 48, 67, 120–1, 140–3, 152
  modernism 38
  moral values 5, 157–8
  morality 6, 11, 28, 31–2, 35, 37, 42, 97, 157, 161–2
  reformists 24, 26
  theology 56
Islamist(s) 9, 17, 25–7, 31, 34–8, 41–2, 44–5, 48–50, 63, 112, 141, 147, 158

jihad 9–11, 20, 23–5, 37, 41, 44, 71, 98, 101, 150

Kazım Nami 25–6, 32
khaki fever 66
Kınalızâde (Ali Efendi) 4
Koçu Bey 4
Kurds 10, 12

martial courts (court martial) 73–4, 78–80, 90, 92, 125, 127, 130, 133–4, 136–7, 151, 154
martial law 17, 71–5, 78, 80–1, 87, 89–92, 95, 124–5
  territories and areas 21, 78–9, 81, 83, 95

Mecca 11
medrese 9, 45
Mehmed Akif 34–7, 158
Meşihat 33, 44
Millî edebiyat 52
mobilization 10, 18, 65, 78, 91, 115, 118, 125, 127, 135, 146
   domestic 11
   efforts 3, 72, 92, 118, 120, 138
   of the home front 68
   mass 115
   total 13, 74
moral
   authority 5–6, 9, 50, 99, 112, 149
   control 67, 95, 99–100, 117, 136
   crisis 1–5, 7–9, 12, 17, 23, 27, 36, 52–6, 58–60, 65, 78, 149–50, 153, 156–7, 161–2
   criticism 5, 160
   decadence 14, 97
   decline 2, 4, 6–8, 15–19, 23, 32, 35–9, 41–4, 49–51, 54–5, 57–58, 60–3, 65, 83–4, 99–100, 105–6, 114–16, 135, 140, 143, 147, 149–52
   degeneration 27, 39, 84, 132, 137–8
   discourse 1, 4–5, 11, 13, 99, 103
   laxity 5, 66, 85, 105, 156
   order 20, 99–100, 126, 142, 149–50
   polarization 4, 9, 159
   renewal 5, 56
Morale laïque 52–3, 55–6
morality
   ascetic 53, 56–7, 60
   debates 2, 6, 12, 35, 108, 150, 152
   discourses 4, 6, 8–9, 26, 77, 84, 98–9, 116, 120, 152
   national 20, 26, 52–4, 61
Mount Lebanon 12
Muallim Vahyi 30
Müdâfaa-i Millîye Cemiyeti (Society for National Defense) 104, 107
Muhammed Abduh 34
muinsiz 118
Mustafa Ali 4
Mustafa Sabri 9, 50

nasihatname 4
national economy 103–4
national family 8, 120

Necmeddin Sadak 39–40, 52–4, 60–2
new life 20, 23, 39–40, 47, 52, 54, 62, 150
New Order (nizâm-ı cedid) 5
non-Muslims 7, 75, 84, 87, 103, 121, 155

örf (mores) 25, 56, 141
Ottoman Family Rights Decree of 1917 (family decree) 9, 13, 117, 138–9, 141–4, 146–8
Ottoman-Muslim 4, 42, 112
   families 120, 140, 143, 147
   identity 2
   intellectuals 9
   intelligentsia 149
   society 32, 44, 54, 150
   women 134

Palestine 11
Patriarchal 115
   family 4, 150
   norms 117
   order 150
Population 12, 14, 17, 42, 66, 103, 115
   Armenian 16
   concerns 7
   control 145
   and decline 7, 17, 122
   Muslim 7, 12, 150
   ratio 147
   urban 12
progress
   of country 6–7, 14–16, 20, 24, 30–2, 34, 38, 40, 49–50, 55–6, 112, 149–50
   economic 100
   moral 63
   scientific 55
prohibition of alcohol 3, 99, 101, 112
Prophet Mohammed 26, 29, 31
prostitution 2–4, 12, 14, 18, 20, 37, 49–51, 68, 70–2, 74–5, 77–87, 91–5, 97, 100, 114, 118, 128, 137, 149, 151, 153, 156
   regulation of 65, 74–6
public morality 10, 17–18, 38–9, 44–5, 49, 65, 75, 77–8, 80, 82–3, 88, 90, 97–9, 111, 114, 122, 149
   protection of 2–3, 9, 18, 65, 70, 74, 94, 102, 108–10, 112–13, 150–1

Quran 25, 29, 31, 33, 101, 113

Recep Tayyip Erdoğan 158–60
Refik Halid (Karay) 52, 61
Russia 10, 13, 24, 85, 154
Russian
   citizens 81, 88, 92–3
   Revolution 13
   troops 11

Sadık Rıfat Pasha 6
Said Halim Pasha 9, 35–7, 155
Sebilürreşad 17, 23, 25, 34–51, 57, 59, 155, 157–8
Selim III 5
Şemseddin Sami 3
sexual assault 134
   and rape 18, 19, 147
   and soldiers' families 13, 19, 116, 123–7, 131–2, 134, 136, 138, 147
Sharia 8, 103, 145
   courts 9
   law 36, 144
Sharif Huseyn 11, 103
social pathology 15
Society for the Employment of Ottoman Muslim Women 77
sociology 15, 25, 37, 52, 54–6, 58, 161
   religious 57
sumptuary laws 5–6, 18, 99
syphilis 11, 43, 77, 84, 127
Syria 8, 12, 92, 103

Takrir-i Sükûn 34
Talat (Pasha) 10, 38, 126, 153, 154

Tanzimat era 6, 26–7, 32, 63, 105, 112, 139, 152
   bureaucrats 5
   elite 5
   literature 59
   reforms 26
total war 11, 13, 16, 76, 117
traffickers 71, 74, 81, 83, 85–8, 91
trafficking in women 3, 17, 83–5, 87–93, 95, 151
Tripoli War 10, 34
Turkey 1, 2, 35, 42–3, 51, 86, 95, 112, 122, 152–4, 156–9, 162
Turkish Hearths (Türk Ocakları) 37, 41, 44–5, 49
Turkish nationalists 17, 24, 27, 36, 39, 41, 44–5, 49, 53, 55, 141

ulema 2, 8–9, 25, 28, 33–4, 46, 99, 101, 162
Uprising of 31 March 8

venereal disease 18, 36, 42–3, 68, 70, 75–7, 82, 100, 127, 146, 149

War of Independence 34–5, 154
war profiteering 18, 40, 54, 58, 60–1, 99, 103–5, 151, 153
women's employment 50, 67, 80
   and campaigns 77

Yeni Mecmua 17, 23, 26–7, 39–40, 47, 51–6, 58, 60–2, 155, 157–8

Ziya Gökalp 15, 20, 24–6, 32, 34, 39, 49, 51–60, 120, 141–2, 161

www.ingramcontent.com/pod-product-compliance
Lightning Source LLC
Chambersburg PA
CBHW062144300426
44115CB00012BA/2029